African literature in defence of history

African literature in defence of history

An essay on Chinua Achebe

Herbert Ekwe-Ekwe

First published in Great Britain and Senegal in 2001 by
African Renaissance
B.P. 5336,
Dakar,
Senegal,
West Africa.

A catalogue record for this book is available from the British Library.

ISBN 1-903625-10-6

© Herbert Ekwe-Ekwe 2001

All rights reserved. No reproduction, copy or transmission of this publication may be made without written permission from the author.

African Renaissance is a member of the Praxis publishing co-operative.

www.nursingpraxis.com

Printed and bound in Great Britain by
RPM Reprographics, Chichester, West Sussex.

To the memory of my father
Humphrey Akpa Ekwe-Ekwe
okaa omee

To overhaul a history, or attempt to redeem it - which effort may or may no justify it - is not at all the same thing as the descent one must make in order to excavate a history. To be forced to excavate a history is, also, to repudiate the concept of history, and the vocabulary in which history is written; for the written history is, and must be, merely the vocabulary of power, and power is history's most seductively attired false witness. And yet, the attempt, more, the necessity to excavate a history, to find out the truth about oneself! is motivated by the need to have the power to force others to recognise your presence, your right to be here. The disputed passage will remain disputed so long as you do not have the authority of the right-of-way - so long, that is, as your passage can be disputed: the document promising a safe passage can always be revoked. Power clears the passage, swiftly: but the paradox, here, is that power, rooted in history, is also the mockery and the repudiation of history. The power to define the other seals one's definition of oneself - who, then, in such a fearful mathematic... is trapped?

James Baldwin, *Just Above My Head* (Corgi Books, 1980)

Contents

1 Retrieval — 1
2 Transition — 55
3 Exposition — 75
4 Involution — 109
5 Reconfiguration — 134

Bibliography — *163*
Index — *174*

1
Retrieval

It was clear from the outset that the progress, or otherwise, of African-centred scholarship was inextricably linked to the radical choices that African peoples across the world had to make in the closing years, months, and weeks of what had been a cataclysmic gorge of 500 years of disinheritance during the course of the last millennium. Pointedly, it was to break out of the enthralling universe of a suffocating Western World cultural and socio-economic tyranny. Molefi Kete Asante had emphasised the thrust of this cultural movement of African renaissance when in *Kemet, Afrocentricity and Knowledge*, he asserted: 'The scholar who generates research questions based on the *centrality* of Africa is engaged in a very different research inquiry than the one who imposes Western criteria on ... phenomena' (emphasis added).[1] '[T]his centrality,' he stressed, 'cannot be left to chance... [I]t must respond to a theoretical framework where each phenomenon is examined within the context of the authentic empiricism so fundamental to the methodology.'[2] 'Afrocentricity,' Asante continued elsewhere, 'is the idea that African peoples and interests must be viewed as *actors* and *agency* in human history, rather than as *marginal* to the European historical experience - which has been institutionalized as universal' (emphasis, again added).[3]

Africa or Africans or indeed African interests as subject(s) and/or agent(s) of History? No intellectual disposition could have been more revolutionary, with its impact and implications most far-reaching. Surely, this was a turning point in the all too familiar truncated trajectory of the age long liberation struggles of African peoples to free themselves from European World

---

[1] Molefi Kete Asante, *Kemet, Afrocentricity and Knowledge* (Trenton: Africa World, 1990). p. 14.
[2] Ibid., pp. 38-39.
[3] Molefi Kete Asante, 'On the Wings of Nonsense,' *Black Books Bulletin*, 16 (1&2), Winter 1993-94, p. 38.

domination. Despite the landmark breakthroughs of the 20th century African liberation projects (partial restoration of independence in Africa/the Caribbean and South America [Guyana, Surinam], the African American Uprisings), African intellectuals in Africa and elsewhere in the world had still not freed African scholarship from the contorted and debilitating caverns of the European World academy. Despite this academy's unenviable role as the cultural trigger that fired on the European conquest and occupation of Africa, not to mention the preceding holocaust and dispersal (the most extensive and enforced exportation of peoples in recorded human history) and the hermeneutic codification of the aftermath, the Janus-faced institution was to masquerade as 'innocent,' 'neutral' and 'universal' (to quote words that it would quite readily inscribe into a crusading motto) during the 30-40 years of (African) post-liberation to spearhead the construction of a so-called 'African Studies' epistemology. This was supposed not only to offer an authoritative guide to what it began to call 'development studies,' regardless of the amazing hint of irony given the centuries of the European conquest and occupation of Africa and the overarching racist architecture of the rationalising scholarship on the enterprise (namely, 'We had conquered and occupied Africa in order to civilise it, develop it'!), but also on *independent*, i.e. pre-conquest, African history. The outcome of this exercise was not surprising. The epistemology was still a trenchantly objectified and dehistorised construct, underlining the point in Chinua Achebe's celebrated essay on Joseph Conrad's *Heart of Darkness*: 'Quite simply it is the [European] desire - one might indeed say the need - in Western psychology to set Africa up as a foil to Europe, as a place of negations at once remote and vaguely familiar, in comparison with which [the European World's] own state of spiritual grace will be manifest.'[4] Achebe continued:

> For reasons which can certainly use close psychological inquiry the West seems to suffer deep anxieties about the precariousness of its civilization and to have the need for constant reassurance by comparison with Africa. If Europe, advancing in civilization, could cast a backward glance at Africa [supposedly] trapped in primordial barbarity it could say with faith and feeling: There go I but for the grace of God. Africa is to [the European World] as the picture is to Dorian Gray - a carrier on whom the master unloads his physical and moral deformities so that he

---

[4]Chinua Achebe, *Hopes and Impediments* (Oxford: Heinemann, 1988), p. 2.

may go forward, erect and immaculate.⁵

Quite clearly, the European World academy and other critical sectors of the European intellectual heritage had bluntly refused to do penance for Europe's 500 year-long crimes in Africa, in the wake of this liberatory epoch of the re-establishment of independence by African peoples. In addition, the academy exploited the unresolved problematic historical and strategic underpinnings of the African freedom movement in a number of regions of the African World. It was therefore able to trap African scholarship and institutions of varying hues to partake in the broad ahistoricity of its 'African Studies' discourses including, perhaps most centrally, in the perpetuation of those gaping fault lines extant in the recasting and reconstruction of society which had emerged across the landscape of the African struggle on the morrow of liberation. The cost to the African World has been grave and devastating. The crisis of the reclamation of the African heritage and interests in the US/Americas and the virtual collapse of the African and Caribbean political economies, ensure, for instance, that the latter two regions have uninterruptedly since 1981 become net-exporters of capital to the European World. An empirical illustration with Africa *itself* is always a pointed reminder of the calamity of this plague of disinheritance of African peoples. This challenges quite graphically a cardinal tenet of 'development economics' which presupposes that capital flows required for African 'development' or indeed any other political economies especially in the Southern World (so categorised as 'developing' or 'underdeveloped' in Western socio-cultural definitions) emanate from the so-called 'developed' economies of the West. Furthermore, this illustration confronts head on the current imagery of a blighted African humanity which the same European World, particularly through its media and academia, propagates with vengeance.

In 1981, Africa recorded a net capital export of US$5.3 billion to the West.⁶ In 1985, this figure increased to US$21.5 billion. Three years later, the crisis of Africa's dispossession worsened. Its net capital transfer to the West was US$36 billion or US$100 million *per day*. By 1995, the levels of this daily dispatch had increased even further, with Africa's net capital transfer to the West

---

⁵Ibid., p. 12.
⁶The revelations, in the 1980s, of the extensive nature of Africa's net capital exports to the Western World were at odds with that decade's Western media demonisation of the African humanity as 'beggarly incompetents'. For an excellent exposition of the issues at stake, see, for instance, Frederick Clairmonte and John Cavanagh, 'Impossible debt on road to global ruin,' *The Guardian* (London), 9 January 1987.

standing at US$100 billion. On the eve of the new millennium in 2000, Africa's net capital transfer to the West reached US$150 billion. It should be stressed that none of these figures included the national accounting of the Arab states in north Africa (namely Morocco, Algeria, Tunisia, Libya and Egypt) but those of the rest of the continent (47 countries and the overwhelming majority of the population) which the West's largely-controlled 'international' financial and cultural institutions (especially the United Nations and its affiliates) as well as Western social sciences so dogmatically categorise as 'sub-Saharan Africa' - a concept which requires some comment given its steadily growing use in these circles. 'Sub-Saharan Africa' is essentially a racist geo-political concept which its users aim repeatedly to create the imagery of the desolation, aridity, and hopelessness of a desert environment. It is definitely not the benign reference to the word 'under' which is but one meaning out of at least three others for the key prefix of the term, 'sub-'. Furthermore, the West uses 'sub-Saharan Africa' in order to create the stunning effect of a supposedly shrinking African geographical landmass in the popular imagination,[7] coupled with its attendant geo-strategic global irrelevance. In effect, this characterisation dovetails dramatically into the overall eurocentric packaging of the Western media and academic typecasting of contemporary Africa. Except this increasingly pervasive use of 'sub-Saharan Africa' is robustly challenged by rigorous African scholarship and publicity work, the West will succeed in the next 10-20 years to effectively replace the name of the continent 'Africa' with 'sub-Saharan Africa' and the name of its people, 'Africans', with 'sub-Saharan Africans' or worse still 'sub-Saharans' in the realm of public memory and reckoning. Furthermore, it should indeed be noted that apart from Tunisia, the remaining four Arab north African states that the West does not refer to as 'sub-Saharan Africa' *not only border* on the Sahara but have at least 50 per cent of each of their territories covered up by this desert. Precisely because of this geographical fact and its obvious implications which, alas, do not impact on the lives of at least 85 per cent of Africans on this continent, each of the latter countries of Morocco, Algeria, Libya and Egypt is scientifically more of a sub-Saharan African state than a Nigeria whose northern borders are at least 500 miles from the Sahara, or a Republic of Congo which is at least 2500 miles from the Sahara or in fact a Zimbabwe, a Botswana, a Malawi, or a Namibia, all of which are at least 3000 miles from the Sahara desert.

It is instructive for any serious student of Africa-European World Relations

---

[7] In contrast, see ch. 4 of this study.

to reflect carefully on the multifaceted consequences on Africa of this (now) *regularised* net capital export to the West sketched above because this is the continent whose humanity is gratuitously derided in Western propaganda publicity as 'helpless', 'hungry' and 'beggarly'. Indeed as we write, the latest World Bank's development survey's focus on Africa (contained in its *The Development Report 2001*) underscores this very ritualised uncritically pontifical testimonials on African poverty that emanate periodically from the West. According to the bank about half of Africa's population of 645 million currently live on the 'equivalent of [US]$1 a day or less';[8] but, even more seriously, as the bank's own forecasts claim, the number of people within this poverty bracket will increase by about 60 million by the year 2016.[9] The World Bank must now know that in its annual surveys on Africa, particularly, it can no longer pretend that it is some disinterested and neutral organisation studying socioeconomic trends run by independent countries, carrying out independently-formulated decisions and policies for their own peoples. The World Bank and the International Monetary Fund, its sister organisation, as well as other closely-related so-called international finance organisations that are dominated by the West, are part and parcel of Africa's present tragedy. In the last 20 out of the total of 40 years of Africa's post-conquest independence, the continent's economy has been virtually run on World Bank/IMF-directed social and economic programmes. During the period, Africa's overall social conditions plummeted catastrophically:

> Living standards ... have fallen 2 per cent annually in the last ten years and are now lower than in 1970; unemployment has quadrupled to more than 100 million, and Africa's potential productive capacity now averages only about 30 per cent across the continent. Real wages have fallen by a third and investment is now less in real terms than ... the 1980s. Indeed, economic growth in many countries has ceased and debt has emerged as the single most important cause of Africa's present inability to develop.[10]

The mainly Western personnel and powerful interest groups that devise these policies, especially the notorious 'structural adjustment programme,' would

---

[8] *AllAfrica* (Washington), 29 April 2001.
[9] Ibid.
[10] Kenna Owoh, 'Fragmenting Health Care: The World Bank Prescription for Africa,' *Alternatives*, 21, 1996, p. 213.

dare not proffer similar initiatives on any economy in the West without contemplating the tragic consequences that encapsulate the very desperate African situation being 'analysed' in such self-effacing surveys. The World Bank-IMF dyad must therefore accept the responsibility of being in the commanding pincer with maleficial African leaderships since the 1980s to create the very tragedy that amounts to its surveys year in, year out. Instead of being transferred to the West as some inexorable feature of international financial transaction, mostly through the levers of the World Bank and the IMF, the unimaginably stupendous African capital assets that we have been describing should have been invested strategically in the radical transformation of the continent in order to achieve the so-called 'development' objective that has eluded most of Africa since the beginning of the restoration of independence in the 1960s - namely, the provision of a comprehensive health programme, the establishment of schools, colleges and skills' training institutions across the board, the construction of a national integrative communication network, and finally, the transformation of agriculture to abolish the scourge of malnutrition, hunger and starvation. To this effect, Colin Powell, the new US Secretary of State, is yet to fully comprehend the current state of Africa-Western World *capital exchange* relations. In his most astonishing advice to Africans during his first visit to the continent following his appointment, Powell said: '[Don't] sit around waiting for money to come your way!'[11]

We still need further discussion on the subject of Africa's net capital transfers to the West, especially considering the minimal profile that it receives in the World Bank annual surveys on the continent. We should focus on the figures of 1985. It is very important to emphasise Africa's 1985 US$21.5 billion net capital transfer to the West because it was the same year that the world was confronted with the depressing television pictures which reported the unfolding Ethiopian famine disaster. The Irish pop musician Bob Geldof launched his 'Live Aid' African famine charity programme in response to the tragedy, with a globally-televised pop fiesta which raised US$75 million. Whatever were Geldof's motivations then to embark on this project, which one must assume would almost inevitably have included some deeply heart-felt concern or indeed sympathy for the dreadful plight of the starving African humanity (which the Western news organisations so dutifully and most unrelentingly inundated television news coverage night after night), the amount he raised 'for Africa'

---

[11]*AllAfrica* (Washington), 29 May 2001.

represented a paltry *0.35 per cent* of the gargantuan sum of US$21.5 billion which was Africa's net capital export to the West that year. Yet, for his broadcast fiesta, Geldof was instantly transmuted from a little known musician playing gigs in Irish pubs to the status of 'Saviour of starving Africa' by the propaganda might of Western media bombast. As a result, the Irish government of the day lobbied seriously for Geldof to be awarded the Nobel Prize for Peace. Quite a few commentators thought that Geldof only narrowly missed the award, but he was knighted by the British government as well as receiving other official commendations from elsewhere in the West.

Thus lost in all the frenzy of the Western publicity surrounding Geldofmania was of course the centrality of the African subject's role in the crucial reckoning of historical accounts - the Africa and Africans that transferred the thundering net capital sum of US$21.5 billion to the West in 1985 were quickly moulded into the enthralling object awaiting the crumbs from Geldof's handout! No one thought it fit to offer Africa some accolade for this extraordinary export of its wealth, say for instance, 'The Burden Prize for Western Wealth'. But as Achebe had noted in the quote (above), the point, for the West, was already made as far as it was concerned in this episode of history: 'Africa is to [the European World] as the picture is to Dorian Gray - a carrier on whom the master unloads his physical and moral deformities so that he may go forward, erect and immaculate.' Herein lies the logic of the apparent Western amorality towards an 'international' economic/financial system which it fully controls and which assigns Africa *the* essentialist role to create such enormous wealth and export it to the European World year in, year out. If this logic is a perverted one, which surely it is, then the following four crucial questions should be directed to the humanity that carries the heavy burden of this role: (1) Why do Africans live to work for the European World? (2) Why do Africans transfer their hard-earned wealth to enrich the coffers and the life styles of the European World? (3) Why should Africa continue to be a critical source for the accumulation of Western wealth? (4) How will the European World's current stranglehold on the human and material resources of Africa be terminated?

These questions and several other related ones will of course be answered in the course of this study especially as we stress that the only way out of Africa's current crisis is for a fundamental continental change in the use of its human resource, geared expressly for domestic goals. This resource, the engine of societal development, must disengage from its present wasteful and inevitably terminal venture of working for the European World. In examining these questions, we shall demonstrate that deeply embedded in the Western intellectual cultural heritage to continue to set Africa up as that totalising reference of the European World's own tapestry of negations, is the Western strategy to foreclose owning up to any responsibilities for its crimes (past and present) in Africa. For the West, its plethoric vilification of the African humanity, whether on the lie that the HIV/AIDS virus emanated from Africa or even the latest in some sections of the British media that the 2001 deadly mouth-and-foot disease that ravaged British livestock may have originated from Africa,[12] represents a compulsive opportunity to be on an *indefinite propaganda offensive* to ward off the punishing judgement of history.

A distinct and apt contemporary variation on the theme of the West's perpetual need to create a European benefactory reference 'for Africa' for reasons just stated, concerns Princess Diana, the late estranged wife of the heir to the British throne. Emerging from an embarrassingly high-profile divorce, it would have been inconceivable that Africa would be left out in any concerted attempt by concerned British officials to embark on the construction of the princess's 'rehabilitation' in British popular consciousness.[13] Indeed, the opportunity came much sooner than even the most crusty of cynics would have contemplated when it was announced dramatically in March 1997 that Diana

---

[12]See, for instance, *Daily Telegraph* (London), 2 March 2001.

[13]It is not without some irony that it was again to Africa that the British royal family organised the first visit abroad for Prince Charles in October 1997, following Diana's tragic death, for yet another episode of character rehabilitation. This time round, it was for Charles to demonstrate that he was an open, caring and sensitive human being, contrary to criticisms that he had been subjected to by some in the (British) media and public soon after the death of his former wife. Their son and heir to the throne, Prince William, has since joined his parents to undertake a trip to Africa! On this occasion, though, the aim is to fulfil another function that the West routinely typecasts Africa which will be discussed in further details later: the animalisation of the continent's social existence. On this visit, according to the London *Daily Telegraph* (4 March 2001), William 'will spend some time on safari and will also become involved in game conservation, learning about African wildlife and environment.' Africa's apparent recuperative powers were equally not lost on former US President Clinton during his embarrassing sex scandal entanglement while in office. In March 1998 Clinton embarked on an extended trip to Africa which provided him with a badly needed breathing space as he awaited a crucial court ruling on one of the numerous sex litigation hearings against him. On the eve of his return from Africa, he received the best news he had sought for months (even if temporary as events later in the year would prove) from his tortured personal life: in the tortuous count for the scores in this round at least, the court found in his favour! Surprise?

would travel to Angola forthwith to demonstrate her campaign to stop the production of anti-personnel land mines. There was scarce mention that Britain was in fact one of the world's largest producers of land mines and that 70 per cent of these mines used in the war in Angola were actually manufactured in Britain. It would then have been far more effective for the ultimate success of the Diana campaign (and also more cost effective) if those who organised the princess's trip had instead meticulously identified the land mines' manufacturing plants in Britain and then arrange for her to visit each of these facilities so as to inform staff and perhaps shareholders of her most laudable initiative and objective.

Throughout the publicity generated by Diana's 3-day Angolan visit which became a top headline news item on British television and other media during its duration, the emphasis on news footage material was on the number of Angolan mines-caused amputee survivors that the princess met. Keeping predictably close to the 'standard norm' of Western news reporting format on African tragedy, these amputees were literally stripped of their dignity, if not humanity, by the offensively-prying and intrusive photographic shots of varying angles of horrific injuries and pain that were clearly bereft of sensitivity. In contrast, when, in a few months later, Diana went to Bosnia on a similar visit to campaign against the use of land mines in war, the press coverage on amputees here had a marked touch of sympathy, sensitivity and humanity that such an occasion understandably deserves. The latter reportage was quite in line with the way that generally the Western media covered the 3-year Bosnia War itself, and also their coverage of human tragedies elsewhere in the Western World or where Europeans or their descendants were caught up as victims such as the Hungerford and Dunblane massacres in Britain, the Oklahoma bombings in the United States, sporadic bombings in Israel, the 1997 devastating floods in east and central Europe, the floods across different parts of Britain in 2000, the 30 year-old war in Northern Ireland, and of course not to mention both the British-originated 'mad cow' and foot-and-mouth epidemics. It is quite ironical that the Western press would be so accused by part of its own public, particularly in Britain, for its insensitivity of intrusive reporting and coverage in news 'packaging', albeit in a different context, in the events leading to the tragic death in an automobile accident in Paris in August 1997 of Princess Diana. But it must not be forgotten that this same public has in the past been hardly critical of similar aloofness and insensitiveness with which its press 'packaged' news on Africa and the African humanity; on the contrary, it has come to accept the rationalisation of that 'packaging' as most aptly depicted in that infamous introductory 'disclaimer' which often precedes the intrusive outcome of African news item on Western television: 'You might find the following pictures distressing ...'

Green beans vs nuclear-war biscuits

If the West's construction of a Princess Diana-benefactory symbolism for African 'helplessness' has such a core defining personage as one who would have been queen of Britain, it is not always the case that this reference has to take the form of highly elevated individuals. Going by a 1997 advertisement in a British newspaper[14] asking for (British) 'volunteers' to work on 'health projects' in rural Tanzania, it is clear that the most lowly in social terms could easily join this hallowed train of Europeans out there to 'save Africa' - if need be, even from itself! To underline the significance of this point, the advertisement assures the volunteers: 'no skills needed.'[15] It surely baffles the imagination to ponder over the sort of 'health projects' in rural Tanzania that these *unskilled* British 'volunteers' were scheduled to work on! Just what were these Britons going to do whilst in east Africa? Was the Tanzanian government aware of the initiative? But then, it is not just Tanzania that has been turned into an all time destination for the West's unskilled, partially skilled, mostly untested, and usually inappropriate humanpower whose highly inflated costs are scandalously paid for by the recipient country regardless. To the contrary, this is the problem that afflicts the entire Africa. Currently, the continent has a staggering population of 100,000 foreign,[16] mostly Western, so-called 'technical assistants' who are found virtually in every conceivable sphere of African social existence. However, it is the presence of a number of these 'assistants' deployed to the key economic decision-making institutions of the state, advising, or as the case might be, even directing the very decapitalisation of the economy under the IMF/World Bank ideological banner of the age called 'Structural Adjustment Programme' that has most symbolised the scourge of contemporary Africa. Astonishingly, part of this outcome was implicitly acknowledged during the course of his term in office, albeit with amazing insensitivity, by none other than Michel Camdessus, the former IMF managing director, who told a church group in the United States that what he termed 'benefits' of his organisation's decapitalisation programme in Africa/Southern World might require the

---

[14]*The Guardian* (London), 16 July 1997.
[15]Ibid.
[16]Joseph Ki-Zerbo, 'Which Way Africa?' *Development Dialogue*, 1995:2, p. 114.

'sacrifice of a generation.'[17] But in a measured response to this outrage, Soren Ambrose, of the US-based 50 Years Is Enough, has argued: 'If the enforced [programme] of "structural adjustment" truly led to higher standards of living for the majority of the people in IMF client countries [in Africa and elsewhere], the pain inflicted might be acceptable. But an internal study, completed by the IMF staff [itself] in September 1997, found that per capita income *stagnated* in countries undergoing structural adjustment from 1981 to 1995. In [Southern countries] free of the IMF, the study found that per capita income *rose*' (added emphasis).[18] Tragically, all this is occurring at a time when 100,000 African intellectuals,[19] the cream of the continent's advanced humanpower development during 1960-1990 (the first 30 years after the restoration of independence) have been literally forced out of their homeland to work in the European World and elsewhere by the very socio-economics of decapitalisation. For Africa, the defining aphorism of this era is a cruelly haunting one indeed: SAP *saps* Africa of its human and material capital and creates the dumping ground on the continent for the European World's unemployed and unemployable.

If the 'no skill needed' advertisement (above) underscores the fact that the West is prepared to sink to any depths in its desire to sustain the construction of its propaganda imagery of a 'benighted Africa,' ever dependent on European 'generosity,' including even that of its unskilled humanpower, the next example is no less farcical. A few years ago, the London *Mail on Sunday*[20] reported what would have been regarded as a most sensational story - that is, if the reference had not been the African humanity. Under the caption 'Cold War Rations Help Feed Starving,' the newspaper stated that tons of 'Cold War' emergency rations, 'some going back 30 years' and stored in warehouses in Britain, were being sent to 'famine hit'-African countries. Two thousand and four tonnes of 'high-protein' biscuits, originally meant for possible British survivors of a nuclear war, had been made available to the Save the Children (STC) charity for shipment to Ethiopia.

How safe were these biscuits for human consumption? Don Redding, an STC official at the time, replied: 'Some are very old, but they are totally edible ... [S]cientific test have revealed that they are still of a high quality. We would not be sending them out to Ethiopia if there was any suggestion [that] they were

---

[17]Quoted by Soren Ambrose, 'Challenging the IMF, Intellectually and Politically,' *International Herald Tribune* (Paris), 29 April 1998, p. 11.
[18]Ibid.
[19]Ki-Zerbo, 'Which Way Africa?' p. 114.
[20]See Mail on Sunday (London), 5 July 1992.

not fit for human consumption.'[21] What was the position of the Ethiopian government on this question, namely the safety or otherwise of these biscuits for human consumption? Incidentally, or should we rather say pointedly, there was no indication whatsoever on this in the report. Possibly, this piece of information was of no interest to the news editor of the *Mail*. So, we pose the question here: What did the Ethiopian government feel about these ancient nuclear-war biscuits? Were these biscuits tested by Ethiopian doctors, nutritionists, public health officials, etc, before Ethiopia supposedly accepted delivery of the products? Were the Ethiopians aware that earlier on in 1992 (the year of this controversy) Russia rejected a consignment of British beef donated by Britain to alleviate food shortages in that country? This was because Russian veterinary experts found the beef unsuitable for human consumption. Quite auspiciously, this Russian rejection came about four years before the worldwide ban on British beef exports because of the deadly 'mad cow' disease. Finally, to return to Save the Children, the following two questions are pertinent on these nuclear-war biscuits: (1) Were there ever any considerations to distribute these products to the hungry and destitute on the streets of London, Birmingham, Manchester, Bristol, Cardiff, Liverpool and other British cities? (2) Why weren't these products sent for instance to Bosnia-Herzegovina instead, where, during the same period in 1992, entrapped citizens in the country's war ravaged cities faced starvation?

Later on in 1992, the Sainsbury's food stores chain unwittingly reminded the world, if such a reminder were still necessary, of the strategic role that Africa plays in European World wealth and wellbeing - exposing, in effect, the silly gimmickry of the nuclear-war biscuit propaganda that had raged just a few months earlier. In huge billboards in a number of London underground railway stations, Sainsbury's told the uncomfortable truth of their efficient delivery system of flying in green beans grown on the Kenyan highlands of east Africa into Britain within 48 hours of being harvested: 'Christmas Is Around the Corner. Some Delightful News For Beans Consumers! Lush Green Beans From The Kenyan Highlands of Africa! Available in your Saucepan Within 48 Hours Of Harvest!' The accompanying photographs of the species of these beans were luxuriantly appetising and could not fail to entice the most modest palate ... But green beans from Africa? Africa of 1992? And more so from east Africa! Indeed, the beans in question were and are still grown in rich agricultural lands located within a 500-mile arc of the epicentres of the devastating famine and

---

[21]Ibid.

human misery that had wreaked Ethiopia, Somalia and Sudan during the period. In these lush lands in Kenya, still 'owned' by influential British families/corporate interests despite 36 years of Kenyan so-called independence, carnations are also grown extensively for export to Britain, Switzerland and other countries in Europe. It must therefore be the most cruel of ironies that as millions of people in the region starved and anxiously awaited food relief from abroad, perhaps including the 30-year-old nuclear-war biscuits from Britain, the Sainsburys of the Western World had, and still have unlimited access to the *African* sources for the cultivation and importation of such highly nutritious foods which locals needed and required as a matter of life-and-death – much more than Londoners and other Britons, 7000 miles away. Six years later, in what was appropriately an update to the African green beans scandal, the British Channel 4 Television broadcast an exclusive report showing the radical expansion of the Kenyan cultivation fields which, in addition to Sainsbury's, now catered for the import needs of three other major British food retailers: Marks & Spencer, Tesco and Safeway.[22] What was particularly grave in Channel 4's research was its finding that in order to support the ever-increasing intensive and extensive nature of the beans cultivation to support demands in Britain, the cultivators were continuously violating strict officially (Kenyan)-stipulated limits of water taken out from the adjoining river systems aimed at protecting the region's precarious ecosystem. The report showed that the cultivators pumped out millions of litres of water (in excess of the limits) from the rivers to their bean fields, thereby threatening the lives and livelihood of African farmers and herdspeople further downstream who had begun to experience acute water shortages.

Critics of the manner of our presentation of these Sainsbury's bean-imports could conceivably argue that the food chain conglomerate was doing nothing wrong in its Africa business other than 'free trade' particularly in this epoch of so-called globalisation. But that would just be begging the question, even though in that process the argument in fact comes full circle as this Africa 'relationship' surely fulfils what the West would indeed call 'free trade' - namely, the latter's conversion of the fertile territories of the world under its hegemony to grow products on the cheap for its own consumption; in the reverse, the essentially complementary direction of this activity, the West sends chaffs of left-over (nuclear-war biscuits and the like) to those invariably made hungry and destitute as a result of the earlier phase of the process. The latter is

---

[22]Channel 4 Television 7.00pm News (London), 5 August 1998.

actuated, quite often, under the cover of glittering publicity of 'carers' and 'saviours' of suffering humanity by the West's ubiquitous media. In effect, the 'Green Bean-Nuclear War Biscuit' dyad, with its evident interlocking dialectical tension becomes a painfully graphic metaphor that succinctly captures the basic historical character of Africa-European World relations - the delicious and highly nutritious green bean is symbolic of the life, life-giving, and socio-economic sustenance of the African component while the nuclear war biscuit is indicative of the dread, scorched, and exhausted wasteland of the European response. African life-giving capacity not only envisions the possibilities of the enormous wealth at the centre of the staggering capital export drama so graphically illustrated above, but also serves as a reminder of the historic role of Africa all along in this dreadful saga of 'contact' with the European World. Indeed, within 300 years of achieving the strategic control of Africa's human and material resources, Europe laid the foundation for the West's political and economic hegemony of the world as we know it presently. This is a fact - 'though largely erased and ignored in Western thought,'[23] as Michel Beaud, the influential French economist, is keen to remind the West. Britain, the first truly effective Western global power, used the gargantuan wealth it acquired during the course of its late 17th century/18th century pre-eminent role in the enslavement and mass exportation of millions of Africans to the Americas to consolidate its conquest of the Americas (especially the north), embark on its conquest of India and other regions of Asia, embark on the subsequent pan-European (Britain, France, Portugal, Belgium, Spain, Germany and Italy) conquest and occupation of a (subsequently) weakened Africa, and lastly, but surely not least in importance, *finance* its 19th century industrial revolution which was the turning point in the development of Western capitalism. During the 300 years of Britain's ascendancy as the world's principal slaver power in Africa and the Americas, leading members of its state establishment (especially in royalty, clergy, parliament, industry, academia, science and the arts) personally and collectively profited enormously from this unprecedented holocaust in human history.[24] This stupendous British fortune and the gullies of socio-economic devastation it unleashed across Africa and the obvious debilitating consequences on survivors in Africa itself, the Americas and elsewhere in the world, ensured that a triumphant Prime Minister Salisbury

---

[23] Michel Beaud, *A History of Capitalism: 1500-1980* (New York: Monthly Review, 1983), p. 44.
[24] Cf. Ronald Segal, 'The chains of shame,' *The Guardian* (London), 17 December 1997, p. G2/2.

would confidently insist in a speech in London in 1898: 'One can roughly divide the nations of the world into the living and the dying... [T]he living nations will fraudulently encroach on the territory of the dying.'[25] Less than 50 years after these remarks were made, the dire consequences of pogroms and holocausts would be felt much closer home to the heart of Europe rather than just the targeted lands further afield in Africa and elsewhere. On this, Sven Lindqvist has solemnly observed:

> I am fairly sure the nine-year-old Adolf Hitler was not in Albert Hall when Lord Salisbury was speaking. He had no need to. He knew it already. The air he and all other Western people in his childhood breathed was soaked in the conviction that imperialism is a biologically necessary process, which, according to the laws of nature, leads to the inevitable destruction of the lower races. It was a conviction which already cost millions of human lives before Hitler provided his highly personal application.[26]

As should be expected, the effect on Africans and their homeland of this earlier holocaust, which remains the worst in history, had the devastating sterility of those ancient nuclear-war biscuits stored in British warehouses: the active human power of millions of future African generations were uprooted and shipped off to the Americas by European slavers to work the cotton, sugar and tobacco plantations, excavate the gold and silver mines, and build new towns and cities in territories being conquered by a rampaging European imperialism. In the process, Africa lost about 150 million of its peoples as slaves, including those who died during the overland journey to slave ships and the voyage to the Americas.[27] Soon, the European powers that formally occupied Africa turned the continent into a reservoir of cheap labour for intensive and extensive agricultural and mineralogical exploitation. The African farmer was converted overnight into a 'cash crop farmer,' a term that at face value had a dubious meaning as it was aimed to describe a farmer who cultivated assorted crops such as cotton, cocoa, palm produce, groundnut, cloves and sisal solely for export to European markets. The farmer who cultivated other crops, but for the home

---

[25] Quoted in Sven Lindqvist, *'Exterminate All the Brutes'* (London: Granta Books, 1997), p. 140.
[26] Ibid., p. 141.
[27] Cheikh Anta Diop, *Precolonial Black Africa* (New York: Lawrence Hill Books, 1987), p. 142.

market which he or she still sold for cash, was not a 'cash crop farmer'! Instead, goes the conquest economics jargon, the latter farmer was involved in 'subsistent farming'. Considering that the overwhelming majority of Africans were, and are still farmers, these millions of people were, as a result of the European conquest and occupation, being culturally alienated at the crucial site of their economic activity with obvious far-reaching implications which are still at the core of Africa's current crisis. If the African labour was not bound for agricultural activity, 'cash crop' or not, it was instead deployed by the occupation state to the ever-expanding European mining corporations dotted all over the continent to extract various types of minerals including diamonds, gold, tin, bauxite, coal, copper, iron ore and petroleum products, again for export to Europe. In effect, African land and property relations, which in most cases were characterised by an age long system of communitarianism, were abolished to make way for private appropriation of land for both plantation agriculture and mining enterprises already referred to, or for the construction of new communication infrastructure, or for the direct population settlement by Europeans as exemplified in east Africa (Kenya), southern Africa (Mozambique, Zimbabwe, South Africa, Angola, Namibia), west Africa (São Tomé and Principé, Equatorial Guinea, Guinea Bissau, Cape Verde) and north Africa (Algeria). In each conquered country, now arbitrarily carved out from hitherto existing African states, the imperial regime imposed its monetary system on society and also ensured that the terms for the exchange of goods and services, fundamental for the logical development of any socio-economic activity or relation, was inextricably tailored to the exigencies of the home market back in Europe.

All forms of taxes were imposed to expedite this European take-over of Africa, and the strategic spheres of the continent's *independent* pre-conquest culture, industrial and other forms of technological creativity therein were curtailed or suppressed. No doubt, the economies that emerged subsequently in Africa, particularly on the eve of the re-establishment of the peoples' independence in the 1960s, were *structurally bereft* of local needs and priorities. Instead, these were mineralogical and agricultural redoubts to service a European home market, and, at the same time, acted as conduits for European immigration. In summary, two distinct consequences on the African humanity can be discerned from the European conquest. First, the destruction/near destruction of local populations (genocide) and the herding of survivors/others into labour reserves/'townships' to make way for direct European occupation (particularly east/southern Africa), and secondly, the overall control of subjugated populations and the conversion of human and material resources to serve imperial interests (rest of Africa).

Merchants of memory erasure & genocide

The nuclear-war biscuit-500 years of Western desolation of Africa is humanity's most intensive and extensive holocaust. Africa and Africans *have yet to recover* from this tragedy. As for the European World perpetrator, its reaction to the holocaust has in the overall been to exercise a haunting silence or as Michel Beaud has noted, attempt to ignore or erase the memory of the episode from formal or informal accounting. A predictable path that Europe uses to pursue this stratagem of African historical erasure is through its scholarship of demonisation or defamation of the African subject of history. On this critical issue, Chinua Achebe has argued and it is crucial to quote him at length:

> [The European conquest of Africa] may indeed be a very complex affair, but one thing is certain: You do not walk in, seize the land, the person, the history of another, and then sit back and compose hymns of praise in his honour. To do that would amount to calling yourself a bandit; and you don't want to do that. So what do you do? You construct very elaborate excuses for your action. You say, for instance, that the man in question is worthless and quite unfit to manage himself or his affairs. If there are valuable things like gold or diamonds which you are carting away from his territory, you proceed to prove that he doesn't own them in the right sense of the word - that he and they had just happened to be lying around the same place when you arrived. Finally if the worse comes to the worse, you may even be prepared to question whether such as he can be, like you, fully human. From denying the presence of a man standing there before you, you end up questioning his very humanity ... [I]n the [European conquest] situation *presence* was the critical question, the crucial word. Its denial was the keynote of [this conquest's] ideology (emphasis added).[28]

Yet, 'every time [the European] sees [the African] face, he[or she] sees a mirror

---

[28]Chinua Achebe, 'African Literature as Restoration of Celebration,' *Kunapipi*, Vol XII, No. 2, 1990, p. 4.

of [their] crime - and [their] guilt conscience can't bear to face it,'[29] as Malcolm X, the perceptive African American revolutionary has observed. In the 1960s, when Malcolm made these remarks, Hugh Trevor-Roper, a British historian who taught at Oxford University, was busy regurgitating what had by then become a standard, albeit worn, 'Deny-the-African Presence' litany by many a scholar of the European academy when he proclaimed, 'African history did not exist.'[30] What was perhaps most disingenuous (about Trevor-Roper's 1963 proclamation) was that this came from an historian who was a living witness to that monumental emergency of a major war and a post-war reconstruction in which his country had been centrally involved through the course of the previous 25 years. If Trevor-Roper had cared to research the facts of this war and its aftermath which were available to even the most casual of observers, he would have found how futile and misleading his African Presence-Denial project was indeed. Instead, he would have realised how he and the rest of his country men and women should for ever be *grateful* to Africa not only for wining that war against Germany, but also for producing the critical resources required by Britain to embark on socio-economic reconstruction subsequently. The fact of the matter is that due to the long stretch of Britain's (as well as other key European World states) disruption, distortion and dislocation of the African *historical process*, following its centuries of occupation of Africa, it was able to expropriate and direct the vast resources of the continent's human and material heritage that it had sequestrated as a result to support its war effort against Germany. One and a half million Africans from across the world (from the African continent, the Americas and the Caribbean and elsewhere) were drafted by Britain, France, Belgium and the United States to fight for the anti-German coalition forces during the 1939-1945 war. Essentially, these African forces were conscripts who were deployed to fight the war of their conquerors and occupiers - effectively, *a war that they had no business fighting in.*

Be that as it may, all accounts record the valiant performances of the African descent contingents in the principal theatres of the war: western Europe; the gruesome Far East campaigns against Japan where African casualties ran into scores of thousands; the battles in north-east Africa in 1940/41 which led to the liberation of Ethiopia from the Italian occupation, and finally the preparations leading to the victorious coalition's landings in western Europe in 1944 which was decisive in the subsequent defeat of Germany. Indeed, the role of Felix

---

[29] Quoted in Marshall Frady, 'The Life and Legacy of Malcolm X,' *The Sunday Times Magazine* (London), 14 February 1993, p. 19.
[30] See Basil Davidson, *The Search for Africa* (London: James Currey, 1994), p. 326.

Eboue, the African Guyanese governor of Chad, in providing logistics in west/central Africa for these 1944 operations and his unequivocal support for the Free French Forces even at a time when influential French women and men (including Francoise Mitterand who would later become state president for 14 years) were collaborating with the German occupying forces in France, were crucial in the anti-German coalition successes at this theatre. The total African descent casualties in the war were 900,000 killed and hundreds of thousands others wounded.[31] Besides providing troops, Africa countries, particularly those in the western part of the continent free from any combat activities, also provided the anti-German allies with rear bases and supply lines especially for the north African and west European campaigns. This accounted for the massive expansion of air and sea port facilities in the west African region in 1940-43.

Moreover, the absence of fighting in the region ensured that Britain, which was now the only effective European occupying power in Africa (with the recent fall of France to the Germans), could offset the sharp drop that occurred in the early 1940s in the global production of palm oil, groundnut, tin and rubber due to the Japanese overrun of south-east Asia. It readily stepped up production of these commodities in occupied Nigeria, Gold Coast (Ghana), Sierra Leone and the Gambia. In similar vein, increases of the production of sugar and bananas were embarked upon in British-occupied Caribbean as part of the war effort during the period. But even more spectacularly crucial was British occupied-Africa's direct financial support for London's war effort which was paid to its sterling reserve. This totalled £446 million by the end of the conflict in 1945.[32] Ten years later or just two years prior to the 1957 liberation of Ghana, Africa's contribution to this reserve increased by at least three-fold to £1446 million. This figure represented over one-half of the total sum of British/Commonwealth gold and dollar reserves which was £2120 million.[33] These sterling balances were in fact a 'form of forced saving'[34] to which Britain had decreed that each of its occupied country in Africa and elsewhere must contribute. 'The ... balances were generally invested in long-term British government securities. In other words ... [the occupied states] were lending

---

[31]Herbert Ekwe-Ekwe, 'Africans and the European Wars of the 20th Century,' *African Peoples Review*, July-December 1995, p. 17.
[32]Walter Rodney, *How Europe Underdeveloped Africa* (London: Bogle-L'ouverture, 1972), p. 188.
[33]Ibid.
[34]Bob Fitch and Mary Oppenheimer, *Ghana: End of an Illusion* (New York and London: Monthly Review, 1966), p. 42.

money to ... Britain. Moreover, the interest rates on these securities were extremely low: 0.5 per cent before 1950; from 2 to 4 per cent after 1952.'[35] These balances were not only a crucial resource for Britain to finance its war against Germany (on the eve of the war, the balances stood at £500 million and was over £3000 million at the end of the conflict[36]) but also for the post-war reconstruction of the 1940s/1950s. In response to the British reconstruction programme, its occupied Nigerian government embarked on an intensification of both the country's agricultural and mineral products - especially palm products, cotton, groundnuts, beniseeds, hides and skin, tin ore and columbite.[37] In 1946, the value of Nigerian exports was £23.7 million.[38] By 1955, it was £129.8 million, and in 1960, the year of the so-called restoration of independence, it was £165.5 million.[39] There was a distinct growth in Nigeria's gross domestic product during the period, an annual rate of 4.1 per cent in 1950/51-1957/58.[40] Indeed, not since 1916 had Nigeria enjoyed a favourable net-barter terms of trade with Britain as was recorded in 1951-1955, and 1958-60.[41] But Nigeria was still a British-occupied country, with a political economy that existed solely to serve British conquest interests in Africa. This was underlined by the fact that a huge sum of £276.8 million, the preponderant chunk of the surpluses that accumulated from this unprecedented boom, was transferred to Britain between 1947-1960.[42] This is not to mention British surpluses enjoyed by the corresponding increases in the value of Nigerian imports from mainly Britain at the time: £19.8 million in 1946, £136.1 million in 1955, and £215.9 million in 1960.[43] Besides, Britain's more advantageous trade relations with Nigeria were further consolidated in 1955 when Europe slumped into an economic recession. The prices that Europeans were prepared to pay for imports of agricultural and mineral products from abroad fell considerably, resulting in an instant blow to the Nigerian economy. Even though

---

[35] Ibid., p. 44.
[36] Ibid., p. 42.
[37] See Bade Onimode, *Imperialism and Underdevelopment in Nigeria* (London: Zed Books, 1982), pp. 47-55.
[38] R. Olufemi Ekundare, *An Economic History of Nigeria: 1860-1960* (London: Methuen, 1973), p. 225.
[39] Ibid.
[40] Quoted in Onimode, *Imperialism and Underdevelopment in Nigeria*, p. 48.
[41] Ibid.
[42] Ekundare, *An Economic History of Nigeria*, p. 226.
[43] Ibid.

its export trade that year increased by 7000 tons in volume, the value fell by £17 million.[44] As for Sierra Leone in the 1950s, its very small economy notwithstanding, it made a contribution of £60 million to the British sterling balances.[45] Gold Coast's (Ghana) total was £210 million by 1955, two years prior to its liberation.[46] The latter's transfer was even more significant for Britain because 70 per cent of this sum was in United States dollars which the Gold Coast earned by selling cocoa to the United States.[47] Britain was badly in need of dollars to purchase US capital goods to reconstruct its war-battered industrial enterprises. Besides Malaya, the Gold Coast made the highest contribution to these sterling balances, including their dollar component, during the period.[48] Bob Fitch and Mary Oppenheimer have observed: 'Much [has been] made of the sacrifices made by the British [public] during the period [of post 1939-45 war reconstruction]. *Yet to a large extent it was the Asian and African ... who played the decisive role and experienced the real "austerity"'* (emphasis added).[49]

The 1939-45 essentially intra-European War was undoubtedly the most serious emergency to confront Britain during its 300 years of global dominance. To defeat its implacable German and Japanese foes, Britain comprehensively appropriated and deployed, *as a central corpus of its war strategy*, Africa's human and material resources - the two critical facets of the African historical process which it had seized for its exploitation as a result of its occupation of the continent. The tragedy for Africa, ironically, was that these African resources played a critical role in Britain's eventual victory in 1945 and the post-war programme of socioeconomic reconstruction as we have shown. It would amount to a staggering case of ignorance if Hugh Trevor-Roper, the Regius Professor of History at Oxford University in the post-war years of the 1960s, was not aware of these indelible African features of Britain's war efforts when he launched his anti-Africa slur at his 1963 lecture. He probably was equally ignorant of the role of Africa, again tragic for the continent, in Britain's victory in the earlier intra-European War of the century (1914-18) when

---

[44]Quoted in Okwudiba Nnoli, 'A Short History of Nigerian Underdevelopment,' in Okwudiba Nnoli, ed., *Path to Nigerian Development* (Dakar: Codesria, 1981), p. 124.
[45]Rodney, *How Europe Underdeveloped Africa*, p. 188.
[46]Ibid.
[47]Fitch and Oppenheimer, *Ghana*, p. 44.
[48]Ibid., p. 45.
[49]Ibid.

Africans lost 40,000 soldiers.[50] But Trevor-Roper would have had to stretch his apparent ignorance beyond comprehension, given the prestige of the chair he held at Oxford, if he didn't know of the following data of the African historical process writ large in the decisive emergence of his country as a global power in the early decades of the 1700s. Britain used the huge capital it accumulated during its acquisition of Africans during the devastating holocaust of the age to finance its industrial revolution as we have already indicated. This was the turning point of the development of Western capitalism. Britain's success on this score cannot be over-stressed. This was a country which prior to the mid-17th century was still a 'cultural and scientific backwater,' to borrow the graphic description made by Christopher Hill, the eminent British historian who is an authority on this period of British history.[51] By the beginning of the 18th century, Britain had established virtual world monopoly in the seizure and transportation of millions of Africans from their homeland to the Americas after displacing the Iberian states of Portugal and Spain. It used the enormous resources that accrued to it as a result to finance its burgeoning scientific and technological enterprises. Soon, Britain became the 'centre of world science.'[52] And to underline the sheer size of the wealth Britain was accumulating during the period, Charles Davenant, a late 17th century economist who studied the comparative worth of the African slave in the Caribbean and a worker in England concluded: '[The labour of this slave] is worth six times as much as the labour of an Englishman at home.'[53] Whilst studying the work of African labour in the Guyanese sugar industry in the 1870s, it did not come as a shock to Joseph Beaumont, the British chief justice of Guyana, that it would take two to three days of work by the 'best English laborer' (in England) of the day to complete a day's work done by a typical African plantation worker.[54] 'We have [in England] no excavating work so heavy as trench digging in Demerara [Guyana],' recalled Beaumont, 'and if the reader were to see a stalwart negro ... sweltering under the blazing sun throughout the day ... standing up to his knees and often to his hips in water, not only lifting (or more properly *wrenching*) 4000 to 5000 spits of dense clay ... throwing these twelve or sixteen feet clear on each side - not with a pleasant hammer throwing swing, but delivered straight from the loins at the end of a seven foot shovel... I venture to

---

[50]Ekwe-Ekwe, 'Africans and the European Wars of the 20th Century,' p. 18.
[51]Christopher Hill, 'Lies about crimes,' *The Guardian* (London), 29 May 1989.
[52]Ibid.
[53]Quoted in ibid.
[54]Alan Adamson, *Sugar without Slaves* (New Haven: Yale University, 1972), p. 112.

think he would not only wonder at but *admire* ... the "lazy nigger"'(emphasis in the original).⁵⁵

Basil Davidson, the indefatigable British historian who has studied and published on Africa with greater breadth and clarity than any of his compatriots, has argued that Trevor-Roper's 'denial of African History' was essentially a 'rearguard action ... to provide his [Trevor-Roper's] own version of Hegel's nonsense of 130 years earlier'⁵⁶ during the great 1960s African battle to free itself from European conquest and territorial occupation. For an exasperated observer watching the African liberation movement unfold, Trevor-Roper hardly showed any originality other than repeat the standard line of a number of European World intellectuals in the past (eg Coupland, Egerton, Seligman, Meinhof, Darwin, Wallace, Knox, Pritchard, Marx, Miravale, Hegel, Hume, Lee, Farrar) who were keen to 'deny the existence of African History' as a way of not confronting the relentless European wars of conquest and exploitation of Africa over the ages. Unlike his predecessors however, Trevor-Roper had just witnessed his country emerge victorious from a major war with a formidable adversary who, perchance, could conceivably have been the victor but for the former's internal dogged spirit of resilience *in addition* to those external historical resources which Britain had unrestricted access albeit, ironically, due to *its own* imperialist occupation of these lands. The African component of this unrestricted space of British expropriation was evidently central. If Germany had indeed won that war, Trevor-Roper would surely have had to contend with a new academic dispensation in which German historians and their allied or sympathetic intellectuals would have quickly decreed the 'non-existence of British History' or alternatively strip that History of its defining thrust and character as a means of institutionalising culturally the German take-over or occupation of Britain into an all-embracing Aryan triumphalist academic orthodoxy. Such a development would be in line with the 'principal characteristic, common to every kind of imperialist domination ... [namely] the denial of the historical process of the dominated people,'⁵⁷ as Amilcar Cabral, the influential African theorist on the subject, is keen to stress. But rather than merely engage in the non-taxing gesture of just repeating Hegel & Co. on their racist and utterly unscientific utterances on African History, Trevor-Roper, in 1963, was keen to influence the general perspective and particularly the charting

---

⁵⁵Quoted by Sidney Mintz, 'Descrying the Peasantry,' *Review*, VI, 2, Fall 1982, p. 210.
⁵⁶Davidson, *The Search for Africa*, p. 326.
⁵⁷Amilcar Cabral, *Unity & Struggle* (London: Heinemann Education Books, 1980), p. 141.

of the historiography of the burgeoning 'African Studies' programmes that were then being set up in a number of universities (and other academic institutions) in the West. The establishment of these institutions had arisen in response to the historic developments being played out in the African liberation process. He had acknowledged in his lecture that British undergraduates were already demanding such 'Studies' but he insisted: 'Perhaps in the future, there will be some African history to teach. But at present there is none; there is only the history of Europeans in Africa.'[58] Forty years on, the scholarship so described as 'African Studies' in the West and the standard format of Western media reporting on African peoples and events affecting them have by and large remained faithful to Trevor-Roper's injunction.

Understandably, this is against the backdrop of the Western World's cultural history's steadfastness to continue to manufacture and market across the globe that 'Africa That Never Was'[59] - to borrow from the apt title of Dorothy Hammond and Atla Jablow's classic. It has been a way of barricading the West from history's judgement and sentence for its crimes in Africa. Almost 30 years to the day after Trevor-Roper's proclamation, the Western reading public (first, in Sweden where it was initially published) was therefore shocked by Sven Lindqvist's book, *'Exterminate All the Brutes'*. Lindqvist, the intrepid Swedish writer and traveller could not have been more successful in his designated task as the notes on the book's dust jacket states: '"*Exterminate All the Brutes*" confronts the roots of European genocide: "the truth that we prefer to forget."' In a painstaking and penetratingly graphic survey, Lindqvist examines one towering authority after another in that much revered pantheon of European World science and philosophy and shows how each of these, over the ages, contributed their thoughts, knowledge and beliefs towards the European *sociopolitical and military obsession* to exterminate Africans and other members of the human race whose homes or lands or countries or continents or resources Europeans craved to seize, as part of their global conquest. All that these European genocidists, or champions of genocide, needed to do to authorise or rationalise such deeds was to decree that a targeted people or targeted peoples were an 'inferior race,' 'savages,' or, alternatively, simply 'brutes'.

Herbert Spencer, the English philosopher writing in the 1850s, recalls Lindqvist, saw the European conquest of the world that had been on-going for 300 years as the 'forces which are working out the great scheme of perfect

---

[58] Quoted in *West Africa* (London), 23-29 January 1989, p. 116.
[59] See Dorothy Hammond and Atla Jablow, *The Africa That Never Was: Four Centuries of British Writing About Africa* (New York: Twayne Publishers, 1970).

happiness, taking no account of incidental suffering, exterminat[ing] such sections of [hu]mankind as stand in their way... *Be he human or be he brute - the hindrance must be got rid of* (emphasis added).[60] Arguing in the second volume of his *Philosophy of the Unconscious*, Eduard von Hartmann, the German philosopher, could not have agreed more with Spencer: 'As little as a favor is done the dog whose tail is to be cut off, when one cuts it off gradually inch by inch, so little is their humanity in artificially prolonging the death struggles of savages who are on the verge of extinction ... The true philanthropist, if he has comprehended the natural law of anthropological evolution, cannot avoid desiring an acceleration of the last convulsion, and labor for that end.'[61] Even though he originally began his research into natural history by questioning the hierarchisation of the species which some scholars of his day were beginning to 'theorise upon' or construct, Georges Cuvier, the French zoologist, ended up doing just that in his 16-volume work, *The Animal Kingdom*. Here, he classified human beings into three races, describing the African category as the 'hordes belonging to this variant of human being [who] have always remained in a state of total barbarism.'[62] Cuvier's conclusions already had an echo from the past. Writing almost a century earlier in *The Scale of Creatures*, William Petty had stressed that there 'seem to be several species even in human beings ... I say that the Europeans do not only differ from... Africans in colour ... but also ... in natural manners and in the internal qualities of their minds.'[63] Charles White, an English doctor and a contemporary of Cuvier's pursued the same theme in his *An Account of the Regular Graduations in Man*, published in 1799, and 'prove[d]' that the European was 'superior' to other races: 'Where shall we find unless in the European that nobly arched head, containing such a quantity of brain ...?'[64] Charles Lyell, the 19th century British geologist, returned to the question of the 'extinction' of 'lower-order' species in his *Principles of Geology*. In a study focused apparently on the 'evolutionary process' evidenced in geological phenomena, Lyell was clearly rationalising the European global conquest story so far: 'Extinct species ... have gone under in the same way, through slow changes of life: floods and droughts, diminishing

---

[60]Herbert Spencer, *Social Statics* (1850), p. 416, quoted in Lindqvist, *'Exterminate All the Brutes'*, p. 8.
[61]Eduard von Hartmann, *Philosophy of the Unconscious*, Vol. 2, p. 12, quoted in Lindqvist, *'Exterminate All the Brutes'*, p. 9.
[62]Quoted in Lindqvist, *'Exterminate All the Brute'*, p. 99.
[63]Quoted in ibid., p. 100.
[64]Quoted in ibid.

access to food, the spread of competing species. The empty places have been filled by the immigration of species adapted to the changed circumstances.'[65]

'Empty space,' 'filled by,' 'immigration of species' and the like would hence become haunting, emotive, euphemisms with which European propagandists would bandy about in the literature, lecture and seminar rooms in a continuing effort to ensure that Europe's wanton destruction of peoples across the world during 500 years of global conquest receives the most minimal scrutiny from the rest of humanity. Fervently pursued simultaneously, these propaganda projects would also step up the rationalisation of the crimes committed, couched in bogus scientific treatise as our examples above attest. Indeed, Charles Darwin, the most influential scholar of the British evolution school would join in the propagation of this treatise. Such was Darwin's admiration for Charles Lyell's *Principles* that, according to Lindqvist,[66] the former took a copy of the book with him during his journey to the south Pacific in 1834. Darwin later wrote to Lyell and informed him that the latter's crucial conclusions on his geological studies were equally applicable to humans, for according to Darwin, 'the less intellectual races [were] being exterminated.'[67] Darwin soon elaborated further on this position in his book, *The Descent of Man* (1871), where he argued: 'At some future period not very distant as measured in centuries, the civilised races of man will almost certainly exterminate and replace throughout the world the savage races.'[68]

This was however hardly an original point to conclude on in this game of leading European thinkers defending mass murders and murderers of human beings as Darwin's most admired teacher, Charles Lyell, had reached a similar conclusion 30 years earlier in his *Principles* in a chapter chillily entitled, 'Extirpation of Species by Man': '[If] the most insignificant and diminutive species ... have each slaughtered their thousands, why should not we, the lords of creation, do the same?'[69] Lyell's contemporary at the time, the anthropologist J. C. Prichard had followed on the same theme of 'extermination' in his widely publicised 1838 lecture which was equally chillily captioned as the above but this time even more focused on humans - 'On the Extermination of Human Races'. Here, Prichard contended that those in the world whom Europeans had

---

[65] Sven Lindqvist's paraphrase of Lyell's conclusions in *Principles of Geology*, quoted from Lindqvist, *'Exterminate All the Brutes'*, p. 103.
[66] Lindqvist, *'Exterminate All the Brutes'*, p. 104.
[67] Ibid., p. 107.
[68] Ibid.
[69] Ibid.

bracketed off as 'savage races' would be destroyed: 'the white is destined to extirpate the savage.'[70] Nothing could be done to save the latter! '[I]nstead,' Prichard urged his audience, made up of scientists and scholars from other disciplines, '[we should] collect in the interests of science as much information as possible on their physical and moral characteristics.'[71] Finally, to underline the ultimate strategic objective of Europe in its quest for Africa, it is important to unmask the masquerade of rationalisations that informs, so cogently, the expressed thoughts and reflections made by its various scholars cited so far on their chosen subject - 'the extinction or extermination of Africans'. W. Winwood Reade, a member of both the Anthropological Society and Geographical Society in London and a corresponding member of the Paris Geological Society provides this in a book on Africa published in 1864 where he warns that 'we must learn to look at this result with composure. It illustrates the beneficent law of nature, that the weak must be devoured by the strong':[72]

> Africa will be shared between England and France ... Under the European rule, the Africans will dig the ditches and water the deserts. It will be hard work, and the Africans themselves will probably become extinct.[73]

In 1899, Jules Meline, the then French agriculture minister, had no doubts about how to begin to implement Reade's reading of the African 'Final Solution' in French-occupied Africa. He warned that France's agro-industrial policy in the conquered territories was geared to stamping out any forms of development in African agriculture and industry that encouraged African independence.[74] Instead, Meline insisted, Africa would 'fulfil by force if necessary, their *natural function*, that of a market reserved by right to [French] industry' (emphasis added).[75]

---

[70]Quoted in ibid., p. 123.
[71]Ibid.
[72]Quoted in ibid., p. 131.
[73]Lindqvist's paraphrase from the original text, quoted in *'Exterminate All the Brutes'*, ibid.
[74]See Femi Fani-Kayode, 'The Nigerian Question,' *The Guardian On Sunday* (Lagos), 21 September 1997, p. 7.
[75]Ibid.

Just genocide

Alas, millions of people in Africa, Asia, Australasia, the Pacific, the Caribbean and the Americas were indeed killed, or, to use the term that so captivated the sensibilities of the array of genocidists profiled above, *exterminated* by Europeans as the latter marched across the globe looting, destroying, occupying and controlling. But contrary to the pretentious musings of these genocidists in London, Edinburgh, Paris, or Berlin, the millions of exterminated Africans, Asians, Pacific islanders and others *did not* die due to some 'natural law' of the 'inevitability' of the 'weak [being] devoured by the strong.' There was nothing *intrinsically inevitable* in the conception, the process, or the outcome of the European conquest of the world. Despite its success, there wasn't anything immanent in the European biological constitution to have guaranteed the outcome of that aggression as the genocidists would wish to claim in their varying treatises. Indeed, Darwin and Co. were at best mischievous journalists who knew, *through their very privileged position in their societies*, that their compatriots in varying works of life (slavers, soldiers, sailors, miners, traders, buccaneers, desperadoes) were carrying out mass murders and pillage across the globe but they were not prepared to report the truth. This was because they were primarily concerned about the effect that a successful outcome of the campaign would have on the position of Europe and the European in the world subsequently - namely, that of global domination. Whilst Darwin and Co. knew that these massacres were unprecedented in human history, they instead chose to rationalise the crimes in the most unscientific ruminations couched under the rubric of 'inevitability'. Theirs was nothing but scientism writ large. As activist propagators of genocide, Darwin and Co. should be recognised for their role in constructing the mask of legitimacy, if not respectability, for the most heinous crimes that have shaped the contemporary world as we know it. If Darwin and Co. were to extend the rationalisation of their ruminations on genocide to include those Europeans in east and central Europe of the 1930s/1940s who would experience at the hand of fellow Europeans, albeit to a more limited extent, what Africans for instance had been subjected to by Europeans for 500 years, they would surely not command the sort of prestige that they continue to enjoy in the intellectual heritage of the European World. Yet their successors who, from the 1890s, went on to 'theorise' on the European-based genocide just referred to, and whose reflections on the subject are an undisguised copy of the former, are reviled and completely discredited by this heritage as the discourses of the latter half of the century have shown. It remains the case though that the contemporary world's sense of justice will continue to be taxed if it is not recognised, in this context, that 'Auschwitz was the modern industrial application of a policy of extermination on which European world domination had long rested.'[76] The European World is therefore mistaken if it thinks that it would have completed its sentence of retribution from the rest of humanity's tribune of justice for its crimes of these past 500 years by merely limiting and concentrating its intellectual and material recompense on the legacy of the Jewish holocaust of the 1930s/1940s as the world has witnessed in the past 50 years. To fully extirpate the ever haunting demons of this epoch of history, the European World will find that it has no other choice but to confront boldly and dispassionately the African holocaust and the holocausts of the indigenous peoples of the Americas and Australasia. The latter constitute the *foundational holocausts* perpetrated by Europe earlier on in the course of the last millennium which indeed made the subsequent Jewish holocaust possible. This confrontation with what happened in Africa and elsewhere is singularly the most important task facing the political and intellectual leadership of the European World in this new millennium.

Some empirical overview of the European global conquest is thus necessary to reinforce some of the issues just raised. The tangata whenua, or the Maori, the indigenous people of New Zealand who presently make up about 10 per cent of a population of 3.5 million, were once the majority people of their islands. Within a century of the invasion of New Zealand, the British had wiped out most of the Maori through direct extermination campaigns organised by occupying troops or other marauding bands of colonists or just singular acts of individuals who turned the massacres into forms of sport, and through the introduction of hitherto unknown diseases in the country such as tuberculosis, diphtheria and measles.[77] Such was the British confidence in the outcome of these extermination campaigns in 1864 that it was openly 'predicted' during an important Anthropological Society conference in London (unabashedly entitled 'The Extinction of the Lower Races') that the Maori would eventually suffer a similar fate of extinction which another conquering band of Britons had earlier carried out on the Tasmanians,[78] just across the Pacific waters nearby. The fact that there are still Maori people in New Zealand, in the world, is an extraordinary feat of human survival. The same conclusion must also extend to

---

[76]Lindqvist, *'Exterminate All the Brutes'*, p. 160.
[77]Lorna Dyall, 'The tangata whenua: Maori people and their health,' *Radical Community Medicine*, No. 28, Winter 1986/7, p. 8.
[78]Lindqvist, *'Exterminate All the Brutes'*, pp. 118-119 and p. 131.

the indigenous population of Australia who had the earth's most enduring uninterrupted civilisation, with a culture that existed for at least 50,000 years[79] in the world's largest island before the cataclysmic outcome of the 18th century British invasion. The British wiped out 80 per cent of this population within 150 years of its occupation of Australia. They achieved this through direct military and paramilitary campaigns, policies of land seizures and starvation, and just as was the case in New Zealand, they also introduced new diseases such as syphilis, tuberculosis, small pox and the common cold which destroyed hundreds of thousands of the people.[80]

Across the Pacific from Australasia to the Americas, the devastation wrought by the European global conquest was equally staggering. In 1581, about a century after the European invasion of that part of the world had begun, King Philip II of Spain confirmed, whilst addressing a provincial advisory body in his country, that about 35 per cent of South America's indigenous population had already been wiped out by both Spanish and Portuguese colonists.[81] Soon, the Dutch, the British, the French and other Europeans would join their Iberian cousins in mapping out chosen sectors in these vast continental killing fields, particularly to the north (what would later be called north America), to perpetrate their own versions of extermination and territorial seizure. In another 50 years, only 3.5 million of this population had survived the genocide.[82] This was out of about 100 million at the outset of the invasion,[83] ensuring that the grand total of the people exterminated was a haunting 97 per cent of the original. The immediate impact of the European seizure of the Americas on Europe's economy back home was unprecedentedly overwhelming. An observer has argued:

> Latin American silver and gold ... penetrated like a corrosive acid through all the pores of Europe's moribund feudal society, and for the benefit of nascent mercantilist capitalism turned [survivors of the indigenous population] and [African] slaves into a teeming [labour

---

[79]Robyn Holder and John Holliday, '"People been dying today": The politics of Aboriginal health in Australia,' *Radical Community Medicine*, No. 28, Winter 1986/7, p. 35.
[80]Ibid.
[81]Eduardo Galeano, *Open Veins of Latin America: Five Centuries of the Pillage of a Continent* (London and New York: Monthly Review, 1973), p. 49.
[82]Ibid., p. 50.
[83]Ronald Wright, *Stolen Continents* (London: Pimlico, 1993), p. 4.

force] of the European economy ... The [occupied] Latin American economy enjoyed the most highly concentrated labor force known until that time, *making possible the greatest concentration of wealth ever enjoyed* by any civilization in world history (emphasis added).[84]

The teeming African labour mentioned in the above quote was of course Africa's initial link to the European global network of genocide that we have so far sketched.[85] Whilst the Americas and Australasia would appear to be the archetypes of the success story of this extermination project on peoples who several of Europe's leading 17th-19th century scholars so loathsomely categorised as 'lower races,' Africa's position on the genocide league table is more slippery to quantify precisely. Indeed by losing at least 150 million people (or 50 per cent of its population) in the holocaust, Africa's total casualty figure including those who died during the overland journey to slave ships and the sea transportation to the Americas was higher than the combined tally of the dead in the Americas and Australasia. But unlike the latter continents, Africa was significantly more successful in its resistance against the European aggression. In juridico-political terms, even if still nominal in certain critical sites and spheres, Africa has recovered all its lands from the aggression that began 500 years ago. This is despite the desperate and quite often staunch attempts made by Europe during the period, especially in the last 40 years, to carve out such 'strategic' parts of Africa as Guinea Bissau, Cape Verde, São Tomé and Principé, Angola, Namibia, South Africa, Zimbabwe, Mozambique and Kenya for the perpetual occupation by European transfer settlers in similar vein to what it did in the Americas and Australasia. Thus, thanks to the valiancy and resilience of Africans both at home and in the diaspora, the African resistance success score board today illuminates with the extraordinary result that makes nonsense of the premise, assumptions and conclusions of the 'high brow' genocidists of the European academy. Seen in this context therefore, Africa's survival of the holocaust places it at a unique position on the league table mentioned earlier.

Equally important in another historical context, this result demonstrates clearly that Africans had learnt a crucial lesson from the outcome of the previous 'season'[86] of foreign aggression on their territory - namely, that an

---

[84]See Galeano, *Open Veins of Latin America*, p. 49.
[85]Cf. John Wills, *1688: A Global History* (London: Granta, 2001).
[86]For the three distinct 'seasons' or epochs of foreign aggression in Africa, see Chinweizu, *Decolonising the African Mind* (Lagos: Pero, 1987), pp. 109-135.

aggressor, irrespective of the time frame of their occupation of society, should be continuously harried by the political and military forces of the resistance until they are forced out of the country. During the course of that aggression carried out by a rampaging Arab/muslim army which attacked the continent from across Arabia in the north east during the 7th century AD (seizing the great African civilisation of Egypt and expanding its initial territorial gain to the north-west Atlantic coast board - the so-called Maghrib), Africa lost one-third of its territory which the Arabs still occupy to this present day. Essentially, this occupation has continued, thanks to the tapering off of the African resistance, and the dispersal of millions of survivors to the neighbouring regions of central, eastern and western Africa. Soon, the Arab/muslims converted their north African occupation and their later cultural hegemony in Sahelian west Africa into a profitable conurbation for the enslavement and export of Africans as slaves, as well as other resources such as gold particularly to the Arab World, Asia and southern Europe. At the height of the occupation, the Arab/muslims exported two million Africans per annum as slaves to the Arab World.[87] They extensively depleted the gold reserves in the Sudan, Mali, Songhai, Kanem-Bornu and elsewhere which were transferred to enrich the bourses and palaces of the Arab World. Considering the magnitude of this export of African resources at the time, it is significant that the Arabs have a saying: 'Against the camel's mange use a tar, and against poverty make a trip to the Sudan.'[88] The role of the Arab World itself in the re-export of the slaves in its territory to southern Europe (in addition to the Near-East and south-west Asia) during the period - a practice which dramatically doubled and in some cases tripled the value of the slaves - was such that in Naples, for example, 83 per cent of the slaves there by the 15th century were Africans.[89] And, contrary to 'conventional' wisdom, African slaves worked Arab/muslim sugar plantations in Morocco as early as the 9th century, almost 600 years before the Americas! Morocco itself would later on in 1593 attack, pillage, and seize prominent towns of Songhai, leading ultimately in its wake to the collapse of the Songhai state, ironically the most islamised of the Sahelian west African states. Parallel to these events in west Africa, Arab/muslim expansionism in east Africa, subsequent to the initial 7th century invasion of the north, soon spread along the Somali, Kenyan and Mozambican coastline, and their occupation of the off-shore island of Zanzibar which they later transformed into a strategic slave

---

[87]Ibid., 129.
[88]Quoted in Diop, *Precolonial Black Africa*, p. 136.
[89]Chinweizu, *Decolonising the African Mind*, p. 129.

colony.

In a surprisingly uncritical contribution to this facet of African history, Ngugi wa Thiong'o, the distinguished African novelist, notes: 'The ties of geography are easier to see ... The Indian Ocean anyway has never been a barrier and for centuries East Africa peacefully traded with ... Arabia before the arrival of the Portuguese who turned this creative trade into a traffic of destroyed cities, cultures and human beings for a little silver to fatten the coffers of bourgeois Europe.'[90] On the contrary. From the above-mentioned coastal bridgeheads of east Africa, the Arab/muslims began to exert enormous influence into the affairs of the existing independent states and principalities of the African hinterland - in east, east-central, central and southern Africa. In the latter two regions, as were the cases in north and western Africa, they pursued a scorched earth programme of brigandage, murders and the enslavement and export of millions of African peoples to the Arab World and elsewhere - a practice that actively went on well into the 16th century when *it*, in turn, was enveloped by the burgeoning European eventual take-over of Africa. Vusamazulu Credo Mutwa, the Zulu historian, recalls the aftermath of the Arab slaving of southern Africa most graphically: 'no less than a hundred [nations and nationalities] were wiped out completely [during the period] in Tanganyika, Kenya, the Congo basin and [Zambia].'[91] The Arab aggression was couched in the language of racist bigotry and underlying africophobism that hauntingly prefigures Europe's own rationalising efforts a few centuries later: 'You *Kafurs* are not people. It is the will of Allah and the Prophet that we catch you and sell you, for you are not people ... you have no souls. Allah gave you to us for servants.'[92] Finally, in east-central Africa in the early 1550s, the Arab/muslims dealt a further blow to Africa's independence. They overran the three successor states of Nubia, essentially the surviving bastions of Africa's ancient Nile valley civilisations, thus extending their territorial stranglehold on the Nile further south to the river's strategic middle stretches. In the end, Africans escaped the blanket *Americanisation* or *Australasianisation* of their destiny by the Arab conquest, 800 years before the Europeans achieved this goal elsewhere in the world as we have shown. This was because Africans were continuously re-grouping and re-defining the future trajectory of their defence, existence, and

---

[90]Ngugi wa Thiong'o, *Writers in Politics* (London: Heinemann Educational Books, 1981), p. 102.
[91]Chinweizu, *Decolonising the African Mind*, p. 129.
[92]Vusamazulu Credo Mutwa, 'The Rout of the Arabi,' in Chinweizu, *Voices from Twentieth-Century Africa* (London & Boston: Faber and Faber, 1988), p. 13.

development by utilising the flexibility occasioned by the sheer size of their (continental) homeland. Furthermore, they were successful in interweaving the arterial cultural fibre that bound their peoples.[93] This was in order to cope with the inevitable social stresses in regions that had become destinations for the migratory shifts of population leaving any territories lost or severely threatened by the Arab/muslim emergency. Even then, the partial success of the Arab *Americanisation* of Africa, albeit in the north of the continent, was a sufficiently timely warning to Africans; they required both eternal vigilance and a totally different mode of resistance to foreign aggression in future, if they were to avoid the possibility of complete expulsion from their homeland or a distinct marginalisation therein. Precisely because the Arab/muslim aggression on Africa *paved the way* for Europe's later attack, underlining the very double-jeopardy character of the African holocaust, it is evident that a key lesson that Africans learnt from the former was crucial in enabling them to organise the permanent but flexible resistance that eventually led to the termination of Europe's occupation when it arose.

As we indicated above, Africa's position on the genocide league table of the global European conquest was unique. This was principally because unlike peoples in the Americas and Australasia, Africans invariably survived the holocaust despite the universally-known documented cataclysmic prognosis of the European genocidist scholars who specialised on the subject. For Africa, it was this outcome that placed into a sharper focus the validity of that historic observation made by Malcolm X which we cited earlier: 'Every time [the European] sees [the African] face, he [or she] sees a mirror of [their] crime and [their] guilt conscience can't bear to face it.' Moreover, it was in Africa, not the Americas nor Australasia, that those Europeans who would later extend this trail of the killing fields of the age into the heart of Europe itself during the 1930s/1940s first staged their extermination enterprise as we now elaborate.

As a nation-state that only came into being in the 19th century, Germany was a late comer to the pan-European global conquest. Yet, significant sectors of the population of German-speaking people, whether as Christians, Jews, agnostics, Prussians, Saxons or natives or citizens from the other princely states that would amalgamate into the union, were actively involved in the 300-year conquest.[94] Particularly, they were engaged directly in the enslavement of

---

[93]Cheikh Anta Diop, *The Cultural Unity of Black Africa* (London: Karnak House, 1989), especially chapters 3 and 6.
[94]See Paulette Reed-Anderson, *Rewriting the Footnotes* (Berlin: Die Ausländerbeauftragte des Berliner Senats, 2000).

Africans by sending evacuation ships to Africa,[95] and also in providing some of the financing for the holocaust especially involving other states and interests. This was in the form of direct capital, including the underwriting of insurance covering slave ships and crew. In the first half of the 18th century, the port of Hamburg was the largest European sugar-refining centre. Significantly, it imported most of its required raw sugar from Britain and France - products that initially originated from these two states' slave plantations in the Caribbean. On completion, Hamburg's highly prized refined sugar was exported back to England and France as well as other countries across Europe.[96] Finally, it should be recalled that Germans were an important source for the millions of Europeans who would emigrate to the conquered territories overseas, especially in the Americas, and who of course readily offered their services to genocidal campaigns against the local populations.

Not long after its emergence as an amalgamated state in 1871, Germany wasted little time in demanding its own *national* share of the globe's lands, two-thirds of which its European neighbours had then conquered after nearly four centuries of expansion (see below). Thanks to the European conqueror-states' conference on Africa which was held in Berlin in 1884-85 and chaired by Otto von Bismarck, the very enthusiastic German chancellor on the subject at stake, Germany's seizure of six African states (Namibia, Tanganyika, Rwanda, Burundi, Cameroon, Togo) was confirmed and recognised by the other victors. Hence, Germany joined Britain, France, Portugal, Belgium, Italy and Spain in creating and turning its own patch of occupied Africa into a 'veritable hells-on-earth'[97] where the very essence of the human rights of Africans was violated with impunity by the imperial regime either through carefully thought-out policies, or just routinely as a feature dictated by the circumstances of the conquest. Germany adapted or re-created on the local African scene (whether in Namibia, Tanganyika or elsewhere) the prototypes of the limitless strands of the degradation of the African humanity that the rest of the European imperial states had operated on a grand scale elsewhere in Africa or in the mines and plantations of the Americas during the course of the previous 400 years. Right

---

[95] Ibid., pp. 8, 10, 12.
[96] Rodney, *How Europe Underdeveloped Africa*, p. 96.
[97] An apt phrase by J. Stengers, 'The Congo Free State and Belgium Congo before 1914,' quoted in Immanuel Wallerstein, 'The Three Stages of African Involvement in the World-Economy,' in Peter Gutkind and Immanuel Wallerstein, ed., *The Political Economy of Contemporary Africa* (California and London: Sage Publications, 1976), p. 42.

from the outset, Germany was determined not to be outmatched by the sheer virulence of the other cases of the European occupation which Africans had been confronting in the southern (British, Portuguese, the Boers), eastern (British), central (Belgian, French, British), and western (British, French, Portuguese, Spanish) parts of the continent. Soon, German officials in Africa were openly boasting about their unrelenting brutality against resisting African populations. In a book published in 1891 with a title and revelations which were even sensational for the times,[98] Karl Peters, the head of the German occupation administration in east Africa, gave haunting descriptive details of some of the massacres which his army carried out in the region:

> I shall show the Vagogo what the Germans are! Plunder the villages, throw fire into the houses, and smash everything that will not burn ... At about three, I marched further south toward the other villages ... [T]orches were thrown into the houses, and axes worked to destroy all that the fire did not achieve. So by half past four, twelve villages had been burned down ... My gun had become so hot from so much firing I could hardly hold it.[99]

The mass murders of Africans that Peters and his army committed during their campaigns were 'considered quite natural'[100] by the German authorities back home. Across the region to south west Africa, the Germans equally 'show[ed]' the Nama, Herero and Berg Damara peoples 'what the Germans are!' In the early years of the new century, Germany perpetrated ghastly pogroms within these three populations, the severity of which it would repeat in central Europe 40 years later. Whilst the European World has determined to keep the knowledge of the nature, extent, and consequences of the latter massacres deeply embedded in both its intellectual and popular consciousness, it has deliberately wished to ignore the former's existence and importance in contemporary global history for particularly two reasons: (1) The Namibian massacres typify other pan-European outrages during the world-wide campaign for territorial seizure. (2) The Namibian genocide, unlike other European-organised massacres in the Southern World during the 400 years period, is the one that has a *direct link* to the German massacres of Jews and other Europeans

---

[98]Entitled *New Light on Dark Africa* and quoted in Lindqvist, *'Exterminate All the Brutes'*, p. 50.
[99]Lindqvist, *'Exterminate All the Brutes'*, pp. 50-51.
[100]Ibid., p. 51.

in central Europe in the 1930s/1940s. Besides the commonality of the nationality of the perpetrators, the arguments rationalising both deeds by German genocidist scholars and other officials are amazingly not dissimilar. Indeed Adolf Hitler and other sympathetic German opinion on the central European pogroms were captivated by the literature and knowledge of how their compatriots in Africa had 'show[n]' the peoples they had conquered about half a century earlier 'what Germans are!'

Alas, an examination of the October 1904 proclamation issued by Lother von Trotha, the general officer commanding the German military forces in Namibia, aimed at breaking the continuing pertinacious and heroic resistance of the Herero people against the German occupation, takes us back again to confront that dreadful word so adored by the genocidist scholars of the European academy - 'extermination'. Von Trotha, who had earlier served in the German military campaign against the Wahehe people in east Africa, captioned his edict to German troops about to embark on another effort to suppress the Herero, 'Extermination Order'.[101] There was no ambiguity in its objective. The Herero people had the option of either been expelled from their own country into the wastes of the Omaheke desert or they would be destroyed by the German military:

> The Herero people will have to leave the country. Otherwise I shall force them to do so by means of guns... [E]very Herero, whether found armed or unarmed, with or without cattle, will be shot. I shall not accept any more women and children. I shall drive them back to their people - otherwise I shall order shots to be fired at them. These are my orders to the Herero people.[102]

The outcome of Thotha's campaign was horrendous. No sectors of the Herero population, nor indeed those of the other nations in the region such as the Nama and the Berg Damara escaped the resultant genocide as the following statistics from Germany's own 1911 census figures for the area show.[103] In that year, there were 15,130 Herero, compared with a population figure of 80,000 in 1904, indicating that at least 80 per cent were destroyed in the holocaust. For the Nama, their population in 1911 was 9,781 people compared with 20,000 in

---

[101] See Horst Drechsler, *'Let Us Die Fighting': The Struggle of the Herero and Nama against German Imperialism* (1884-1915) (London: Zed, 1980), p. 156.
[102] Ibid., pp. 156-57.
[103] Ibid., p. 214.

1904, recording a 51 per cent German annihilation score. There were no detailed, broken down, figures for the Berg Damara, but the Germans reckoned that about 30 per cent of them were killed in the pogrom. In another move that would have a direct bearing on a crucial sphere of German war policy in east and central Europe in just another 25–30 years, von Thotha set up what his records termed, quite non-fortuitously, 'concentration camps' for those who survived the initial massacres. In these death camps between 1904 and 1907, 45 per cent of both Herero and Nama internees were killed.[104] In a set of decrees enacted by Thotha in 1907, Africans were barred permanently from owning land and cattle in the country and were expected to carry a pass from the age of seven. Finally, it should be pointed out that by using the term 'concentration camps' to describe the death reserves that Thotha had sent survivors of the Namibian genocide, the German commander was incidentally *Teutonising* into operation, a counter insurgency occupation terminology which Spain had invented and used widely in Cuba in the 1890s; which was copied by the United States in its own suppression of indigenous peoples of the country, and which was utilised by the British in their own expansionist wars in Southern Africa later on in that century and at the onset of the new one.[105]

German genocidist scholars and commentators were ecstatic in heralding the imperialist fortunes of their country from its African exploits, coming so soon after the emergence of the German state.[106] Alexander Tille, an avid student of British ideology on imperial conquest had synthesised the 'extermination' arguments proffered by Spencer and Darwin with the so-called 'superman morality' ideas of Friedrich Nietzsche, the German philosopher, to champion the 'validity' of imperialist aggression by those he described as the 'stronger race' against the 'lower race'. In a study published in 1893, Tille was emphatic about his position: 'All historical rights are invalid against the rights of the stronger... [For it is] the right of the stronger race to annihilate the lower... [W]hen that race does not maintain its ability to resist then it has no right to exist, for anyone who cannot maintain himself must be content to go under.'[107]

Friedrich Ratzel was even more robust about his views than Tille and he was profoundly influential in shaping Germany's conquest policies later. Ratzel, a geo-zoologist who had in the past been very critical of the European-organised conquest across the world, became a founding member of the Pan-German

---

[104]Ibid., p. 213.
[105]Lindqvist, *'Exterminate All the Brutes'*, p. 150.
[106]See Drechsler, *'Let Us Die Fighting'*, pp. 7-9.
[107]Quoted in Lindqvist, *'Exterminate All the Brutes'*, p. 148.

League, a pro-German expansionist organisation, and published a revisionist book in 1897[108] in which he accepted the cardinal argument of the rest of the European genocidists - namely, that the destruction of those in the world that they had tagged 'lower races' was 'inevitable'. What was also of importance in Ratzel's new publication, especially for the future political developments in Europe, was that he included Jews and Romanies in his typology of 'lower races' who were 'condemned to annihilation.' Just as his counterparts elsewhere had to *deny the historical heritage and achievements* of their targeted victims (Africans, Australasians, peoples in the Americas) in order to rationalise the 'inevitability of their extermination,' Ratzel was keen to dismiss the evident contributions that Jews had made in German and other European societies, parts of which accounted for the usually populist sentiments expressed in the country that '[Jewish] position in German cultural life was far too dominating.'[109] For Ratzel, Jews and Romanies were 'scattered people with no land,'[110] a label which essentially disenfranchised them in Germany, with the horrendous consequences implied. Aware that there were then few parts of the world outside Europe that the varying European imperialist states were still to seize as theirs (a pointer to what Germany felt had placed them at a 'disadvantage,' given their late entry in the conquest bid), Ratzel argued that Germany would have to consider the conquest of territories in Europe *itself* if it felt that it required land for the expansion of its populations or for resources necessary for its growing industry. He concluded: 'Border colonization is also colonization. Occupations near at hand are more easily defended and assimilated than distant ones. Russia's spread into Siberia and Central Asia is the most important example of this type of colonization.'[111] Ratzel, in effect, developed the 'theoretical' outlook of *Lebensraum* (taken from *Der Lebensraum*, the title of his book on the subject published in 1904) or 'living space' which would be an important plank of Germany's expansionist policy in central and eastern Europe in the 1930s/40s under Adolf Hitler. Indeed whilst the latter in 1924 was writing *Mein Kampf*, his political treatise for what he envisaged was the future of Germany, he had access to Ratzel's copious studies on the extermination of peoples and imperialist expansionism ... It was now becoming apparent that 400 years after it had begun, the chickens of the European expansionist march across the world had, *at last*, come home to roost. As Sven Lindqvist has

---

[108]Ibid., p. 145.
[109]Ibid.
[110]Ibid.
[111]Ibid., p. 146.

succinctly concluded in the quote we earlier referred to, 'Auschwitz was the modern industrial application of a policy of extermination on which European world domination had long since rested.'[112]

A summary of this global control should now be made. By 1800, about 300 years after the conquest began, Europe laid claim to 55 per cent of the world's total territorial land space.[113] The significance of this claim is crucial because on the eve of the outset of the conquest, Europe was a little less than 35 per cent of the earth's lands[114] even though it had both the world's highest population density and its fastest growing people. By 1878, Europe had conquered 67 per cent of the globe's lands[115] and by 1914 (at the outbreak of the imminent five years' major war of its principal powers), it had extended its aggression to cover the occupation of 85 per cent of the world's territory.[116] Significantly, the progress of Europe's global conquest coincided broadly with the extraordinary increase in its population. Between 1650 and 1850, Europe's population increased from 103 million to 274 million.[117] What was however staggering was that during the subsequent 50 years, i.e. between 1850-1900, Europe's population increased from 274 million to 423 million[118] - an increase of 70 per cent! Global conquest had now enabled Europeans, for the first time in their history, to create a vast territorial 'outlet' for its 'surplus' human beings who many a continental philosopher or statesperson would not fail to acknowledge had lived a life that was 'poor, nasty, brutish, and short.' Cecil Rhodes, one of the leading conquerors of southern Africa, recalls, with historic significance, the outcome of a rally of the unemployed he attended in London in 1895:

> I was in the East End of London ... yesterday and attended a meeting of the unemployed. I listened to the wild speeches, which were just a cry for 'bread! bread!' and on my way home I pondered over the scene and I became more than ever convinced of the importance of imperialism ... My cherished idea is a solution for the social problem, i.e., in order to save the 40,000,000 inhabitants of the United kingdom from a bloody

---

[112]Ibid., p. 160.

[113]Harry Magdoff, *Imperialism: From the Colonial Age to the Present* (New York and London: Monthly Review, 1978), p. 29.

[114]Ibid.

[115]Ibid.

[116]Ibid., p. 35.

[117]Rodney, *How Europe Underdeveloped Africa*, p. 106.

[118]Ibid.

civil war, we colonial statesmen *must acquire new lands to settle the surplus population, to provide new markets for the goods produced in the factories and mines.* The Empire, as I have always said, is a *bread and butter question. If you want to avoid civil war, you must become* imperialists (added emphasis).[119]

Suddenly, the spoils of empire provided people in Europe, especially the unemployed and unemployable and those millions perpetually bonded to a callous aristocracy and proto-bourgeoisie with an incredible advancement in their standard of living. This also *included* the option of emigrating to any of the innumerable selection of countries and principalities across the world - from the Americas in the western hemisphere, through most of Africa and Asia, and into Australasia that made up this vast inheritance of conquest. Indeed between 1820 and 1920, 55 million Europeans emigrated to these conquered lands of the Southern World[120] - establishing, in effect, the highest number of the voluntary movement of a people from one continent to another ever embarked upon.

Popularising scientism

This record of phenomenal mass migration by Europeans from their homeland to those conquered territories across three other continents of the world was crucial evidence, if this was needed, of the immediate and direct impact that Europe's unprecedented success as a global occupation force had had on its population, its society. It also appeared to give credence to the 'scientificity' of the genocidal ruminations of its esteemed scholars who so willingly offered the requisite cultural/intellectual rationlaisation for the event - after all, millions of Europeans were now heading to replace, essentially populate the 'empty spaces' vacated by millions and millions of Africans, Australasians and the indigenous peoples of the Americas who had been destroyed or banished to concentration camps in the wake of the holocaust.

This event of conquest and global domination still required to be explained, if not understood, within the broader sectors of European cultural life. Once again, Britain, which was the hub of the intellectual activity of the genocidist scholars as we have shown, led the way to the popularisation of the varying

---

[119] Quoted in Vladimir Lenin, *Selected Works* (Moscow: Progress Publishers, 1977), p. 225.
[120] Magdoff, *Imperialism*, p. 32.

facets of the latter's 'extermination' theses and their consequences. Writers such as Nicholas Monsarrat, Robert Ruark, John Buchan, Edgar Borroughs, R. M. Ballantyne, G. A. Henty, Bertram Mitford and Rider Haggard who are today usually classified harmlessly in many a school or public library as 'adventure storytellers' would be joined by even the so-called 'more innovative' writers such as Joseph Conrad, Rudyard Kipling, Joyce Carey, Elspeth Huxley and Karen Blixen to bring to their readers in Britain and across the world, 'in imaginative form, the ideas and debates being conducted in scientific circles at the time regarding the nature of society in general and of "primitive" society in particular.'[121] These writers are, as their 'scientific' counterparts, unashamedly racist apologists of the European genocide and conquest abroad and the literature they produced has largely formed the basis of the contemporary European World 'intellectual' construction and representation of the history and destiny of African peoples and the other victims of the holocaust. In effect, Britain emerged from this exercise with the unenviable position as the creator, cardinal codifier, and central publicist of European racism as an ideology. As Peter Fryer has shown, British institutions such as the church, school, publishing and the press played a pivotal role in this popularisation of conquest and territorial occupation:

> Public enthusiasm for the British Empire was whipped up by the churches; by the schools (free compulsory education was introduced in 1870); by the comics and adventure stories produced for children and young people (a tremendous expansion in the production of juvenile literature occurred in the 1870s and 1880s); by the new cheap and sensationalist press (the halfpenny London daily was launched in 1896); by the music halls, popular plays, musical comedies and popular songs. These were the main transmission belts for the mythology of imperial glory and heroism and racial superiority.[122]

As should be expected, the dehumanisation or demonisation of the African and other victims of the European genocide world-wide by these new apologists of the crime was the fulcrum on which the construction of this 'mythology of

---

[121]Brian Street, 'Reading the novels of empire: race and ideology in the classic "tale of adventure",' in David Dabydeen, ed., *The black presence in English literature* (Manchester: Manchester University, 1985), p. 104.

[122]Peter Fryer, *Black People in the British Empire: An Introduction* (London: Pluto, 1989), p. 55.

imperial glory' and conquest was anchored. As with the underlying premise of the genocidist scholars themselves, the 'novelists of empire' were also concerned to rationalise the holocaust as 'inevitable', affecting 'primitive' or 'lower race' peoples. Equally, they had little sympathy but derision for the survivors whose survival as we indicated earlier was a devastating blow to the 'theorisation' of the genocidist scholars. It is therefore not surprising that as the most distinct survivors of this holocaust in the world today, Africans have had the most unsurpassingly brutalised representation in these novels. Rather than an occasion of great celebration for the extraordinary triumph of human resilience, the characterisation of Africans in novels (and other writings) offers the typical European writer focusing on this subject the opportunity to construct stereotypical, strait-jacket, de-historicised objects of individuals and events. In examining a selection of the key texts in the literature that specifically target the African humanity, six broad leitmotifs can be isolated as the interest of pursuit to which these novels are usually contextualised: (1) The denial of history or the historical process in the African environment (Haggard, *King Solomon's Mines*; Haggard, *She*; Haggard, *Allan Quatermain*; Buchan, *Prester John*; Mitford, *The Weird of Deadly Hollow*; Conrad, *Heart of Darkness*; Carey, *Mister Johnson*; Blixen, *Out of Africa*; Huxley, *The Red Strangers*; Huxley, *A Thing to Love*). (2) Africophobism or a frenzied hatred of the African race (Haggard, *King Solomon's Mines*; Haggard, *She*; Haggard, *Allen Quatermain*; Buchan, *Prester John*; Mitford, *The Weird of Deadly Hollow*; Conrad, *Heart of Darkness*; Carey, *Mister Johnson*; Blixen, *Out of Africa*; Huxley, *The Red Strangers*; Huxley, *A Thing to Love*). (3) Juvenilisation of the African subject of history (Haggard, *King Solomon's Mines*; Haggard, *She*; Haggard, *Allan Quatermain*; Buchan, *Prester John*; Mitford, *The Weird of Deadly Hollow*; Conrad, *Heart of Darkness*; Carey, *Mister Johnson*; Blixen, *Out of Africa*; Huxley, *The Red Strangers*; Huxley, *A Thing to Love*). (4) The animalisation of the African subject of history (Haggard, *King Solomon's Mines*; Haggard, *She*; Haggard, *Allan Quatermain*; Haggard, *Allan's Wife*; Haggard, *The People of the Mist*; Buchan, *Prester John*; Mitford, *The Weird of Deadly Hollow*; Conrad, *Heart of Darkness*; Carey, *Mister Johnson*; Blixen, *Out of Africa*; Huxley, *The Red Strangers*; Huxley, *A Thing to Love*). (5) Approval/rationalisation of Europe's perpetration of the African holocaust (Haggard, *King Solomon's Mines*; Haggard, *She*; Haggard, *Allan Quatermain*; Haggard, *Allan's Wife*; Haggard, *The People of the Mist*; Buchan, *Prester John*; Mitford, *The Weird of Deadly Hollow*; Conrad, *Heart of Darkness*; Carey, *Mister Johnson*; Blixen, *Out of Africa*; Huxley, *The Red Strangers*; Huxley, *A Thing of Love*). (6) Triumphalism and the centrality of the European as the actuating source and reference in history (Haggard, *King Solomon's Mines*; Haggard, *She*; Haggard, *Allan Quaterman*; Buchan, *Prester John*; Mitford, *The Weird of Deadly Hollow*; Conrad, *Heart of Darkness*; Carey, *Mister Johnson*; Blixen, *Out of Africa*; Huxley, *The Red Strangers*; Huxley, *A Thing of Love*; Alan Paton, *Cry the Beloved Country*).

The classification above is of course purely for analytical purposes as it is clear that no single leitmotif provides an exclusive or exhaustive focus in any given novel. More often than not most of these themes or indeed all of them are played out in the piece of literature concerned. So, in classifying a particular novel under a leading theme as we have shown, our interest has been to stress how dominant these leitmotifs of racist reductionist characterisation are at work in the writer's conception. What should also be obvious by now to the reader is how these leitmotifs, well over a hundred years after their initial codification in European letters, continue to be the defining parameters within which the European World academia and media engage Africa and African peoples in whatever subject or discipline of discourse.

Whilst a few European World contemporary critics of this literature bemoan some of the standard epithets of reference to the African in the texts just cited ('primitive', 'savage', 'underdeveloped', 'tribe', 'dark', 'native'),[123] or alternatively evaluate such characterisation as the 'imperial narratives ... conventional for its time in its strategy and objectives,'[124] it does not fail to amaze how limited the distance the critics themselves have covered in constructing their own language of identification or referencing of the African that is *really* different from the 19th century orthodoxy. A number of them now consider the use of epithets such as 'ethnic', 'ethnic minority' (especially when referring to Africans domiciled in Europe or north America) and 'ethnography' as 'more polite, less offensive' ways to describe or write about the African humanity but some[125] often use these 'new' terms interchangeably with the

---

[123] See, for instance, Street, 'Reading the novels of empire,' pp. 95-111 and John McClure, 'Problematic presence: the colonial other in Kipling and Conrad,' in Dabydeen, ed., *The black presence in English literature*, pp. 154-167.

[124] Terence Rodgers, 'Empires of the imagination: Rider Haggard, popular fiction and Africa,' in Mpalive-Hangson Msiska and Paul Hyland, eds., *Writing and Africa* (London and New York: Addison Wesley Longman, 1997), p. 112.

[125] See, for instance, Terence Rodger's aching apologia for the European conquest ('Empires of the imagination,' pp. 103-121.) which reads more like a Haggard piece published posthumously. See also Gareth Griffiths, 'Writing, literacy and history in Africa,' in Msiska and Hyland, eds., *Writing and Africa*, pp. 139-158 and Frances

Haggardian/Conradian/Buchanan 'tribe', 'tribal', 'black tribal' and 'uncivilised', ensuring that the latter must be seen as durable foundation blocks on which the hermeneutic typologisation of the African must remain cast! Yet, for these critics, the supposedly new language of 'ethnic'/ 'ethnicity'-referencing just leads to a tortuous dead-end of lack of progress in confronting the salient issue about Africa that has still not be posed in their discourses and which we shall be elaborating on soon.

It remains the fact that the 'ethnic' and 'ethnicity' coordinates of African representation in these studies and elsewhere are still basically those of the 'tribe' and 'tribal' mapping: racist. To underline the racial/cultural exclusivity of the use of 'ethnic' and 'ethnicity' by these critics, it should be noted that in both official and popular parlance, no members of the 'majority' population in any country in Europe or north America would be said to belong to the linguistic opposite terminology: 'ethnic majority'. Thus, if one were to ignore for once the deep reservoir of history as a source of strident Africophobism in the European World, there is no doubt that the language of anti-Africanism so prevalent in the West's academia and media fuels the popular racism in society. This was demonstrated so sharply a few years ago in an opinion poll survey across the 15 countries of the European Union where an average of one-third of the population declared themselves as 'racist,' an outcome that some observers even thought was an underestimate.[126] Kimani Nehusi[127] has shown that 'ethnic' has its root in the Latin *ethnicus*, which means 'heathen' or 'pagan'. He adds: 'This term ["ethnic"] always carried a strong connotation believed by some of the supposed "inferiority" of "heathens" and "pagans" and assumed "superiority" of Jews... and christians. This was a short step away from a belief in white "superiority" and the "inferiority" of others.'[128] Even the term 'Black' as it is used in the literature to refer to, or define African peoples (especially in the West and even in Africa in countries where there is some permanent European domiciliation such as South Africa and Zimbabwe), hardly possesses concrete historical/cultural or geographical scientific validity, except to the extent that it is a political term of power classification for those considered 'not-white'. Pointedly, peoples of Asian origin in Britain and

---

Mannsaker, 'The dog that didn't bark: the subject races in imperial fiction at the turn of the century,' in Dabydeen, *The black presence in English literature*, pp. 112-134.
[126] See *The Sun* (London), 20 December 1997.
[127] Kimani Nehusi, 'Why "Ethnic Minority" is Racist,' *African Peoples Review*, Vol. V, No. 2, May-August 1996, p. 20.
[128] Ibid.

elsewhere in the European World have consciously broken out of this 'white'/'black' debilitating power dichotomy and declared themselves 'Asians' - a culturally and more scientifically valid independent referencing. Thus, the overriding concern of the typical European critic interrogating the African presence in history becomes a simplistic curiosity to *negate* the clusters of profiles and paradigms which he or she, before hand, considers to be 'white'.[129]

Indeed, just as the definitive drive of the Haggardian or Conradian caricature, to designate the clearly historical African as 'Black', an utterly non-historical construct, is only intelligible as a 'not-white' derivative in the evaluative schema of characterisation by these critics. It is clear by now for Africans living particularly in the West whose political leaders during the great African American uprisings of the 1960s 'owned up' the 'Black' appellation as a racial/cultural identifier aimed at 'neutering' the term's pervasive negative European connotations ('blackmail', 'black sheep', 'black eye', 'black economy', 'black mass', 'black day', 'black Monday', 'black Wednesday', 'black market', etc, etc), that they must break out of this binary bind of eurocentric construct and embrace their Africanness unambiguously.

It mustn't be ignored or forgotten that there are no *white* people who live on this planet; therefore, the appropriation of the colour 'white' by peoples of European descent to describe themselves has been an age old aesthetic and political illusion which they are perfectly entitled to make. But for African peoples, it is not only a folly but undoubtedly suicidal for them to appear to exist merely as the negation of an illusion whatever might be the underlying short-term political expediency. The fact is that juxtaposed on an evaluative plane of discourse, there is no way that the dual *historical* referents 'African' and 'European', for instance, or indeed 'African' and 'Asian', negate each other; to the contrary, each constituent of the couplet is a subject of history, equally and wholly, and interacts as such with the other without any illusions of subjectivity occasioned by the signification of phenotype. When it is borne in mind that the latter unscientific typecasting on a global scale has, in the past 400 years, been the overriding preoccupation of European World typologists, Africans accept it and its consequences at their own peril. Therefore, what an epithet of identity that is *not* 'African' does in the referencing of someone of African origin, *wherever he or she lives in the world*, is that such a label

---

[129]Cf. Chinua Achebe 'Impediments to Dialogue between North and South,' in Chinua Achebe, *Hopes and Impediments: Selected Essays 1965-87* (Oxford: Heinemann International, 1988), pp. 14-19 and Toni Morrison, *Playing in the dark: Whiteness and the literary imagination* (London and Basingstoke: Picador/Pan Books, 1992).

obliterates any meaningful, or easily discernible historical *and* geographical heritage of the African humanity. Accordingly, Mwalimu Shujaa and Kofi Lomotey have argued that 'African identity is embedded in the continuity of African cultural history and that African cultural history represents a distinct reality, continually evolving from the experiences of all African people wherever they are and have been on the planet across time and generations.'[130] Stuart Hall, the African Caribbean sociologist, is therefore mistaken to think that the diaspora African community in Britain/Western World should abandon their African heritage as part of belonging to some new configurated anthropological tapestry of Britishness/Westerness.[131] Earlier on, Hall had recalled: 'I was never taught [whilst growing up in Jamaica that] I had any African blood in me. It was completely suppressed.'[132] Why someone who makes such an astonishing acknowledgement, with evident regret, would wish to embark on an illusory political project which will further obliterate his *African* identity is indeed most uncertain, if not alarming. Or, is it perhaps the residual consequences of the 'suppress[ion]' of the Africanness in Hall that continues to wreak further havoc of cultural identity? What is however certain is that the tragedy of 'hybridisation' keenly sought by some African diaspora intellectuals in the West presently has taken its heavy toll in fomenting confusion, desperation, and hopelessness in the African descent community especially the young who confront the daily emergency of suffocating racism in schools, playgrounds, work places and elsewhere in society. It should now be abandoned especially in the light of its most zaniest cases yet when (1) Paul Gilroy, another African Caribbean sociologist, begins a study on Africans living in the European World by declaring that he, Gilroy, is 'striving to be both European and black'[133] and (2) Darcus Howe, the African Caribbean journalist, shocked his readers in an interview by claiming that rather than striving to be one, he was already British(!): 'Not only do I *feel* but I *am* British' (emphasis in the original).[134] Peregrine Worsthorne, the British journalist who is not famous for the most progressive of views on Africans in his writings, appears

---

[130] Mwalimu Shujaa and Kofi Lomotey, 'Afrocentric Education,' *African Peoples Review*, Vol V, No 2, May-August 1996, p. 18.
[131] See Martin Jacques and Stuart Hall in conversation, 'Les enfants de Marx et de Coca-Cola,' *New Statesman* (London), 28 November 1997, pp. 34-37.
[132] Ibid., p. 34.
[133] See Paul Gilroy, *The Black Atlantic* (London and New York: Verso, 1993), p. 1.
[134] See Peregrine Worsthorne, 'What my new (black) friend told my relatives about their manor house,' *The Spectator* (London), 11 April 1998, p.30.

to have redeemed himself for once when he correctly offers a diagnosis of how very long indeed the Halls and Gilroys and Howes of the African World still have to wait before being accepted as European and British and something other than *themselves*, which they aspire to become: '[I]t will take several more generations before whites can accept this proposition, and if and when they eventually do accept it, the re-education process experienced in the course of bringing this change about will have fundamentally changed the British character '[135] For his own insight on this crisis of racial identity, Molefi Kete Asante, the astute African American scholar, firstly quotes the famous Wolof aphorism, 'wood may remain in water for ten years but it will never become crocodile,'[136] and then goes on to reflect on the anguish and futility of the quest for race transmutation by this grouping of African intellectuals in the following evocative sketch:

> No white Britishers are striving to be 'white and British'; this type of striving is peculiar to Africans. No French people are striving to be 'white and French' and no whites in Ghana are striving to be 'white and Ghanaian'. As far as I can tell, no white in America [nor Jamaica, nor Guyana, nor Trinidad] of English or German background is rushing to give up his or her heritage in Europe. No other people except Africans are so eager to give up their traditions in order to be dominated by others. I see no evidence of Europeans who have lived in Africa [or the Caribbean] for generations seeking to deny their European heritage. Nor do I find whites who allow others to dominate their thoughts.[137]

For Homi Bhabha, the Asian hybriditist critic of the European novels of conquest and the resultant African resistance scholarship, England does not 'organically' replicate the Conradian welcoming 'home' of rectitude that we shall soon be reflecting upon, even if his wish to be some variant of a Conrad is a much sought after politico-literary objective. After all, Bhabha's Indian sub-continental home of departure, an outpost of the British empire, is not analogous to the Polish central/eastern European 'corporate body' from where Conrad left for western Europe with the ultimate destination for England. It would therefore appear that the only portal open for entry for the unwanted

---

[135]Ibid.
[136]Molefi Kete Asante, 'Finally, Afrocentricity Operationalised,' *African Peoples Review*, Vol III, No 3, October-December 1994, p. 3.
[137]Ibid.

folks of empire who are struggling to be 'European and [themselves]' is clearly marked 'Hybridisation' which is nothing else but a euphemism for racial/cultural assimilation. Quickly past this gate therefore, hybriditist criticism, as typified for instance by Bhabha's *The Location of Culture*, insists that History is divorced from the proceedings of the new times, a kind of era-less era as the only imaginative way forward to face the future is to abolish the past - and present, for that matter - with all its contesting and contestable interpretations! Amazingly though, the conqueror's interpretation, i.e., the European conqueror, emerges from this apparent whirlwind of change remarkably unscathed. Bhabha no doubt finds the resistance discourse, particularly that mounted by the African, destabilising to his project because, to paraphrase Chinua Achebe, '[people] chastened by the humiliation of defeat often have deeper insights to report than [their] conqueror[s].'[138] So, History, according to the conqueror's account, remains the cardinal and defining reference in Bhabha's construction. For instance, and this is immensely crucial to the task, Bhabha does not interrogate Conrad's stark role in contributing to the European literary architecture *rationalising* the African holocaust. The critic's mission instead appears modestly unambitious: he is dazzled by the Polish traveller's tenacity to punch his way into that British choir of choristers, singing ecstatically for that imperialist world at the turn of the 20th century covered up in the *red* colour of blood, death and deprivation from the Bahamas, in the western hemisphere, to Bangladesh, in the east.[139]

In Bhabha's approach to the resistance literature against this mayhem, any remaining doubt about what his hybriditist criticism really stands for evaporates. Here, the great African interventions to meditate on the variegated shades and spheres of the holocaust become unrecognisably muffled in an adventure that has indeed turned into 'the mal-location of culture.'[140] Frantz Fanon, the liberation philosopher and theorist, is 'safely' deculturalised and dehistoricised so that *Black Skin, White Mask* and *Wretched of the Earth* appear, 30-40 years later, as disfigured Disneyland tracts. The shredding of *Beloved*, Toni Morrison's towering portrait, into frizzy, ephemeral, spatio-temporal non-referents of episodes, ensures that students of the holocaust will have to spend

---

[138]Quoted in Ezenwa-Ohaeto, *Chinua Achebe: A Biography* (Oxford: James Currey, 1997), p. 224.
[139]Homi Bhabha, *The Location of Culture* (London and New York: Routledge, 1994), pp. 106-7.
[140]Pointedly, see Bhabha's reviews of Frantz Fanon and Toni Morrison in *The Location of Culture*.

quite a while to pick up the bits and pieces, and reconstruct the canvass to make some sense of two key historic defining features of the landscape: (1) Why Sethe's 'infanticide' is an integrative corpus of the broad front of African resistance during the period. (2) Why Beloved is the incantatory voice of re-call - the *sankofa* of 'rememoration' that harkens unto the survivors, through the timeless medium of ancient Africa's heuristic narrative syntax, the triumphant news of *her own very* survival:

> I AM BELOVED and she is mine. I see her take flowers away from leaves she puts them in a round basket ... All of it is now it is always now there will never be a time when I am not crouching and watching others who are crouching too I am always crouching ... We are not crouching now we are standing but my legs are like my dead man's eyes ... I cannot find my man the one whose teeth I have loved a hot thing the little hill of dead people a hot thing the men without skin push them through with poles ... in the beginning the women are away from the men and the men are away from the women storms rock us and mix the men into the women and the women into the men ... I cannot lose her again my dead man was in the way like the noisy clouds when he dies on my face I can see hers ... I am standing in the rain falling the others are taken I am not taken ... I see me swim away a hot thing ... I am alone I want to be the two of us I want the join I come out of blue water ... I am not dead I am not ... Sethe's is the face that left me ... she is my face smiling at me ... now we can join a hot thing[141]

Dinesh D'Souza's *The End of Racism* belongs to the same genre of recent hybriditist writings by neo-Conradian practitioners who are intrinsically motivated to 'shock and sell' their wares of blatant Africophobism. These have been politically and financially supported by the likes of the US-based John Olin Foundation and the American Enterprise Institute. What is amazing though is that considering the noisy publicity that marked the release of D'Souza's book, there is hardly any new insights made by the author into the subject of European racism except that this is merely an opportunity for him to rehash the standard sound bites of Africophobism which one would easily pick out listening to a Conrad or a Haggard or Blixen or a Buchan megaphone: '[African] civilizational deficiencies,' '[African] dysfunctional culture,'

---

[141] Toni Morrison, *Beloved* (London: Pan Books, 1988), pp. 210-13.

'[African] arrested development,' 'slavery has proved to be the transmission belt that nevertheless brought Africans into the orbit of modern civilization and western freedom,' etc., etc. It is highly unlikely that if D'Souza were European, he would have received the robust support that he is currently getting from anti-African institutes and circles in the United States to propagate over and over the same material that has been the hallmark of genocidist writing on Africa for generations. This simply would not have created the impact required! The fact that an Asian, coming from the so-called 'emerging zone' of global economic power, is saying it is expected to energise the sentiment with the urgency of drama which should give fresh respectability to the earlier European rationalisation of the African holocaust. It is significant that towards the end of the last century and in these early years of a new one, Asian diaspora writers in the West are steadily taking over the role of trumpeting the European conqueror's version of the history of the African holocaust, very much in the tradition of V. S. Naipaul.[142] They have obviously been elated by the ecstatic, but quite often exaggerated views in the West about the socio-economic performances of the Asian 'tiger economies,' and of Asian émigrés in Europe and North America - references which are frequently used as new fronts for anti-African commentaries. It must never be forgotten though that Africa's encounter with Europe is a completely different history from that of Asia's encounter with Europe. Asia has not been the target of the extensive holocaust of 500 years that Africa has had to endure from the European World ever since. Besides, the very genesis of Africa's current turmoil is traceable to that *other* encounter - when the great African civilisation of Egypt was overrun by Arab/muslim expansionism earlier on in the last millennium as we have already noted. Indeed as Europe's own 'relay race' of the occupation of Africa got underway, it readily used Asian 'indentured' labour in parts of east and southern Africa (as exemplified by the British particularly in Kenya, Uganda and South Africa) as a crucial *pliant middle social stratum of non-Africans* to consolidate its control of the African humanity.[143] It allowed the Asians, who had access to

---

[142]For a recent excellent critique of Naipaul's writing on Africa, see Chinua Achebe, *Home and Exile* (Oxford: Oxford University, 2000), pp. 84-91.
[143]Historically, the situation in the Caribbean was slightly different from Africa. The Europeans had largely destroyed the indigenous population of the Caribbean during the course of their conquest of the region and the British/European strategy of effecting social control, following the liberation of African slaves, was to treat the latter as the 'indigenous' population against the imported Asian 'indentured' labour middle stratum. They reckoned that the Asians were 'pliant' and therefore more accommodating to the

capital which was denied to Africans, to run the retail economy and set up schools and other cultural institutions and services, and in so doing prospered, becoming the wealthiest grouping of Asians *outside* their Asian homeland during the period. In effect, Asians, as a privileged social group within these states, constituted another critical obstacle to African liberation. Africans would still not have access to capital in their own homeland right up to the eve of the restoration of independence in most cases. This Asian 'sandwich privilege'[144] would become a serious political issue on the morrow of the restoration of independence in these countries. The strategic role of Asian capital in the economies of contemporary Kenya and Uganda, and the recent debates in South Africa on Asian complicity and privilege in the European-'apartheid' conquest state underscore the enormity of this facet of African history.

Understandably, therefore, most Asians had cultivated a more intimate loyalty to the British crown than to the newly liberated African state where they had lived for decades. With the increasing politicisation of the African and Asian domiciliation in Britain itself since the 1960s, the British have again sought to play the card of Asian 'sandwich privilege' in ways and means not dissimilar to the experiences in Africa. Even though continental African émigrés are currently the most highly educated racial community group within Britain[145] and African Caribbeans in the past 40 years have been in the vanguard, leading the decisive social struggles for change in the position and opportunities for these émigrés (as well as raising fundamental issues of social justice that have impacted on the British population as a whole),[146] the Asian group of immigrants in the country has undoubtedly emerged as the most comprehensive beneficiaries of new accesses to employment, industry, and influence created as a result. Only recently, Herman Ouseley, an influential African Caribbean leader in Britain and the former head of the country's Commission for Racial Equality, openly attacked the British government of 'favouring British Asians over African-Caribbeans.'[147] He concluded, with a striking reminder of the British post-conquest policies in Africa (and the Caribbean) in times gone by,

---

staus quo (Cf. Harry Goulbourne, *Ethnicity and nationalism in post-imperial Britain* [Cambridge: Cambridge University, 1991], p. 49.).

[144] See Jennifer Okpong, 'The Asian Sandwich Syndrome,' *African Peoples Review*, Vol V, No.3, September-December 1996, p. 19.

[145] Charles Hymas and Lesley Thomas, 'Africans move to the top of Britain's educational ladder,' *The Sunday Times* (London), 23 January 1994, p. 5.

[146] Goulbourne, *Ethnicity and nationalism in post-imperial Britain*, pp. 40-50.

[147] *Sunday Telegraph* (London), 22 April 2001.

that contemporary Britain has a 'pecking order, almost a hierarchy, of [constituent racial groups].'[148]

Presently, another interesting but controversial link between Africa and Asia that many observers and commentators tend to ignore concerns the subject of the re-investment of Africa's scandalous capital out-flows (see above) that have largely decapitalised the latter's economy in the past 20 years. It is in the so-called Asian 'tiger economies' that Western banks and other Western-controlled financial institutions such as the IMF and World Bank have invested these staggering sums of money. They have taken advantage of the region's pro-Western authoritarian regimes (particularly during the dictatorships of the regimes in Indonesia, South Korea and the Philippines) and its cheap and controlled labour force. The grave financial and economic turmoil that has struck south east Asia since the last quarter of 1997 has been the inability of the overrated 'tigers' to meet particularly their short term 'debt servicing' obligations to Western creditors.[149] Only the most obsequiously insular of an observer would fail to detect the gaping and arresting irony of recent history on this score: huge capital assets wrenched from Africa by Western financial and economic interests in the name of 'structural adjustment' forced on the continent have been invested willy-nilly in an Asia which can't pay back quickly enough to guarantee even higher profit margins and dividend outlays for banks and stocks in New York, Washington, London, Tokyo, Frankfurt, Paris and Zurich. In its wake, south east Asia currently faces unprecedented grave social dislocations in many an economy. First, there is an impending environmental catastrophe caused by the reckless and unregulated destruction of millions of acres of lush forestland in the region by foraging transnational corporations expropriating logs and minerals, and ever expanding plantation acreage for animal husbandry and the cultivation of assorted crops for export. Secondly, following the May 1998 dramatic fall from power by President Suharto of Indonesia, and the equally dramatic overthrow of his successor in June 2001, the long term survivability of some regimes in the region are at stake as millions of people lose their jobs due to widespread business collapses, lightening currency devaluations, phenomenal hikes in food prices and other essentials, and extensive constriction of state expenditures in crucial public services and the like, thanks to the now notorious precepts of the International Monetary Fund intervention. Most of Africa since 1980 has been subjected to

---

[148]Ibid.
[149]Cf. Ambrose, 'Challenging the IMF, Intellectually and Politically,' p. 11.

54 African literature in defence of history

the enthralling consequences of these precepts being foisted on Asia by no other than the same IMF and its allied financial institutions, creating the decapitalisation of Africa[150] that helped to finance the much heralded Asian 'miracle' which increasingly is appearing more as the Asian mirage.

---

[150]It is difficult to exaggerate Africa's pivotal role in this arena of capital appropriation for the West. Reflecting on French specific interests, Jacques Godfrain, who was until lately head of the French foreign ministry, has observed: `A little country, with a small amount of strength, we can move a planet because [of our] ... relations ... with 15 or 20 African countries.' (See Tom Masland, `African Duel,' *Newsweek* [New York], 30 March 1198, p. 19.) Former French President Mitterand was even more categorical on the subject as he contemplated the future: `Without Africa, France will have no history in the 21st century.' (Quoted in Masland, ibid.)

2
Transition

It is therefore to the recognisable voices of the 18th and 19th century, the megaphone of Africophobism, *rather than* their late 20th century/early 21st century D'Souza-Bhabha replicas, that Terence Rodgers directs us 'occupy... the dominant and most telling ground in the recent history of [European] literary constructions of Africa.'[1] This is true, but there isn't in this 'construction' anything enduringly imaginative or creative but rabid racism, ever wrestling with the opportunity to rationalise a holocaust which was perpetrated by Europe.[2] This is why Rodgers cannot treat Haggard's writings on Africa with the kind of detachment and respectability which his survey envisions. Haggard is intrinsically part of the problem. Besides his peccant chronicles, Haggard served the British occupation in South Africa which was one of the most sordid African experiences of the episode. Haggard's definitive project, just as other genocidist writers, is to demonstrate how a 'confident and expansionist [Europe is] encountering... and overcoming ... Africa.'[3] He is just like a German Nazi operative who would embark on romanticising his role in the Jewish death camps and writing prodigious chronicles of 'imagination' on Jewish people aimed at rationalising the event. Talking of Jews, it is significant that the only criticism that Terence Rodgers makes of Haggard is the 'persistent anti-Semitism in his work ...'[4] Nothing else! In this context of bewildering omissions in scanning the landscape of history, one is reminded of the engaging effort by Arno Mayer's *Why Did the Heavens Not Darken? The 'Final Solution' in History* in which the author investigates the genocides of the past 1000 years

---

[1]Rodgers, 'Empires of the Imagination,' p. 118.
[2]Cf. Dan Izevbaye, 'History's Eye-Witness: Vision and Representation in the works of Chinua Achebe,' in Edith Ihekweazu, ed., *Eagle on Iroko: Papers from the International Symposium, 1990* (Ibadan: Heinemann Educational Books, 1991), p. 22.
[3]Rodgers, 'Empires of the Imagination', p. 106.
[4]Ibid., p. 112.

that are deemed comparable to that of the Jews in Europe in the 1940s. Astonishingly, there is no mention of the African holocaust in this text even though it claimed *25 times more human lives than* the Jewish holocaust. In the same vein, it is astonishing to state the least that *Newsweek*, the US newsmagazine, can assess perspectives of two very similar crimes against humanity - one African, and the other Jewish - in the same edition but arrive at sharply contrasting conclusions.[5] *Newsweek* does not invoke or allude to some 'political correctness' in the case of Jews demanding, justifiably, justice, even if 'long delayed,'[6] from those sectors of corporate America such as Ford, Chase (precursor to Chase Manhattan) and General Motors which collaborated with their German oppressors during the European wars of 1939-45, but have no qualms in making such outrageous imputations in their coverage of stories concerning justifiable African demands for justice in (1) recovering their lands seized by European aggressors and conquerors in Zimbabwe[7] and (2) resisting racist literature in American schools.[8] It is surprising that *Newsweek* appears to ignore that there is a clearly discernible *connecting thread* that links those three stories in that edition - these crimes against humanity share one origin or emanate from one common source: the European World. Unlike *Newsweek*, Clare Short, the British secretary of state for international development, is very conscious of this thread of history but even then wrestles vigorously to sever it, such is the sensitivity of European World public figures (and cultural establishment especially the media and academia) to quash any opportunity to confront the subject of the African holocaust. Similar to *Newsweek* though, Short chooses Zimbabwe on which to air her views! In a letter to the Zimbabwean government over the latter's legitimate goal to recover Zimbabwean lands still controlled by European families and other conqueror interests in the country, despite 20 years of the liberation of Zimbabwe, Short made the most distorted claim of recent British history and politics when she asserted that her Labour party government had 'no ties' to the British conquest of Africa.[9] The claim was aimed at justifying the effort by the Blair administration that came to power in 1997 to renege on successive British government commitment (made during the 1979-1980 talks in London between

---

[5]*Newsweek* (New York), 14 December 1998.
[6]Michael Hirsh, 'Dirty Business,' ibid., p. 26.
[7]Marcus Marby, 'The Tough Go Shopping,' ibid., p. 49.
[8]Lynette Clemetson, 'Caught in the Cross-Fire,' ibid., pp. 82-83.
[9]Chris McGreal, 'Clare Short letter riles Zimbabwe,' *The Guardian* (London), 22 December 1997.

the then British government and contending Zimbabwean liberation movements) to provide capital to Harare to enable it embark on the perverse project of paying these conqueror interests (who had committed heinous crimes in Africa) for African lands recovered from them. Presumably, Short is unaware that there was a Labour party government in office in her country during the 1960s (headed by a man called Harold Wilson) which carefully connived with the European minority population in Zimbabwe when the latter made a so-called independence declaration of the country, aimed essentially at destroying the course of African liberation which was already underway. Africans still had to fight for a further 20 years to free themselves from the British conquest as a result of that declaration. If Short does not know of the Wilson administration and its policy on Zimbabwe, it would be extremely surprising for her not to be familiar with that most revered of Labour party governments of all time - the Clement Attlee government that took power in 1945 soon after the major war of the previous six years. Despite that government's extensive progressive domestic programme of social reconstruction culminating in its creation of the 'welfare state' in the country, its foreign policy during the period did not incorporate Britain's voluntary abandonment of the occupation of any of the countries in Africa (nor indeed anywhere else in the Southern World). In keeping with the sentiments expressed during the course of the war by Winston Churchill,[10] the former prime minister, the Attlee government bluntly opposed the liberation of Africa. Furthermore, as we have already shown, Britain wrenched huge capital outlays from occupied Africa such as in Nigeria, Ghana and Sierra Leone for the post-war reconstruction of Britain. Surely, contrary to her assertion, Short serves in a government that is both organically and ideologically *tied up* with past British regimes of overseas conquest and expansion. In the end, Clare Short and all those who wish to preserve in perpetuity the European World economic (and political) control of Africa must contend with an outcome that even the most cynical observers can no longer disregard: sometime, indeed in the not too distant future, a Zimbabwean government and other African governments which face similar problems, will fully recover African lands seized from their owners.

Still on the subject of justice and restitution, or at least part of it, we should recall here that in a characteristic keenness to impress his American guests

---

[10] Winston Churchill had declared then that he 'had not become the King's First Minister in order to preside over the liquidation of the British empire' (See A.N. Porter and A.A. Stockwell, *British Imperial Policy and Decolonisation, 1938 - 1941. Vol I: 1938-51* [Basingstoke and London: Macmillan, 1987], p.103).

during President Clinton's February 1998 visit to Kampala, Ugandan President Yoweri Museveni dismissed as 'rubbish,'[11] persistent African dual demands for the European World to unambiguously acknowledge its perpetration of the African holocaust *and* pay Africans the 'long delayed' reparations for the crime. Museveni insisted that these African demands should be directed instead to those African monarchs who collaborated with the Europeans at the time. Why the focus should be on the collaborators *only* without including those who bear *primary responsibility* for perpetrating the holocaust is not at all clear in the Museveni logic, except of course that it ensures that the European World is let off the hook of responsibility! Why would *any* African, particularly a head of state, wish to do that? A case could indeed be made for Museveni, or any others for that matter so inclined, to add to the current African list of restitution demands from the European World to include *all known* African collaborators (individuals, institutions) of this crime who still remain unpunished even though it shouldn't be forgotten that the very rich history of popular resistance in Africa against the holocaust involved the benchmark uprisings, overthrows, and the exiling of monarchs and other categories of African leaders who colluded with the principal agents during the period. What this means in effect is that there are very few African collaborators who have not been held to account for their role in the holocaust. In the end, we return to the principal culprits of the crime to pay reparations for their deed. Germany, which participated in the African holocaust, albeit to a lesser extent when compared to Britain, United States, France, Spain and Portugal, has already established a commendable track record in its payment of reparations to Jews during the past 50 years for the genocide that it carried out on the latter in the 1930s/40s. Germany is fully aware of the range of some Jewish *own collaboration* with German forces and security apparatus during that holocaust including cases of Jews who not only worked as commandants and officials in the concentration camps in central/eastern Europe (where fellow Jews were sent to their deaths) but also as very senior officers in the German armed forces.[12] Some even had to falsify their Jewishness in order to ensure that their conditions of service in the German military, especially promotions and attendant privileges, were not jeopardised in any

---

[11]Carol Castel, 'Clinton's Historic Visit,' West Africa (London), 6-26 April 1998, p. 387.

[12]See, for instance, Tom King, 'Jews who wore a Nazi uniform,' *The Daily Telegraph* (London), 2 December 1996, pp. 4-5. See also John Keegan, 'Why men of Jewish blood shed it for Adolf Hitler,' in ibid., p. 20.

way.¹³ All wars and all crimes of genocide in history against a people often have some form of complicity or collaboration from some among the targeted population. Understandably, Germany has not allowed this collaboration by some members of the race or people that it subjected to nearly a decade of such a horrific crime to distract it from its responsibility to 'own up' to its role as the primary and principal culprit of the event and pay reparations accordingly. Similarly, there is no compelling argument for Germany, Britain, United States, Spain, Portugal, France, Belgium, Italy, Holland, Switzerland and other European World nations and interests who were the principal architects and beneficiaries of the African holocaust (whose duration was *several decades* longer than the Jewish one) to be distracted from accepting their responsibility for this crime and pay reparations to Africans wherever they are on earth. This is the case even if it can be established that some Africans collaborated in the event.

Alas, the attempt to obliterate the scientific authentication of Africanness in human history has been part of the cardinal goal of the European genocidist scholars and their literary allies as we have demonstrated so far in this study. Hardly any of the contemporary critics of the 'writings of empire' has interrogated this feature of the enterprise. But more importantly, none of these critics has questioned the underlying import and objective of this literature - namely, the *triumphalisation* of the European genocide and conquest of Africa. 'It should be recognised,' as Abena Busia notes cogently, 'that the "Africa" being discussed [by these scholars and writers] has very little to do with any Africa Africans themselves, from whatever part of the continent, might recognize as "home".'¹⁴ There are few strands in this body of European discourse which operate from the position that a heinous crime has been committed here and that some restitution is urgently required from those responsible for it. In rare moments when a few critics appear to be disposed to such an inquiry, what can at best be described as a sleight-of-hand tendency of equivocations, geo-historical spatial limitations, and the banality of parcelling out the crime so that it is shared equally by perpetrator and victim alike emerge as the guide rules.

Terry Eagleton, arguably Britain's leading marxist literary critic, begins his discussion of Conrad's *Heart of Darkness*¹⁵ by reminding us of crucial features

---

¹³King, ibid., Keegan, ibid.
¹⁴Abena Busia, 'Manipulating Africa: the buccaneer as "liberator" in contemporary fiction,' in Dabydeen, ed., *The black presence in English literature*, p. 168.
¹⁵Terry Eagleton, *Criticism & Ideology* (London: Verso, 1978), pp. 130-41.

of the novelist's social and national background which cannot be ignored as this constitutes an important component in the formulation of an overall critique of the novel. Conrad was a Polish aristocrat who went into self-imposed exile in western Europe in 1874 when he was 17. He had left his country because it was then dominated by neighbouring czarist Russia. As a young boy, he had accompanied his father, a hero of the Polish resistance against Russia, into an internal exile (in northern Russia) ordered by the czarist regime. Away from Poland, Conrad first went to France where he joined the merchant marine and worked as a sailor, travelling around the world. Twenty years later, he settled in England. He took up British citizenship with the anglicisation of his name from Teodor Josef Konrad Korzeniowski to Joseph Conrad and devoted his time to writing. He published several novels and short stories and one of the latter, *Heart of Darkness*, was published in 1902. For Eagleton, Conrad was a dedicated Polish nationalist who felt that despite the hegemony exercised over it by Russian imperialism, Poland remained a 'corporate body' or 'an organic living thing'.[16] The self-imposed exile, Eagleton continued, had 'affirmed his freedom from an intolerably claustrophobic imperialism'[17] through his work as a sailor and writer. The latter profession, underpinned by his British naturalisation, would catapult Conrad to the heights of Victorian English letters but on terms that at best appear deeply ironical, as Eagleton acknowledges: '[the] ideological conjuncture in Conrad's texts is determined in the last instance by the imperialist character of the English capitalism he served ...'[18] Surprisingly, Eagleton does not interrogate this irony in its *crucial* African context where the implementation of Conrad's ideo-political 'shifts' of admonitions, sympathies and alignments for conquerors and conquered alike are dramatically played out. Instead, Eagleton is content to find an explanation for this in what England offered the Polish exile - a home, away from the 'European [continental] political turbulence.'[19] Conrad himself had argued elsewhere that England was the 'only barrier to the pressure of infernal doctrines born in [European] continental backslums... [the bulwark against the force that] tends to weaken *the national sentiment, the preservation of which is my concern*' (added emphasis).[20] But this 'barrier' or 'bulwark' was exactly what neither England/Britain nor indeed any other European country was for Africa

---

[16] Ibid., p. 132.
[17] Ibid., p. 133.
[18] Ibid., p. 134.
[19] Ibid., P. 133.
[20] Quoted in ibid.

at the time Conrad was writing *Heart of Darkness*. On the contrary. Just like Russian imperialism's ruinous stranglehold on his native Poland, Britain, Conrad's newly adopted home, was part of the pan-European imperialist force, in fact a pivotal force for that matter, which was not only 'weaken[ing]' but obliterating the 'national sentiment' of many an African state and society. Conrad, one would think, was therefore well-placed to map out the connecting threads of conquests and *human* subjugation on the universal dashboard facing him. Of course, he never made that connection between his plight as an exile from a subjugated homeland and the plight of Africans being subjugated by the jackboot of British/European imperialism. That would have been to expect Conrad to embark on the impossible! He would not have transmuted from a nondescript Slavic Konrad to a Conrad of English Letters if his task was not to champion the most important battle that faced the central powers of the European World of his day: the subjugation of the African and the outlandish popularisation of the resultant holocaust. This was exactly what Conrad achieved in *Heart of Darkness*.

Eagleton also never makes the connection of the devastation of these two imperialisms on their respective Polish and African victims in his reading of Conrad. His reluctance to dwell on the irony in Conrad raised earlier on becomes obvious in his discussion: his lavish sympathy for the plight of Poland contrasts sharply with his *approval* of British/ European imperialism in Africa. Eagleton achieves the latter by intuitively latching on to the standard anthropological rationalisation for Europe's occupation of Africa when he notes that the European task was to mould 'politically amorphous ... societies into truly "organic" units.'[21] No doubt, Eagleton expects his readers to be familiar with this rationalisation which they would also note contrasts sharply with Conrad's Polish 'organic living thing'! The allegiance of the marxist critic to British/European imperialism in fact deepens with what he claims is the 'message' of *Heart of Darkness* which appears, paradoxically, as a variant of 'blame-the-criminal/blame-the-victim' solution: 'Western civilisation is at base as barbarous as African society...'[22] If indeed that was the case, why did Europe then invade Africa? 'Barbarous Africa' should surely have been left alone by 'Barbarous Western civilisation'! Why would Europe wish to mould supposedly 'politically amorphous' societies that were 4,000-10,000 miles away from it? Was Russian civilisation at base as 'barbarous' as Polish society? Eagleton

---

[21] Ibid., p. 135.
[22] Ibid.

never poses these questions either. For him, these questions on Africa would be irrelevant, as the key to the understanding of Europe's conquering escapades in Africa *lies* in the treatise of the genocidal scholars and writers to which both the *Heart of Darkness* and the basis of Eagleton's own non-disapproval of it belong.

Karl Marx, whose intellectual work in England spanned the era when the final phases of the architectural layers of this treatise were being constructed in 19th century Europe, is hardly more condemnatory of the African holocaust. On the contrary, he either makes a parody of the event whilst in fact engaged in very related philosophical, political or economic discussion of the European World[23] or, more subtly, does not disapprove of it because he sees it as merely representing a negation of freedom in a dialectical 'reality' of antagonism.[24] Yet, unlike his contemporaries and most of the Eagletons of late 20th century European World scholarship who work under the overarching discipline of marxian discourses, Marx at least acknowledges that the wealth of the European World is built overwhelmingly on Africa.[25] But this most acute philosopher who called for the overthrow of European World capitalism by, and for a European World proletarian state-rule, would not countenance the liberation of this subjugated African humanity precisely because the latter's liberation would amount to a collapse of *this* European wealth. Underscoring Marx's argument of not dealing with the African liberation as the quote further down indicates, is that he, and his fellow European scholars, writers and commentators on the subject, does not deal with the African as a *human being*. This is the crux of the matter - a point that Joseph Conrad popularised in that most notorious introspection on africophobia for which the *Heart of Darkness* has since remained typecast and on which, we dare note, underline, centrally, this book's undiminishing popularity within the European World academy. As the fictional Marlow, no doubt Conrad's voice, recalls his voyage up the River Congo to meet Kurtz (at the ivory trading post), he once contemplates some kinship with the Africans along the route (who have in the mean time been the focus of his unrelenting megalomaniac racist outpourings) but quickly rejects the idea: ' No,

---

[23]See, for instance, Karl Marx, *Capital, Volume 1* (Harmandsworth: Penguin Books, 1976), p. 915 and p. 1014.

[24]Karl Marx and Frederick Engels, *Selected Works (In one volume)* (London: Lawrence Wishart, 1977), pp. 664-65.

[25]Ibid., p. 665. See also, *Marx, Capital* Volume 1, p. 337 and p. 934 and Marx, *The Revolutions of 1848: Political Writings, Volume 1* (Harmandsworth: Penguin Books, 1973), p. 296.

they were not inhuman. Well, you know, that was the worst of it - this suspicion of their not being inhuman ... what thrilled you was just the thought of their humanity - like yours - the thought of your remote kinship with this wild and passionate uproar. Ugly.'[26] For Marlow's Polish exile-British domiciled creator, History, as it were, catches up with him on the Congo but he fails to make the 'connection' *between* him and those Africans there being annihilated by two ruthless imperialisms from continental Europe - French and Belgian. Conrad also reminds his readers of how conversant he was with the chilling captions of the debates raging in Britain (and elsewhere in Europe) during the time by genocidist scholars writing and lecturing on the 'extermination of lower races' when he makes his *own* contribution to the record by ensuring that in Kurtz's final exhortation in his prepared report at his trading station, the latter proclaims: 'Exterminate all the brutes!'[27] It is this declaration that Sven Lindqvist, the Swedish writer, adopts as the title of his book to which we referred earlier. The tragic weakness of an otherwise profoundly illuminating and engaging book on the European execution of the African holocaust is evident in Lindqvist's use of Conrad's *Heart of Darkness* as the anchor for his sustained study without for once noting that the 'thoroughgoing racist,'[28] as Chinua Achebe aptly describes Conrad, is *directly implicated* in the African holocaust as those writers, scientists and statespersons so critically profiled in *'Exterminate All the Brutes'*.

Similarly, as we have already hinted, Marx, the German exile domiciled in England, does not recognise the humanity that is African. The African is coterminous with the slave, Marx argues instead, the artefact of economic production and vice-versa: 'What is a Negro slave? A man of the black race. The one explanation is as good as the other.'[29] The above schema is of course unscientific and seriously flawed in logic as Marx uses the concept 'negro,' an a-historical creation of the European oppressor, as a given referent from which he wishes to derive the historical African.[30] The fact is that the African enslaved

---

[26]Joseph Conrad, *Heart of Darkness and Other Tales* (London: Pickering and Chatto, 1993), p. 38.
[27]Ibid., p. 55.
[28]Achebe, *Hopes and Impediments*, p. 8.
[29]Marx and Engels, *Selected Works (In one volume)*, p. 79.
[30]Molefi Kete Asante is therefore correct when he notes: 'A slave is one who has been reduced to an artifact of an oppressor's creation and changed into something defined, fabricated, and marketed by the will of another as being useful for the oppressor's purposes, thereby losing one's own material and creative terms. Only in this context can

by the Europeans in the Americas and elsewhere is a *subject* of history. Whilst the slave-status has turned this African into some kind of 'capital,'[31] he/she is an unusual 'capital' different from the machinery and other 'categories' Marx cites below; this African is essentially *human, a human being*, and therefore the subject of the possibilities of an historic liberation to terminate the state of their subjugation then, or in the future, *whatever may be the consequences* to the oppressor - including the very one Marx refers to here in his 1846 letter to P. V. Annenkov which was later incorporated in his book, *The Poverty of Philosophy*:

> Freedom and slavery constitute an antagonism. I need not speak of the good and bad sides of freedom nor, speaking of slavery, need I dwell on the bad sides. The only thing that has to be explained is its good side. We are not dealing with indirect slavery, the slavery of the proletariat, but with direct slavery, the slavery of the black races in Surinam, in Brazil, in the Southern States of North America. Direct slavery is as much the pivot of our industrialism today as machinery, credit, etc. Without slavery no cotton; without cotton no modern industry. Slavery has given value to colonies; the colonies have created world trade; world trade is the necessary condition of large-scale machine industry. Thus, before the traffic in Negroes began, the colonies supplied the Old World with only very few products and made no visible change in the face of the earth. Slavery is therefore an economic category of the highest importance. Without slavery North America, the most progressive country would be transformed into a patriarchal land. You have only to wipe North America off the map of the nations and you get anarchy, the total decay of trade and of modern civilisation. But to let slavery disappear is to wipe North America off the map of nations.[32]

In the end, the marxist intellectual project, the most radical critique of existing European World global hegemony from within does not differ radically in its essence from its other more 'conservative' theoretical/political cousins on its

---

we truly understand the dangerous implications of the loss of terms. European slavery maintained the most brutal, total, and repugnant form of human reduction transforming the "organic materiality" of Africans into what was essentially an inorganic violence.' (See Asante, *Kemet, Afrocentricity and Knowledge*, p. 192.)

[31]Marx, *Capital, Volume 1*, p. 337.
[32]Marx and Engels, *Selected Works (In one volume)*, p. 665.

position on the crucial subject of the African holocaust. Nah Dove, in her recent excellent discussion on marxism and the African liberation concludes: 'Although [Marx] challenges the abusive and exploitative nature of European class oppression, he fails to understand [t]he nature of the racialised power relations and the racist oppression so critical in the construction of capitalism [and] [t]hat the resistance of African peoples and other nations and peoples against [European World] supremacy is an essential ingredient for social change.'[33]

Davidson's challenge

Finally, an examination of a European scholar on African history and the holocaust whose work distinctly stands apart from the rest in this grim 300 year-old catalogue of authors whose searing title could as well be 'Why We Support the African Holocaust, Conquest and Occupation'. Basil Davidson has been one of the major prolific writers on Africa in the past 50 years. His goal has been the quest for truth on Africa and about Africa, away from the malignity and slander of European academe and media on the subject. This mission has undoubtedly received a lot of resentment from the sturdy guardians of the 'writings of empire'. In a recent review of Davidson's work, Michael Bygrave notes that '[i]n Britain, Davidson is the often-overlooked fourth man in the group that includes his contemporaries and fellow historians, Christopher Hill, Eric Hobsbawm and E. P. Thompson ... These men's committed ... approach to writing history opened up the ... chauvinist world of British professional historians ... But whereas the others wrote about the British or European past, Davidson studied Africa ...'[34]

Davidson is one of the very few contemporary European World historians who has consistently emphasised Africa's seminal contributions to human civilisation, especially since its founding of Kemet (or ancient Egypt), the now-widely acknowledged humanity's first civilisation. He has again returned to this topic in a publication of his recent essays.[35] He has also been forceful in his discussion of the African holocaust throughout his studies. In a commemorative

---

[33] Nah Dove, 'Contra Marxism,' *African Peoples Review*, Vol IV, No. 3, July - December 1995, p. 3.
[34] As quoted in the *James Currey Publishers, New Books and Back List Catalogue* (Oxford), 1998, p. 7.
[35] See Davidson, *The Search for Africa*, pp. 318-333.

essay to mark 500 years after Christopher Columbus's infamous trans-Atlantic voyage, appropriately captioned 'The Curse of Columbus,' Davidson argues: 'Columbus was the father of the [African] slave trade to the Americas; and this trade, far more than any other consequences attached to his name, may be seen - it seems to me without the least manipulation of the evidence - as composing the true curse of Columbus.'[36] Occasionally though, the imposing architectural edifice of the Davidson *construction* wobbles, such is the hurricane-force wind pressure to pursue the truth about African history! In *Africa in History*, one of Davidson's most often-quoted books, the author employs the space of several pages of text documenting very graphically the atrocities perpetrated on conquered Africans by the Portuguese, French, Belgium and German occupation regimes during the second phase of the Africa holocaust.[37] For instance, he recalls that 14,000 ('official' figures), if not 20,000 Africans (quoting the independent studies and more reliable estimates of Catherine Coquery-Vidrovitch, the French historian), died during the construction of the Congo-Ocean railway in French-occupied central Africa between 1921 and 1932.[38] As for Germany, Davidson reviews that country's seizure of African lands and other property in Tanganyika and Cameroon, as well as providing statistical details of the German pogrom carried out on the Herero and Nama peoples of Namibia. For him to however conclude his focus on Namibia by stating that 'Nearly 75,000 had paid the price of imperial prestige,'[39] amounts to an astonishing understatement if this were the epitaph on such a devastating pogrom.

But it is on Britain, the leading conqueror force in Africa, that Davidson's approach to his overview of the pan-European occupation of Africa becomes markedly different. Here, he covers the British examples with carefully sanitated phraseologies that essentially bother on meaninglessness. Some examples from *Africa in History* are necessary to illustrate the point. In spite of clear-cut British atrocities in Kenya, the following is Davidson's quaint review of this occupation of east Africa:

> [T]he process of imperial enclosure was more often coercive than not, and that in no few cases it was violently destructive. These things may

---

[36]Ibid., p. 335.
[37]Basil Davidson, *Africa in History* (London: Granada Publishing, 1978), especially ch. 7.
[38]Ibid., pp. 266-67.
[39]Ibid., p. 273.

be disagreeable to remember. Yet no history can quite pass them by without a word, for the violence and destruction were also an influential part of the scene: their consequences, in fact, are with us to this day. They should not be allowed to obscure the humanitarian and civilising efforts of many excellent men and women nor sully the reputation of many colonial officials and soldiers whose principal sins were no worse than Victorian smugness, ignorance, and insensitivity to the claims of pre-industrial peoples. Nor should they, perhaps above all, form any reason for modern Africans to 'blame their condition' only on the failings or excesses of colonialism.[40]

At no place in his discussion does Davidson detail empirically the systematic expulsions of Africans from their homes and farmlands and their incarcerations into concentration camps euphemistically termed 'reserves' in the lexicon of the occupation, nor does he focus acutely on the British seizure of this now designated 'empty space' for European settlement and expropriation. Instead, Davidson exonerates these perpetrators of crimes against the African humanity on the grounds of 'Victorian smugness, ignorance, and insensitivity ...' For him to reduce the subject of the loss of a people's homeland as a result of a brutal foreign occupation to the ephemeral status of 'claims of pre-industrial peoples' is indeed astonishing. Would it have been different if the Gikuyu or Luo were industrial peoples? If Germany had succeeded in occupying Britain either during the 1914-1918 or 1939-45 intra-European Wars, how would British claims to the conquest differ from those of the Gikuyu or Luo, or the Igbo, Ibibio or Yoruba of west Africa (other examples of Britain's African conquest)? Just what amounts to the 'humanitarian and civilising efforts' of the British conquest on the lives of the surviving Gikuyu, Luo, Massai, Kipsigi, Nandi and other nations and nationalities in the region - jettisoned to concentration camps to singularly slave away for the occupation until their death? What really are the 'failings or excesses' of the British conquest? Finally, what is the agreeable or acceptable threshold to which 'modern Africans' should blame British/European brutalities of conquest on their contemporary 'condition'? As Davidson switches his review to southern Africa, that region of extensive British strategic experimentation on racial separateness and hierarchisation in the 19th century/early 20th century (effectively preceding Germany's 1930s/40s efforts in east and central Europe by at least 50 years), he could not have been

---

[40]Ibid., p. 270.

more amazingly bland: 'Forced labour practices might be less frequent here, but the end-result was to prove even worse than for the Africans of the French and other equatorial lands in the Congo Basin and its periphery. As the imperial structures took shape, Africans found themselves increasingly deprived of their best land, and often enough of all their land.'[41] Elsewhere, still on the subject of southern Africa, Davidson laces that blandness with courteous sensitivity whilst responding to the outrageous defence of British imperialism which was made by Alfred Milner, a one-time British chief representative in South Africa (and activist proponent of evolving apartheid during the early years of this century). Milner had described the British occupation as some '... moral [order] even more than material,' to which Davidson notes: 'Yet a disrespectful eye would have noticed that it was all one in the end.'[42]

Evidently, what emerges in this Davidson 2-track approach to European atrocities in occupied Africa is a tame, placid one for Britain, and a critical, rigorous one for the rest. No doubt, this smacks of a selective, *and* convenient reading of history. This could lead some people to reflect on the pointed observation made by John McClure elsewhere that if there is any relevance of Conrad's *Heart of Darkness*, it is that 'no European can be trusted to represent the [African].'[43] Seen either way, this observation is of course patronising as African existence and progress is not dependent on some European representation! European historians, writers, artists or journalists whose subject or focus of work is Africa should therefore not be expected to be involved in their vocation, *even whilst their quest is transparently informed by the search for truth*, because they would 'be trusted to represent the African' any more than African historians, writers, artists or journalists working on the European World should expect to 'be trusted to represent' the European. As a result, serious epistemological problems arise if there are any doubts about the following key propositions: (1) Europeans make their history; they ultimately write their history and represent the totality of the legacy of that history. (2) Africans make their history; they ultimately write their history and represent the totality of the legacy of that history. Given the obvious tragic circumstances of the history of Africa in the past half of a millennium, the African endeavour in accomplishing this task is not only extremely urgent but it also amounts to a far-reaching reconstruction programme.

---

[41] Ibid., p. 268.
[42] See Basil Davidson et al, *Southern Africa: The New Politics of Revolution* (Harmondsworth: Penguin Books, 1976), p. 24.
[43] See McClure, 'Problematic presence,' p. 162.

It would appear that Basil Davidson himself may have been reflecting on some of the issues just raised when he recently alluded to objections made by some commentators and viewers a few years ago over his presentation of an African History series on British television which was subsequently telecast on several television channels across the world.[44] The subject at stake was not strictly speaking a case of 'representation,' as one does not have to be a *representative* of some targeted social, national or racial audience in order to present a television programme on them. Davidson had therefore done nothing inappropriate to have made the broadcast and he was surely not 'representing' Africans in carrying out the task! Some had wondered why *an* African historian was not invited to write and present the programme and one critic specifically suggested that the series should have been broadcast by Cheikh Anta Diop, the African polymath whose scholarship in the last 50 years has comprehensively revolutionised the study of Africa and its peoples. Davidson's view on the latter suggestion was to indicate that Diop 'spoke no English.'[45] This was true, just as it was true that Diop 'wrote no English,' but neither of these should have been a totally convincing reason for Diop not to have presented the series - provided the programme organisers really wanted him to do so. Diop spoke (and wrote in) several other languages including Wolof and French and where required and necessary, his audience would have adequately followed his television lectures in any of these languages through that ancient device known to human beings called translation (it is through this process that most of the world have been able to access Diop's extensive research on Africa which was originally largely available in the French), which, in the contemporary age, has even been so technically perfected that it has become an indistinguishable feature of television viewing across the world. So, for our purposes, the following are more important questions to be posed on the 'controversy' generated by this television programme: (1) What did the organisers set out to achieve? (2) Did they consider inviting *an* African to write and present the programme? (3) Did they invite *an* African to present the programme? (4) Did they feel that *an* African *should* present the programme?

There are several African historians on both sides of the Atlantic who have spent most of their academic and intellectual lives writing and lecturing on European History. If the television series we have been discussing were on European History instead, would the programme organisers have invited one of

---

[44] See Davidson, *The Search for Africa*, p. 318.
[45] Ibid.

these African experts to write and present the series? Undoubtedly, the answer to this question must be 'most unlikely,' and the public at large, *particularly in the European World*, would not find such a decision controversial. No, not at all. Indeed, it is to the contrary decision, namely inviting *an* African expert to present such a programme that they will find most controversial! If the same perceptions and considerations that lead to the *expected* outcome in our last question do not extend to cover the grounding on questions 2, 3, and 4 (above), then it is clear that for the programme organisers of the series in question and similar features on Africa that are occasionally broadcast on Western radio and television, the teaching, writing and propagation of African History are not endeavours seen or felt to be actuated on the same level playing field as that of the European. In that case, Africans' current resolute demand for justice and reciprocity becomes more complex and complicated than just whether or not African History 'could be written [and broadcast] only'[46] by *an* African historian as Davidson has tended to limit the problem.

All considered though, Basil Davidson's scholarship on Africa is an unrivalled challenge against the tradition of those members of the European World intelligentsia (respectable men and women, some of whom are even revered in their various disciplines) who in the past 300 years have pursued a frenzied campaign to malign and vilify Africa and Africans in order, primarily, to avoid confronting the European perpetration of the most horrific and enduring genocide of the last millennium - the African holocaust. It should be recalled, as David Dabydeen has stressed,[47] that besides the obvious state, quasi-state or proto-state operatives of the day (namely the politician, the soldier, the merchant and the buccaneer), the European conquest of Africa and the rest of the world was the *work* of its intelligentsia - the poet, the novelist, the anthropologist, the philosopher, the historian, the biologist, the naturalist, the journalist ... Our study so far has demonstrated this role to be true. Davidson no doubt recognises the crucial importance of this role of the European intelligentsia and as such one should see the untiring *counter-thrust* of his scholarship as the foundation on which a seriously committed, alternative, European scholarship of recompense on Africa should be built. This is the only meaningful and productive path open for future European scholarship on Africa. Some might perhaps find the use of the term 'recompense' in this context unsettling, but that can only be the definitive outcome of a process in academe

---

[46]Ibid.
[47]David Dabydeen, 'This land is our land,' *New Statesman & Society* (London), 1 November 1991, p. 19.

and the media aimed at chipping away the age long chunks of lies and slander on Africa and Africans. Logically, this process opens up an additional front for the European intelligentsia to apologise for its *own* contributions to Europe's crimes in Africa, and throw its influential weight on current African demands for all-state apology and payments of restitution from the European World for these crimes and their incalculable aftermath.

Dimensions & extensions

It is significant that the scholar whose work of the past five decades opened up this historic possibility for the European intelligentsia to redeem itself from its role in Africa, is British. This is because, as we have shown, Britain is the principal beneficiary of the African holocaust. The ideology of Africophobism, which is aimed at explaining away the holocaust or perpetuating the outcome of it, was developed and largely codified in Britain. Within seven months of taking power in May 1997, the new Labour party-government in Britain which has declared that its relation with the rest of the world would be guided by what it calls 'ethical foreign policy,' chaired an international conference in London to discuss outstanding areas of European reparations to Jews over the Jewish holocaust of the 1930/40s. Yet, four years after its first term in government and a successful re-election in June 2001, there is no intention whatsoever from its officials including the prime minister and foreign secretary over extending this initiative to confront, in its entirety, the African holocaust which is to Britain what the Jewish holocaust is to Germany. On the contrary. By May 2001, any illusions that the chief architect and principal beneficiary of the African holocaust would embark on apologising and recompensing Africans for this monumental crime against humanity was put paid by the British position at a preparatory meeting for the August-September 2001 international conference on racism in South Africa. Britain led a pan-European World grouping of delegates that included the United States to oppose these historic African demands.[48] A legal opinion sought to explain the British response to the subject with telling insight: 'For nations such as Britain and Portugal, for instance, to agree to a resolution with that wording [that the African holocaust was a 'crime against humanity'] would be like signing an admission-of-guilt affidavit that

---

[48] *Daily Telegraph* (London), 22 May 2001.

could and probably would be used against them in any action for reparations.'⁴⁹

So, on this all important African subject, as it has been the case for successive British governments since the 16th century, it's business as usual for the new government: no acknowledgements, no apologies, no restitution. As if to underline the saliency even in contemporary British social life of the peccant language of the genocidist scholars of old on the African humanity, a British member of parliament would in the era of his country's so-called 'ethical' international relations warn his compatriots in an extensively publicised radio interview that they risked the 'mongrelisation' of Britain with the presence of what he described as 'massive immigration' of African and other Southern World people in the country.⁵⁰ Very few observers were shocked by the parliamentarian's choice and use of such racist language of discourse in the year 2001. This was due centrally to the identity of the population group that was the target of the outrage. Bill Morris, the country's African Caribbean senior labour leader, explains why such a comment could have been made by a highly-placed public figure without showing any feelings of sensitivity towards African descent people: '[Britain] is [a] land where ordinary [African descent populations] wake up every morning to listen on the radio to descriptions of themselves that they do not recognise.'⁵¹ In what appeared initially as an unrelated development as the ramifications of the 'mongrelisation' outrage spread in Britain, Jews who had to contend with the implementation of this epithet of hate and death in the death camps and chambers of east and central Europe 50 years ago, were treated to George Turner's informative 3-part survey of the state of Jews in the contemporary world.⁵² Turner reviews the contributions that Jews have made to the world, the long stretch of history of discrimination and violence, and the tragedy of the holocaust they were subjected to by Germany half a century ago and concludes his study by noting: 'The rest of us owe the Jews an irredeemable debt, and we ought never to forget it.'⁵³

Turner's was a distinct antidote to this season of racist nightmare that engulfed Britain. From all indications, it is still going to take a while yet for a similar serious survey on African people and history to be written by a Western

---

⁴⁹Ibid. For an excellent analysis of the legal issues at stake here, see Geraldine Van Bueren, 'It's Britain's guilty secret', *The Guardian* (London), 25 May 2001.
⁵⁰*Daily Telegraph* (London), 29 March 2001.
⁵¹*Daily Telegraph* (London), 29 April 2001.
⁵²See *Daily Telegraph* (London), 10 April, 11 April & 12 April 2001.
⁵³*Daily Telegraph* (London), 12 April 2001.

writer and published in a comparable mainstream Western medium of publicity as the Jewish example above, and with a conclusion that is as unambiguous as 'The rest of us owe Africans an irredeemable debt, and we ought never to forget it.' Even though such an acknowledgement of historic truth has still not been forthcoming from the West, the latter cannot delay much further to confront the fact that if there are any peoples in human history positioned on the apex of those owed the most 'irredeemable debt' by the West, such an unenviable position is surely occupied by Africans. We have demonstrated this clearly in this study. It is not fortuitous that Turner's excellent survey and conclusion on Jews in the contemporary world was published during that season of anti-African racist vituperations in Britain. Africans and Jews share the same source for the mayhem that has afflicted their respective recent histories. We have shown that there is a clearly discernible link between the earlier, more prolonged, more extensive, and therefore more devastating African holocaust, and the Jewish holocaust of the 1930s/40s: the mindset (more applicable to the African than the later as evidenced in the ideas and policies of successive statespersons - popes, bishops, priests, kings, queens, presidents, prime ministers, chancellors, etc – and the thoughts and writings of intellectuals of varying hues), corporate interests (several of today's very powerful Western names in banking, insurance, manufacturing and commerce were created by the staggering wealth generated by the enslavement of millions of Africans during the holocaust) and the socio-political institutions and systems that were responsible for perpetrating the crimes of history affecting these two peoples all emanated from one source – the European World. What has remained outstandingly significant to date has been the very contradictory responses of this source of so much devastation and anguish to the dual sectors of the gruesome heritage: for the Jews, the West accepts unfettered responsibility (hence, the Turner-type surveys), whilst for the African there is either outright denial or just a deafening silence on the subject, punctuated by periodic racist slurs and diatribes or, worse still, the rationalisation of the holocaust itself. In a way the halo surrounding Western penance and sense and state of restitution to Jews in the past 50 years, must act as a compulsory reference to the parameters and depth of commitment that the West will surely have to embark upon sometime in the future to redress the 'irredeemable debt' it owes Africa and Africans.

It is evident why the West has still not confronted its responsibility in perpetrating the African holocaust as it has done on the Jewish one despite the organic link between the two. Chinua Achebe, Africa's most outstandingly consistent writer and intellectual on the African holocaust and on the grounding for the continent's liberation and renaissance, provides the most elaborate panoramic and definitive reason for this. This is found in the quote which we have already cited and part of which we must again refer to here:

> [O]ne thing is certain: You do not walk in, seize the land, the person, the history of another, and then sit back and compose hymns of praise in his honour. To do that would amount to calling yourself a bandit; and you don't want to do that. So what do you do? You construct very elaborate excuses for your action. You say, for instance, that the person in question is worthless and quite unfit to manage himself or his affairs. If there are valuable things like gold and diamonds which you are carting away from his territory, you proceed to prove that he doesn't own them in the real sense of the word – that he and they just happened to by lying around the same place when you arrived. Finally, if the worse comes to the worst, you may even be prepared to question whether such as he can be, like you, fully human. From denying the presence of a man standing there before you, you end up questioning his very humanity.

Building on the intellectual foundation that maps out an unambiguous affirmation of the African heritage and historical process that was laid down 200 years earlier by Olaudah Equiano (another distinguished Igbo intellectual and author of the engaging *The Interesting Narrative of the Life of Olaudah Equiano or Gustavus Vassa the African*, published in 1789), Achebe has ensured that everything he has written from *Things Fall Apart* (1958) to *Home and Exile* (2000) is a treatise of this affirmation and the reconstruction of Africa after the devastating holocaust. It is to the examination of this Achebean *oeuvre* that we must now turn.

3
Exposition

Deep in the shed

Contrary to the nightmare that is the European World's elaborate construction of *that* Africa that merely serves its continuing reluctance to acknowledge and do penance for its perpetration of the African holocaust, African History in fact imposes itself doggedly and triumphantly on the human landscape of time and space as we have so far demonstrated in this study. For Chinua Achebe, the African *recall* and *rendering* of this history, including the ruthless disruptions from the European invasion, is a remarkably straightforward, disarmingly effortless, and a non-convoluted task. It is this that makes *Things Fall Apart* the classic that it is.

'Okonkwo was well known throughout the nine villages and even beyond.'[1] This 11-worded dramatic opening statement of the novel on the life and times of Ogbuefi Okonkwo of Umuofia is as defiant as it is engaging in establishing the African *presence* in History, right from the outset, after 'all the nonsense of Hegel,' and that of the other men and women who make up the raging army of eurocentric fabricationists and distortionists. Quite simply, if someone does not know of Okonkwo and his land and his people and his humanity, then they are surprisingly ignorant, or, worse still, pathetically ignorant, or just a mindless mischief maker. Chinweizu, Onwuchekwa Jemie and Ihechukwu Madubuike have roundly criticised Charles Larson's disquiet[2] over what the latter considers

---

[1] Chinua Achebe, *The African Trilogy: Things Fall Apart, No Longer At Ease, Arrow of God* (London: Pan Books, 1988), p. 17. Subsequent page details of citation made from any of the three novels in this trilogy will be quoted directly in the text preceded by *AT* and a colon.
[2] See Chinweizu, Onwuchekwa Jemie and Ihechukwu Madubuike, *Toward the Decolonization of African Literature, Vol I* (Enugu: Fourth Dimension, 1980), pp. 128-31.

as Achebe's limited 'characterisation of Okonkwo'[3] in *Things Fall Apart*. Understandably, Larson cannot co-exist with the Okonkwos of the African World; he prefers, instead, to interact with the African 'removed from history' by the European conquest,[4] as Walter Rodney would graphically put it. This is essentially why Larson is highly infatuated by Joyce Carey's characterisation of that lobotomised African called Mr Johnson in the latter's racist novel of the same title. Unlike Mr Johnson, Okonkwo is a *subject* of history and Larson cannot fail to recognise the import of this in that thundering opening statement of *Things Fall Apart* which could not have been any more definitive: 'Okonkwo was well known throughout the nine villages and even beyond.'

Despite the centuries of hostility directed by the guardians of eurocentricism on the African humanity, the African story does not require some pretentiously nor ornamentally turgid sociological or narrational *oeuvre*. Thus, Robert Wren is correct when he observes that '... much of Achebe's fiction, like the greatest fiction, has something of the compression of poetry, which says much in little.'[5] In contrast, Kole Omotoso is obviously unconvincing in his *Achebe or Soyinka?* where he asserts that the so-called 'complexity' or 'obscurity' of Wole Soyinka's literary contribution to this history of Africa is dictated by the latter's conviction that the Yoruba 'encounter' with the European World, unlike those of other Africans such as the Igbo, was a 'mere episode, a catalytic episode only.'[6] It is this 'mere episode,' Omotoso contends, that provides Soyinka with the 'area of his creative activity.'[7] He adds: 'The Yoruba ... accepted the negative [the genocide?/the exportation of peoples?/the occupation?] and saw something positive. They would attempt to compromise and accommodate, perhaps "shop around" among the offerings of both cultures and hope to put together something new out of the encounter ...'[8] Specifically indicating what he considers to be the *difference* in the Igbo experience to the European

---

[3]Charles Larson, *The Emergence of African Literature* (London and Basingstoke: Macmillan, 1978), p. 33.
[4]See Rodney, *How Europe Underdeveloped Africa*, p. 246.
[5]Robert Wren, *Achebe's World* (Harlow: Longman, 1990), p. xi.
[6]Kole Omotoso, *Achebe or Soyinka?* (East Grinstead: Hans Zell, 1996), p. 17. For more sanguine efforts in the past by some African scholars to defend the so-called 'obscurity' contributions of Wole Soyinka to this epoch of African history, see for instance Stanley Macebuh, 'Poetics and the Mythic Imagination,' *Transition*, 50, 1975-76, pp. 79-84 and Niyi Osundare, 'Words of Iron, Sentence of Thunder: Soyinka's Prose Style,' *African Literature Today*, No 13, 1983, pp. 24-37.
[7]Omotoso, *Achebe or Soyinka?*, p. 17.
[8]Ibid., p. 11.

conquest, Omotoso notes: 'The Igbo saw the British coming as an encounter with a strange Difference, an Other, a Contradiction, an encounter that can only be negative in terms of the effects on Igbo culture and its ways.'[9] Omotoso does not however specify what he means by the Yoruba acceptance of the 'negative' component or spheres of the conquest. The conquest broadly had three distinct junctures - namely, the genocide, the dispersal or the exportation of peoples, and the occupation of the lands of those who remained. Which of these have the Yoruba 'accepted'? Just one of the three, or two of the three, or all of them? What exactly does it mean for an African people to 'accept' *any* or *all* of these 'negative' attributes of a devastating holocaust? Apart from perhaps the Akan, the African holocaust had the gravest impact on the Yoruba. Arguably, more Yoruba than any other Africans, *including* the Igbo, were exported to the Americas and elsewhere by European slavers during the period. As J. S. Ade-Ajayi and Robert Smith have shown, the turbulent Yoruba civil wars of the 19th century were essentially sustained by these exports.[10] The consequences on the Yoruba nation were horrendous. It is therefore an outrage for any scholar, particularly a Yoruba for that matter, to describe this history as 'mere episode, a catalytic episode only.' If anyone elsewhere in the world were for instance to use similar phrases to describe the Jewish holocaust, a genocide far less in extent to the African on such critical spheres of comparison as the sheer brutality and dehumanisation of the episode, the numbers of people exterminated, the duration, and the overall impact on the course of human history in the last 500 years, not only would they be branded, correctly, 'anti-semitic,' and their career irrevocably blighted if they happened to be an academic, but they would run the risk of prosecution in many a European World country!

Such is the tragedy of the contemporary African World reality that phrases that depict this crass dismissal or marginalisation of the most prominent feature of the African history of the last millennium can be penned with scant critical unease by an African scholar. If indeed Soyinka's literary response to the African holocaust or his 'area of ... creative inquiry' is based on a flimsy patchwork of 'mere episode, a catalytic episode,' then Omotoso's *Achebe or Soyinka?*, contrary to the express intention of the author, not only reinforces the *grounds* for the main thrust of the African-centred critique of Soyinka's work which was articulated so forcefully nearly 20 years ago in *Toward the*

---

[9] Ibid.
[10] J. S. Ade-Ajayi and Robert Smith, *Yoruba Warfare in the nineteenth century* (Cambridge: Cambridge University, 1964).

Decolonization of African Literature, but it in fact opens up, albeit unwittingly, one, if not two possible avenues of explanation that account for the 'obscurity' preoccupation of Wole Soyinka. First, Soyinka's literary contribution to this epoch of African history, whether 'obscure' or not, has always been based on the playwright's limited reading or understanding of this history ('mere episode'). This, no doubt, amounts to a disquieting, if not an astonishing conclusion. Alternatively, Soyinka is fully and competently aware of *this* history, but prefers the limited, narrow reading that Omotoso suggests because it gives the playwright the opportunity not to confront his past! It therefore follows, thanks to *Achebe or Soyinka?*, that the unduly-discussed architectural 'obscurity' of Soyinka's work becomes nothing more than the dramatist's device to take refuge in resupinated diversions as Africa's great intellectual battles of the age rage, while others instead resolutely and valiantly deploy in trenches here and there for the continent's defence.

'Who can deny that of *all peoples*,' Cheikh Anta Diop once observed solemnly, 'Africans have been the greatest victims of aggression, racism and oppression? The consequences can be seen today in the state of underdevelopment and technical backwardness of African societies'(emphasis added).[11] The apogee of this devastation of a heritage for each and every African nation or people, without exception, was the '*loss of national sovereignty*' (emphasis in the original).[12] Five hundred years later, and into a new millennium, the aftermath of the African holocaust is all too familiar for anyone, anywhere, to interrogate: the mass impoverishment of African people wherever they are in the world and the extensive devastation of their continent coupled with the blunt refusal of the European World, the authors, perpetrators and beneficiaries of this genocide, to accept responsibility. This is the legacy that Africans are currently wrestling with. Positioned top on the priority of action is of course the unfettered recovery of African sovereignty. This requires two fields of activity that are by no means mutually exclusive: (1) the retrieval and reaffirmation of African History especially in the wake of centuries of eurocentric distortions, fabrications, and evasions which constitute the primary focus of this study and (2) the safeguarding of the vast African human and natural resources for the extensive reconstruction required following the holocaust. African resources must hence be used exclusively by Africans for the benefits of Africans themselves.

---

[11] See Carlos Moore, 'Conversation with Cheikh Anta Diop,' *Presence Africaine*, Nos 3/4, 1993, p. 418.
[12] Ibid., p. 381.

So, in pursuance of the reconstruction of African History, African intellectuals must be uncompromising and untiring in setting the records straight. They would need to confront eight fundamental questions during this endeavour: (1) What were the salient socio-economic features and processes in Africa *prior* to the epoch of the conquest and loss of national sovereignty that constitute the subject of their reconstruction? (2) Who carried out this conquest? (3) What were the objectives? (4) What were the outcomes? (5) How has the conquest shaped the contemporary world? (6) How did Africa that is the subject of their reconstruction *respond* to this conquest and loss of national sovereignty? (7) What *Africanness* can they reclaim under the encrusted layers of this conquest, the dispersal, and occupation? (8) How has Africa which is the subject of their reconstruction been *coping* with this History during the age of the Re-establishment of National Sovereignty which began in the mid-1950s?

This reconstructionary process is not only liberatory on a personal level but it provides the scholar with the possibilities of having the outcome of their work become an invaluable contribution to the ever expansive library of African-centred historiography worldwide. Furthermore, the rigour of the project battles head on with the varying influences and guises of eurocentricism which have tried in the past to limit, distort or indeed obliterate the total picture of the African holocaust in order to let the European World off the hook of culpability. Such guises have ranged from the 'mere episode, a catalytic episode only' genre to the current fad that parades under the flag of the 'end of history'. The African story must be told unequivocally with confidence, commitment and courage. It is the heuristic foundation of the all-embracing African-centred historiography that effects the rupture that African discourses must make from the enthralling grip of eurocentric control. Chinua Achebe has observed: '[p]eople create stories create people; or rather stories create people create stories.'[13] 'Narratives,' Dan Izevbaye has therefore argued, 'are a cultural necessity because they are the means of bringing a meaningful structure to bear upon reality. Narratives are the signs of the order that human consciousness has harvested from the chaos of the past. The cultural importance of narratives is evident in the amount of material and intellectual resources that are invested in their preservation.'[14] Thus, the compulsive tight economy of words that Achebe deploys in his narrative in *Things Fall Apart* underlines the urgency of this task of African-centred reckoning of history - girded by the rich poetic and cultural

---

[13] Achebe, *Hopes and Impediments*, p. 112.
[14] Izevbaye, 'History's Eye-Witness,' pp. 22-23.

assuredness of Igbo life and living: 'among these people a man was judged according to his work and not according to the worth of his father' (*AT*: 20). Indeed by the end of chapter one, which is just about four and one-third pages long, the author establishes a discerning profile of Okonkwo, the main protagonist in the novel: his upbringing and family ties, his friends, his achievements, and a fascinating overview of the juridico-spiritual and political economic foundation of Umuofia. We can fully recognise Okonkwo for who he is without any ambiguities. If someone doesn't, that state of ignorance is theirs and theirs alone!

Okonkwo's 'fame rested on solid personal achievements' (*AT*: 1). He achieves his goals in life very quickly. He overturns his poor and wretched family inheritance from a lazy father by becoming an industrious and wealthy farmer whilst still a young man, and by raising a respectable large family. Politically, he emerges as one of the distinguished leaders of Umuofia, a position acquired as a result of being a valiant general of his people at war, an envoy-extraordinary to the neighbouring *mba* (or states) during times of emergency, a recipient of several titles of high honour, and a steadfast defender and upholder of the values and traditions of Umuofia. Okonkwo has indeed 'cracked his own palm-kernels himself,' as his people would say, 'rather than having this done for him by some benevolent spirit (sic)' (*AT*: 34). His rags-to-riches success story is aptly summed up in the Igbo adage: 'Looking at a king's mouth, one would think he never sucked at his mother's breast' (*AT*: 34).

Achebe's project here is of course not the evocation of a romantic blast of Umuofia history. The contradictoriness of Umuofia's social existence is laid bare for sure. In Okonkwo's struggles to succeed to overcome poverty, we examine simultaneously the background highlighting the blight of poverty and deprivation and the modes or modality of overcoming it, as well as the attendant Umuofia attitudes to socio-economic differences, opportunities and progress. No more illustrative example than Unoka's, Okonkwo's father, will suffice! He is heavily indebted, poor, and an unsuccessful farmer. Why? He is 'lazy and improvident and was quite incapable of thinking about tomorrow' (*AT*: 18). But Unoka surely has other talents to offer society! He is after all a cultural worker - flutist and dancer especially during those three months' 'season of rest' (*AT*: 61) after the end of the yam harvest and the beginning of the new planting season. He would travel around Umuofia and elsewhere performing with various dance troupes and exchanging and learning new compositions. But his entertaining skills do not help to improve his standing in society because 'his wife and children had barely enough to eat' (*AT*: 18-19). Indubitably, the accomplishment of this crucial family task is a benchmark for measuring the relevance and the success of the choice of one's occupation or indeed vocation in Umuofia. The family is very important in Umuofia, typifying African social existence. It is celebrated as not only the ensemble of the synthesisation of the love and affection between husband and wife/wives, but also the incorporation of the two different families that predicate on the 'union', and, by extension, the two lineages from whence the 'contributing' families emerged in the first place. As a result, the role of the man, the husband, in providing the financial supportive mechanism for the sustenance and progress of the family is crucial in the Umuofia sociological order. Thus, his musical talents notwithstanding, Unoka is pronounced 'a failure' (*AT*: 18) precisely because of his inability to fulfil this family task. We should recall that when Olaudah Equiano, the prominent Igbo ex-enslaved public person, intellectual, African liberationist and explorer describes his people as 'a nation of dancers, musicians and poets'[15] in his celebrated 18th century autobiography (*The Interesting Narrative of the Life of Olaudah Equiano or Gustavus Vassa the African*), he is of course not writing about the Unokas in society, as he adds pointedly that Igboland grows assorted foods and fruits and raises varieties of livestock.[16] For Umuofia, therefore, a person's overall success in society demands a more multidisciplinary capability infused with *social responsibility* (particularly in supporting one's family/community), which would make an Okonkwo, not Unoka, a 'loafer' (*AT*: 19), a preferred model for progress. Yet, the existence and in fact the extent of Okonkwo's breadth-taking triumph over the acute social deprivation he inherits at birth cannot be fully comprehended without our insight into the Unoka legacy. Indeed, the dialectical complexity and resonance of the Unoka-Okonkwo dyad in the novel underscores that salient plank of Igbo philosophy which contends that 'Wherever Something stands, Something Else will stand beside it.'[17] Furthermore, in reflecting on the sharply contrasting careers of this father and son and their social standing in Umuofia, it is obvious to note that Umuofia is a meritocratic society - even if for some individuals success is achieved, in the final instance, with the assistance of a 'benevolent spirit.' Later, we shall be returning to this subject of 'meritocracy' in Igboland to determine how this heritage fares in the wake of the late 19th century/early 20th century British conquest and occupation, and how it literally battles for its survival

---

[15]See Paul Edwards, ed., *Equiano's Travels* (London: Heinemann Educational Books, 1967), p. 3.
[16]Ibid., pp. 4-8 especially.
[17]Chinua Achebe, *Morning Yet on Creation Day* (London: Heinemann Education Books, 1975), p. 94.

during the post-conquest epoch of the Igbo presence in the haunting quagmire that is the Nigerian federation.

In the meantime, one cannot ignore, with a deep sense of irony, that in the Western sociological stereotyping of the African, especially its male in the contemporary European World, the Unoka-type profile of indolence and 'entertainer' (especially in sport activity or non-durable popular music) is preferred and assiduously cultivated in children's literature, in schools, in the media (particularly television) and through other agencies of cultural life. Where or when serious African classical musical creativity for instance openly challenges these underlying racist sociological assumptions, the responses from the guardians and commentators of Western cultural institutions are often swift and predictably invidious, a position aptly typified by the British jazz critic and poet, Philip Larkin, which we should examine at some length given the importance of the subject in contemporary cultural life.

Larkin is very unhappy of the phenomenal revolution in jazz, African American classical music, which began with bebop in the 1940s and reinforced by free jazz in the 1950s/1960s with the following astonishing reflections:

> The tension between artist and audience in jazz slackened when the Negro stopped wanting to entertain the white man ... The jazz band in the night club declined ... [J]azz moved, ominously, into the culture belt, the concert halls, university recital rooms and summer schools ... Men such as Ornette Coleman, Albert Ayler and Archie Shepp, dispensed with pitch, harmony, theme, tone, tune and rhythm, were copied by older (Rollins, Coltrane) and young players alike. And some of them gave a keener edge to what they were playing by suggesting that it had some political relation to the aspirations of the Black Power movement. From using music to entertain the white man, the Negro had moved to hating him with it.[18]

Essentially, it was the deeper *africanisation* of jazz which went in tandem with the great African revolt in the US and elsewhere during the period that most upset Larkin. Against the background of the throbbing liberatory lines of the compositions and performances of earlier epochs such as Duke Ellington's 'Black, Brown and Beige' and Charlie Parker's 'Now's The Time,' leading jazz

---

[18] Philip Larkin, *All What Jazz* (London: Faber and Faber, 1985), p. 24.

musicians at the time made seminal compositions and albums that became instant standards of interventionist engagement with the revolutionary politics of the age. These included Ellington (*Money Jungle*), Miles Davis ('So What'), Max Roach (*We Insist!: Freedom Now Suite, Deeds Not Words,* 'Man from South Africa'), Sonny Rollins (*The Freedom Suite*), Jackie McLean (*Let Freedom Ring*, 'Appointment In Ghana'), Andrew Hill (*Point of Departure, Black Fire, Shades*), Charles Mingus (*Pithecanthropus Erectus, Meditations on Integration, Right Now,* 'Fables of Faubus', 'All The Things You Could Be By Now If Sigmund Freud's Wife Was Your Mother', 'Lock 'Em Up'), Oliver Nelson (*Straight Ahead, Blues and the Abstract Truth*), Albert Ayler ('Truth is Marching In'), Lee Morgan ('Zambia', 'Mr Kenyatta', *Search For The New Land*) Eric Dolphy (*Out To Lunch*), Mal Waldron (*The Quest, Free At Last*), Tony Williams (*Spring*), Archie Shepp (*Freedom, Yasmina/Poem For Malcolm*), Alice Coltrane (*Ptah The El Daoud*), George Russell (*Ezz-thetics, Outer Thoughts*), Thelonious Monk (*Evidence, Misterioso*, 'Straight, No Chaser', 'Invitation'), Booker Little (*Out Front*) and Ornette Coleman (*Change Of The Century, Tomorrow Is The Question*). A brief reflection on the prodigious contribution of John Coltrane, perhaps the most influential musician during this cultural renaissance, is vital in excoriating the gaping africophobist grounds of Larkin's irrepressible attack.

Coltraneology

It is worth recalling that prior to forming his own band in 1957, John Coltrane had spent his first eight years as a professional musician playing in a number of bands of the be-bop movement, most notably the Dizzy Gillepsie big band and the Johnny Hodges combo. But it was during his tenure in the tenor saxophone chair in the Miles Davis Quintet, first in 1955-57, and in the expanded sextet during 1958-1960 (incorporating Cannonball Adderley on alto saxophone), that the world began to take notice of who would soon be the most iconoclastic jazz saxophonist since Charlie Parker. At the time with Davis, Coltrane had moved from the standard be-bop scalar improvisation genre to exhaust the possibilities embodied in chord variations of standard compositions - his 'sheets of sound' phase.[19] *Giant Steps*, one of Coltrane's memorable 1957 albums as leader, typifies this shift. Next, of course, was the sextet's experimentation with modes

---

[19]Dean Tudor and Nancy Tudor, *Jazz* (Littleton: Libraries Unlimited, 1979), p. 170.

with few chord changes beginning with the 1958 *Milestones* to the exquisite *Kind of Blue* in 1959. Coltrane would use this experimentation on modal jazz as his launching pad for continuous melodic excavations to produce a range of albums in the subsequent five years including the following landmark signatures: *My Favorite Things, Coltrane Jazz, Bye Bye Black Bird, Live at Birdland, The Avant-Garde, Brazilia, Afro Blue Impressions, Impressions, The Legend, A Love Supreme, Live at Village Vanguard, Transition, Ascension, Live at Seattle* and *Africa/Brass*. Following *A Love Supreme* in 1964, Coltrane gave notice of his abandonment of most rules that had governed jazz compositions to date. Coinciding with the great African American liberation movement of the era, the free jazz interplay threaded stretched but interrupted melodic lines, entombed harmonic hubs, and pushed the saliency of the instantaneity that is often the hallmark of jazz creativity to the fore. It should however be stressed that the relevance of the three 'phases' of Coltrane's musical career just sketched lies more for its analytical import rather than any rigid ruptures in what is on the whole a clearly coherent testament of an odyssey. A continuing thread that runs through the inner workings of coltraneology is its preoccupation with African-centredness. While ill-health and sudden death in July 1967 denied Coltrane his well-advanced plan to visit and study in Africa, the motherland evoked, centrally, the musical imaginations and cathartic probes of his ten years (1957-1967) as band leader or leading soloist in other groups. In the 1957-59 period, Coltrane's interpretations of African themes in two critical 1957 personal albums, as well as a couple of 1958 albums made by a sextet led by trumpeter Wilbur Harden are instructive. The Harden albums are appropriately entitled *Dial Africa* and *Tanganyika Strut* and the tracts therein have a telephonic urgency of an African continental directory: 'Dial Africa,' 'Oomba,' 'Gold Coast' and 'Tanganyika Strut'. The tracts 'Dakar' and 'Bakai' from Coltrane's own albums complement these African references. None of these compositions is actually Coltrane's, but the tone colours of his solos and exchanges with other horns (conferencing with the dual baritone presence of Cecil Payne and Pepper Adams on 'Dakar'; the enduring two-cornered dialogue with baritone saxophonist Sahib Shihab and trumpeter John Spawn on 'Bakai,' and the majestic interchanges with Harden and trombonist Curtis Fuller on those other entries in the Harden phonebooks), and the underlying rhythmic foundations of the music here, are richly embellished with African ornamentation.

In the 1960-67 period, African themes become more programmatic in the Coltrane trajectory. Coltrane reels off several compositions that focus on identifiable African persons, places and events: 'Ogunde,' 'Tunji,' 'Africa,'

'Liberia,' 'Dahomey Dance,' and 'Kulu Se Mama'. No doubt the 1961 big band (15 members) performance of *Africa/Brass*, with the breadth-taking orchestration by his friend and multi-intrumentalist Eric Dolphy, is a dress rehearsal of the Africanised spiritual music which we referred to earlier, and which would be most pronounced in Coltrane's output in the last three years of his life, beginning with the December 1964 *A Love Supreme* and continuing with the eschatological treatise called *Stella Regions* which was initially recorded in February 1967 but not released until 1995 - 28 years later! *Stella* tracts such as 'Seraphic Light,' 'Sun Star,' 'Configuration,' 'Tranesonic' and 'Stella Region' itself underline the exploratory, and quite often incantatory transcedental African spirituality which all along defined Coltrane's music, but particularly in the last three years of his life beginning with that much discussed, much reflected upon, and most expressive majestic rendering for the gods called *A Love Supreme*. While *Interstellar Space* which was recorded a week after *Stella* is a duo performance with Rashied Ali on drums (thus giving Coltrane all the space to evoke and configure the tapestry of sound that elucidate the planetary references to 'Mars,' 'Venus,' 'Jupiter,' 'Saturn' and 'Leo'), the proceedings in *Stella* are executed more conventionally in the quartet mode: the Master on tenor saxophone; Alice Coltrane, piano; Jimmy Garrison, bass, and Ali, drums. The outcome is nonetheless the same. The interrogative tension and quest in 'Seraphic Light,' 'Sun Star,' or 'Tranesonic' are not too dissimilar from the throbbing and exhilarating escapades in 'Mars,' or 'The Father and the Son and the Holy Ghost' movement in *Meditations* (recorded 1965) or the transfigurative and triumphant 11-member ensemble walkout in *Ascension* nor does the sensuousness and serenity in 'Venus' not as evocative as the sketch of 'Iris' in *Stella* or 'Serenity' in *Meditations* or indeed 'Psalm' in *A Love Supreme*. The point is that whatever the personnel line up, Coltrane's music has an integrative spiritual coherence about it which is easily traceable to his upbringing in North Carolina (United States) in the 1930s where his grandfather was a politically conscious and active minister of St Stephen's African Episcopal Zion Church in Hamlet.[20] Consequently, the themes on Africa, African Essence and African Reality, become the propelling force in Coltrane's seminal musical quest for life's meaning and in his enduring contribution to the great African liberation struggle on both sides of the Atlantic.[21]

Finally, moving away from music to axiology and aesthetics, a now familiar

---

[20] Bill Cole, *John Coltrane* (New York: Da Capo, 1993), pp. 24-25.
[21] Cf. ibid., p. 51.

Western response to crucial African liberatory projects is again expressed ritualistically without due critical analysis. For instance, it is not surprising that Terry Eagleton, the marxist literary critic we encountered earlier whilst discussing Joseph Conrad racist literature on Africa, appears completely unaware of the *cultural import* for African liberation of that defiant and assertive African American declaration, 'Black is beautiful', that blazed the struggles of the 1960s. For Eagleton, this affirmation is 'rhetorical' and cannot be taken as 'true' on its face value.[22] Even more emphatically, he does not think that the 'truth' of the declaration could be 'proven' except it can be demonstrated that none of the attributes that constitutes the broad range of the converse of the affirmation can be shown to be 'false' especially that which predicates on the racist society which triumphalises those indices that it terms 'white'.[23] At the end, Eagleton fails to make any headway in his attempt to interrogate the 'validity' of the African conviction of this historic axiological affirmation. This is because the basis of his inquiry remains trapped in the same reductionist binary linguistic bind of discursive universe which, *a priori*, defines the racist society that consigns the African humanity's presence as the cluster or clusters of 'negations' to the presumed status of Europeans. It does not occur to Eagleton that Africans in the United States or indeed anywhere else in the world could proclaim that the 'African is beautiful' without necessarily foreshadowing a discourse that elicits a parallel or comparative insight on the views or experiences of Europeans or any other peoples for that matter on the specific subject at hand, or on the broader issue of 'beauty'. When, for instance, the Igbo say 'Nwanyi a manma' ('This woman is beautiful'), or give a baby girl the name, Amaka ('beauty'), they are imposing an authoritatively exclusive cultural judgement on an axiological or aesthetical appreciation of human taste and experience which is bound to differ somehow from their Ibibio or Bini neighbours, not to talk of that of the Scots who live 6,000 miles away from them or the Iroquois who are 4,000 miles further away. Elsewhere, Molefi Kete Asante refers to the popular African American expressions, 'beauty is as beauty does' and 'she's beautiful because she's good'[24] to underscore the multifaceted and more complex meaning that a particular culture could independently derive and practicalise upon from a concept that would otherwise appear to have incontestable 'universal' intelligibility. It is now clear, if ever any further

---

[22]Terry Eagleton, *Walter Benjamin or Towards a Revolutionary Criticism* (London: Verso Editions and NLB, 1981), p. 112.
[23]Ibid., pp. 112-113.
[24]Asante, *Kemet, Afrocentricity and Knowledge*, p. 11.

evidence was required, that the eurocentric denials of African affirmation are pursued at multifocal spheres or sites of activity and that the cultural arena, which these varied examples above aptly attest to, are highly *targeted and prized* ones, often treated as the linchpin to neutralise the possibilities of a complete African recovery and reconstruction.[25]

The father and the son and the spirit and society

Chinua Achebe's early introduction in *Things Fall Apart* of the story of Ikemefuna, the young hostage-of-war from the neighbouring state of Mbaino who is in 'custody' in Umuofia as a condition of averting war between the two communities, is another plank that the author constructs for the interrogation of the complex and contradictory social inheritance of Umuofia. The drama surrounding Ikemefuna, the 'ill-fated lad' (*AT*: 21), is excruciatingly tense as he is in fact brought to Umuofia by no other than General Okonkwo who headed the delegation that lodged the Umuofia war ultimatum at Mbaino. In the meantime, it is in Okonkwo's household that Ikemefuna is domiciled, living there at the behest of the leadership of Umuofia, until his 'final fate,' invariably certain, is determined by the same leadership, one of whom is Okonkwo. Ikemefuna is loved in his new home and receives the same parental care and support as Okonkwo's other eight children. As far as he is concerned, *Okonkwo is his father*. Tragic as it is, this drama is a singularly crucial sub-plot in *Things Fall Apart* because its outcome impacts directly, and, in some cases, indirectly, on the key socio-cultural motifs explored in the novel which help to illuminate our greater understanding of the lives of the people of Umuofia. These include the subject of *chi*, or personal god, the position of the other gods/goddesses/deities and their influence on the individual(s) and the environment, the relationship or balance between personal initiative/individual rights and public responsibilities or expectations.

Three years after his arrival from Mbaino, a decision is finally taken on Ikemefuna's future by the leaders of Umuofia. A curious, if not extraordinary intervention occurs soon after this decision is made known. The highly respected Ogbuefi Ezeudu, himself a senior member of the leadership, and in

---

[25]It is in this context that the thrust of Ngugi wa Thiong'o's observations on the saliency of this cultural site of subjugation are enduring despite some unease expressed by Abdul JanMohamed (see Abdul JanMohamed, *Manichean Aesthetics* [Amherst: University of Massachusetts, 1983], P.186.)

effect an *assessory* to the decision, visits Okonkwo and warns the latter in no uncertain terms:

> That boy calls you father. Do not bear a hand in his death. Yes, Umuofia has decided to kill him. The Oracle of the Hills and the Caves has pronounced it. They will take him outside Umuofia *as is the custom*, and kill him there. But I want you to have nothing to do with it. He calls you father (emphasis added; *AT*: 55).

What does one make of this intervention? How does Okonkwo react to it? By indicating that the execution of Ikemefuna would be carried out 'as is the custom,' it is clear that Ezeudu does not question the legitimacy of the deity's directive. But that does not stop him from advising, or rather instructing Okonkwo not to participate in the killing of the young man. Is Ezeudu then challenging the gods? Does he have to challenge the gods? If so, why? What is really at stake?

There is no evidence in the novel of any direct *personal* interest that Ezeudu has in the Ikemefuna episode. We do not know if the ogbuefi attended the Umuofia emergency meeting which decided on the dispatch of an ultimatum to Mbaino. Such was the importance of the meeting that barring ill-health or other serious personal problem, Ezeudu would have been there, joining the other titled and distinguished persons in the land in attendance. No reference of his contribution in the meeting is made, but then apart from Ogbuefi Ezeugo, the 'powerful orator [who] always... speak[s] on such occasion' (*AT*: 23), no other speaker is mentioned by name even though there must surely have been several other contributors considering the gravity of the subject matter of the gathering. It is rather obvious that in the absence of any decisive dissenting views at the meeting, given the clear-cut nature of the Mbaino 'aggression' (the murder of the Umuofia woman in an Mbaino market - *AT*: 23), the narrative does not wish to over-labour the text with a profile of the rest of the contributions. The final outcome - the ultimatum to Mbaino - is therefore unanimous and its implementation 'follow[s] the normal course of action' (*AT*: 23-24), a clear reference to Umuofia's famed military pre-eminence in the region. The other point to note, which would have been fully considered by Ogbuefi Ezeudu prior to delivering his dramatic warning to Okonkwo, is that Umuofia's revered Oracle of the Hills and Caves, the deity that oversees the nation's war and peace options during periods of emergency, is also the ultimate deciding authority on the future of the young man from Mbaino.

Indeed, Ezeudu himself mentions the deity by name for having 'pronounced' the death sentence, as he instructs Okonkwo not to participate in carrying it out. In effect, Ezeudu authenticates the veracity of the source of the sentence - an important god in the land, a god of justice who in the past has stopped even the formidable Umuofia from waging any wars that it, itself, considered 'unjust' or 'a fight of blame' (*AT*: 24). *So, the Oracle of the Hills and Caves is definitely not a god that one would wish to challenge, not least by the respected Ogbuefi Ezeudu.* On the contrary, Ezeudu gives his controversial advice to Okonkwo well aware that the latter's non-participation in Ikemefuna's execution does not in any way undermine the implementation of the deity's edict. Thus established, he could point out that there is no where in the edict that states that Okonkwo should personally partake in the execution. In that case, Ezeudu's advice is aimed at ensuring that Okonkwo, another respected member of the Umuofia society, does not feel that he has to exercise *his personal* responsibility to public duty, even if it is fully justified in the prevailing circumstances ('Umuofia has decided to kill him'), by contributing to the fulfilment of the directive of the gods. As far as Ezeudu is concerned therefore, Okonkwo's role at this occasion is complicated by the rather *personal dimension* of the subject matter ('That boy calls you father') which no doubt originates from Okonkwo's public responsibility of taking care of Ikemefuna on behalf of the people of Umuofia (*AT*: 24-25). In effect, it is this personal dimension of the Ikemefuna episode which Ezeudu feels takes precedence over other considerations, particularly as it enables Okonkwo, in concert especially with his *chi* which could not conceivably order or approve of someone killing their child/children, not to partake in the forthcoming execution under the aegis of wishing to carry out some community responsibility.

It is important to raise the subject of *chi*[26] at this stage of the discussion because it is the reference that helps us to appreciate more fully the importance

---

[26] '*Chi*' is undoubtedly the most dominant concept in Igbo religion/spirituality that has attracted innumerable debates, expositions and discourses among Igbo writers, historians, philosophers, theologians, clerics and the like. See, for instance, Donatus Nwoga, *The Supreme God as Stranger in Igbo Religious Thought* (Ekwereazu: Hawk, 1984), Achebe, *Morning Yet on Creation Day*, Victor Uchendu, *The Igbo of South Eastern Nigeria* (New York: Holt, Rinehart and Winston, 1965), Elechukwu Njaka, *Igbo Political Culture* Evanston: Northwestern University, 1974), Francis Arinze, *Sacrifice in Ibo Religion* (Ibadan: Ibadan University, 1970), Christopher Ezekwugo, *Chi: The True God in Igbo Religion* (Alwaye: Pontifical Institute of Philosophy and Theology, 1987) and B. I. Chukwukere, 'Chi in Igbo Religion and Thought: The God in Every Man,' *Anthropos*, 78 (1983), pp. 519-534.

of the Ezeudu intervention and the interplay of the 'personal' and 'public' gods in Igbo spirituality/religion. It is true that Ezeudu does not mention the word *chi* any where in his unambiguously brisk instruction to Okonkwo not to participate in the impending execution of Ikemefuna, but he does deal with the subject, albeit indirectly, in that his famous injunction: 'That boy calls you father. Do not bear a hand in his death.' By emphasising the personal implication for Okonkwo, if the latter were to participate in the death of Ikemefuna, Ezeudu essentially shifts the legitimate directorial responsibility of the unfolding execution drama away from the corporate leadership of Umuofia to Okonkwo personally. But Okonkwo could not justify such a responsibility on personal grounds either in the text of the edict of the Oracle of the Hills and Caves or, more importantly, according to the scruples of his inner being, or that 'unique god-agent'[27] in him which the Igbo call one's *chi*. For Okonkwo, his disposition to partake in the execution rests firmly on a *social responsibility* which, he reasons, equally applies to any other adult member of the Umuofia population: '... someone had to do it. If we were all afraid of blood, it would not be done' (*AT*: 62).

Ezeudu is therefore well assured as he embarks on his magisterial intervention at Okonkwo's residence that no one's *chi* would order them to kill their child. On the basis of this alone, it should constitute sufficient moral grounds for an interlocutor to warn a person contemplating on embarking on committing such an act, *whatever* may be the motivations or impulses, that 'This boy calls you father. Do not bear a hand in his death.' By emphasising the word 'whatever,' we are assuming that among a range of possibilities that would incorporate the motive or impulse to commit such a murder, there must surely include the most grave scenario yet where a god, including perhaps the indomitable Oracle of the Hills and Caves, could, for instance, order someone to kill their child! Indeed, Obierika, Okonkwo's closest and 'greatest friend' (*AT*: 105), a person 'who thought about things' (*AT*: 105), and the authorial voice in the novel,[28] anticipates such a possibility when in his own admonition of Okonkwo's involvement in the death of Ikemefuna, he insists that 'if the Oracle said that my son should be killed I would neither dispute it nor be the one to do it'(*AT*: 63). In essence, there appear to be no grounds on which the people of Umuofia would make an exception on this score of personal responsibility and judgement, despite Okonkwo's more flexible position on the

---

[27] Achebe, *Hopes and Impediments*, p. 39.
[28] Cf. Biodun Jeyifo's interesting appraisal, 'For China Achebe: The Resilience and the Predicament of Obierika,' *Kunapipi*, Vol XII, No 2, 1990, pp. 51-70.

subject that 'someone had to do it' (*AT*: 62). To underline the seriousness of the situation, Obierika invokes the retributive justice of the earth goddess, *ani*, as he warns his friend: 'If I were you I would have stayed at home. What you have done will not please the Earth. It is the kind of action for which the goddess wipes out whole families' (*AT*: 63). It seems paradoxical that Obierika has had to refer to *ani*, another deity in the Igbo pantheon, as a way of counterposing Okonkwo's own preferred, open and non-personalised interpretation of the Ikemefuna death directive from the Oracle of the Hills and Caves. On the contrary, this is a deft move by Obierika who must be aware that his friend could not fail to recognise that with his reference to *ani*, the goddess that oversees society's moral order, he, Obierika, is clearly hinting that by participating in the execution of Ikemefuna, Okonkwo may have committed the abominable crime of *nso-ani*, or taboo-to-earth, whose punishment invariably carries a *direct* personal censure.

Derek Wright completely misses the complexity of this facet of Umuofia society when he alleges that Obierika and Ezeudu's position on the subject constitutes a contrivance which rests on the following maxim: 'offend neither the gods by hindering nor one's own conscience by helping.'[29] Nothing could be further from the truth. What these two respected members of Umuofia's leadership are highlighting in their respective interventions on this issue is a cardinal feature in Igbo religion/spirituality which expects a person to worship all the gods in the Igbo pantheon equally all the time, in contrast to the liberty of selectiveness which exists among other nations and peoples. Hence, the Igbo adage: 'You may worship Udo to perfection and still be killed by Ogwugwu.'[30] Okonkwo could thus feel that he has dutifully carried out the decree of the Oracle of the Hills and Caves as we have seen, but risks unmitigated sanctions from say, *ani*, the earth goddess, if his action(s), whilst implementing the directive of the oracle, are in breach of *ani*'s moral code! Okonkwo is however quick to discount committing any such breaches: 'The Earth cannot punish me for obeying her messenger ... A child's fingers are not scalded by a piece of hot yam which its mother puts into its palm' (*AT*: 63). Yet, Okonkwo would probably still recall, with some foreboding, the story of the dramatic reaction of Obiako, the Umuofia palm wine tapper, who had felt no obligation to carry out the instruction of the oracle who had asked him to sacrifice a goat at the

---

[29]Derek Wright, 'Things Standing Together: A Retrospect on *Things Fall Apart*,' *Kunapipi*, Vol XII, No 2, 1990, p. 79.
[30]Quoted in Chinua Achebe, 'Words of anxious love,' *The Guardian* London), 7 March 1992, p. 21.

behest of his late father: 'Ask my dead father if he ever had a fowl when he was alive' (*AT*: 30). Whilst Okonkwo's friends found this episode quite hilarious as one of them recounted it during a discussion session (*AT*: 30), Okonkwo himself did not appear amused. The reference to a father who did not own 'a fowl' was bound to remind Okonkwo of his own father, Unoka, but the fact that Obiako was indeed clearly defying an entreaty from the gods could not have been lost on Okonkwo's steadfast cultural sensibilities. Besides the obvious underlying humour in the tale and the implied reference to Unoka's poverty, which only an Okonkwo would have hardly been unconscious of, Okonkwo may have missed the most striking lesson of the Obiako episode which uncannily relates to his psycho-social predicament in the wake of Ikemefuna's death. This has to do with that flexibility which the Igbo impose on their relationship with their gods and in their pursuit of life's quests and goals through the distinct role of the *chi*, or the individual's exclusive personal god-agent.

So, let us finally return to Ezeudu's visit to Okonkwo ... It is now evident from our discussion that the ogbuefi would have similarly asked Okonkwo not to participate in the killing of Ikemefuna even if the directive from the oracle had been more specific in naming Okonkwo as the would-be executioner. This is so as long as Ezeudu can establish that there exists an organically-immutable link between the issue at stake and Okonkwo ('That boy calls you father') which in itself opens up the latitude or creates the space for the activation of that crucial *personal* judgement or initiative required in such grave matters. In contrast to the Jewish historical experience, for instance, Abraham is unquestionably prepared to carry out his god's explicit instructions asking him to kill his son Issac as 'burnt offering' to him (god),[31] but only stops short of carrying out the execution when the same god intervenes by providing Abraham with a lamb for the sacrifice. Yet, contrary to Ernest Emenyonu's intriguing observations on the subject,[32] both Okonkwo and Abraham's impulses and motivations to obey the instructions of their varying gods to carry out the task of a ritual sacrifice, are lodged in the same hermeneutical universe of service that is solely dictated by faith. Where the critical difference lies in the two belief systems here is on the measure or range of personal initiative that a believer has to negotiate in carrying out the obligations inherent in their relation to their gods. The Igbo definitely have a greater leverage than the Jews to manoeuver on this score and it is this feature rather than any supposed authorial contrasting

---

[31]*The Holy Bible* (authorised King James version), Genesis, ch. 22,v. 2.
[32]Ernest Emenyonu, *The Rise of the Igbo Novel* (Ibadan: Oxford University, 1978), p. 120.

hints at the 'implicitly preferable'[33] scriptures of the christian 'New Testament' that is paramount here. Given the opportunity therefore, Obierika would have clearly warned Abraham not to sacrifice his son Isaac in a 'burnt offering' precisely because the latter 'call[ed] you father'! In contrast to the Jews, christians appear more prepared to liberalise the power relationship between their god and the individual on this subject somewhat. The god head of the 'trinity' who clearly has the power to stop the impending death of his son Jesus on the hills of Calvary allows the latter, himself a member of the 'trinity' - and therefore god, to decide for himself whether he would go ahead with this sacrifice of crucifixion for the redemption of humanity. The power/spiritual status of Jesus as god in the christian hierarchy is crucial in him 'being allowed' to determine this grave feature of his fate, a role that is unlikely to have been allocated to an ordinary mortal!

To that extent, the christians share with the Jews a pertinent existentialist basis of god-individual relationship which ensures that the gods have the overriding power to decide on such issues of life and death. Not for the Igbo would such an initiative to act or not to act on these matters be *removed from* personal judgement and initiative and left solely in the hands of the gods. For a people who are prepared to 'discipline' or 'do away with' gods who have 'failed to serve their functions,'[34] or who indeed *create* new ones if they find existing gods inadequate for their purpose, this is not surprising! Donatus Nwoga, the Igbo escathologist, puts the case quite cogently: 'The strength of this point lies in the fact that the basic relationship between an Igbo person and another Igbo person, or between the Igbo person and [their] god is one of *contractual relationship*. The Igbo ... will serve [their] god but that god had better also do that thing for which it was established and/or recognised' (emphasis added).[35]

Yet, for Okonkwo, the need for him to 'do away with' any of his gods does not even arise at this occasion. No god has asked him personally to murder any of his children, *including indeed* Ikemefuna, the 'boy who calls [him] father.' This is the crux of the Ogbuefi Ezeudu intervention. Okonkwo of course ignores Ezeudu's advice and goes ahead and partakes in the execution of Ikemefuna.

---

[33] For this interpretation, see Donald Weistock and Cathy Ramadan, 'Symbolic Structure in *Things Fall Apart*,' in C.L. Innes & Bernth Lindfors, *Critical Perspectives on Chinua Achebe* (London: Heinemann Educational Books, 1979), p. 132.
[34] Nwoga, *The Supreme God as Stranger in Igbo Religious Thought*, p. 30.
[35] Ibid., p. 30.

Ironically, though, Okonkwo's involvement in Ikemefuna's murder is not motivated by any feelings that *he* is under the obligation of the god(s). While he fully respects the traditions of Umuofia, his character is not driven by any fears of the gods of his people but rather, crucially, on not being appraised by the Umuofia public as having 'inherited' the lazy, unsuccessful attributes of his father, Unoka (*AT*: 25). To that extent, Okonkwo does not doubt the validity, if not the sincerity, of the distinction that Ezeudu makes between personal accountability and social/community responsibility.

Love supreme

Evidently, *Things Fall Apart* is replete with a string of dialogues and snippets or fragments of off the cuff conversations involving influential members of Umuofia's political and cultural life which Chinua Achebe skillfully employs in his narrative to explore or highlight varying spheres of Igbo philosophical and historical heritage. We shall soon be discussing other subjects in this schema of an inheritance including, crucially, women and gender relations, exile, the nature of the British invasion of Igboland, the people's resistance to that invasion, and the ultimate loss of Igbo national sovereignty. Before that, though, we should examine other features of Igbo history and sociology attested to by some of these conversations but which might not readily appear as important especially in the event of a less critical reading of the text.

'Who taps your tall [palm] trees for you?' Obierika finally asks his friend Okonkwo a question (*AT*: 64) that is for once far removed from the existentialist debates on life, the individual, the community, death, responsibility, and the gods which have been the hallmark of their earlier conversations (and those involving Okonkwo and Ezeudu) and to which we have already shared much critical review here. 'Umezulike,' replies Okonkwo briskly (*AT*: 64), to which Obierika retorts: 'Sometimes I wish I had not taken the *ozo* title ... It wounds my heart to see these young men killing palm trees in the name of tapping' (*AT*: 64). Okonkwo, ever critical of youth who show slackness in upholding tradition and history, agrees broadly with his friend's observations but in his usual steadfast defence of the juridico-sociological *status quo* of Umuofia, he quickly cautions against any changes in the regulations overseeing the lives of those who acquire the prestigious *ozo* as he declares: '[T]he law of the land must be obeyed' (*AT*: 64). Once again, such an assertion provides Obierika, ever the contemplative intellectual, with the occasion to ruminate over the contentious subject of tradition, rationality and continuity. To underscore his dramatic questioning of how Umuofia 'got that law' (*AT*: 64) on the *ozo* and the palm tree in the first place, Obierika reminds Okonkwo that there are some peoples and regions elsewhere in the Igbo nation where those who take the *ozo* '[are] not forbidden to climb the palm tree' (*AT*: 64). A sceptical Okonkwo is very much aware of this and couldn't have been presented with a greater opportunity to drive home his point: 'In these other [lands] you speak of, *ozo* is so low that every begger takes it' (*AT*: 65). Surprisingly, or so it appears, Obierika concedes: 'I was only speaking in jest ... In Abame and Anita the title is worth less than two cowries. Every man wears the thread of title on his ankle, and does not lose it even if he steals' (*AT*: 65). So, the two friends end their conversation in full agreement with each other on a subject that at the outset appears quite controversial with the possibilities of ending on a note of disagreement similar to the deliberation on Ikemefuna!

We seem to be left bewildered by the unexpected, anticlimactic end to this humorous dialogue ... But we soon regain our composure as it dawns on us that in the typical Achebean deftness to convey complex sociological or historical information in easily comprehensible style and with the most economic use of words, the author is alluding to spheres of differentiation in cultural life within an Igboland that would otherwise be categorised academically as culturally homogeneous. Both the dreaded, corrupt, and despised court messengers or *kotma* and the often mischievous and overzealous (language) interpreters employed by the fledging British occupation regime and the church would also be the focus of widespread parody of some of these forms of cultural diversity. Right from the outset, the conquest regime's recruitment policy for these two crucial posts concentrated on people from states and communities that it had *already* overrun as the invasion got underway. The British occupation objective was obviously aimed at constructing an alternative security allegiance network that would rely on these subjugated 'outsiders' as well as the internal culturally-alienated *efulefu* to undermine the statutory independence of the individual Igbo village state. The interpreters' often different accents from the Igbo spoken in Umuofia as well as among its immediate neighbours, and their use of words that at times assumed a completely different meaning with the slightest inflection in the voice, do indeed add some exhilarating humour to the narrative in *Things Fall Apart*. The following quote highlights a typical speech mannerism of one such interpreter working for a British church official in a public meeting at Mbanta: 'Instead of saying "myself" he [the interpreter] always said my "buttocks"' (*AT*: 120). A sarcastic remark from someone in the crowd no doubt heightens the humour further: 'Your buttocks understand our language' (*AT*: 120). Yet, belying all the humour is the underlying fact that besides their security role, these interpreters and their *kotma* counterparts represent a critical counter-cultural facet of the occupation's mission to undermine the cohesive cultural tie that characterises the autochthonous independent fabric invested in the typical Igbo village state. This British task was not easily achieved, though. It was clear that the immense flexibility inherent in the Igbo state system ensured that the Igbo resistance to the invasion was drawn out indeed - well into the 1930s, 40 years after the initial assault! Thus, unlike most of its neighbours who had more centralised pre-conquest political formations (e.g. the Bini, Yoruba, Igala), the Igbo defence of the overall stretch of its homeland, on both sides of the River Niger, lasted for many more years. As a result, a leading British military commander during the period noted the following observations in his memoirs which we shall be elaborating upon in the next chapter: 'Igboland had proved the most troublesome area in all Nigeria.'[36]

Ogbuefi Obierika must be some specialist in the sociology of cultural diversity as he later returns to the subject during crucial discussions with his would-be in-laws on the impending wedding of his daughter, Akueke. Contrasting Umuofia's bride-wealth transfer tradition with those of Abame and Anita, Obierika informs his audience that the latter 'do not decide bride-price as we do, with sticks. They haggle and bargain as if they were buying a goat or a cow in the market' (*AT*: 67). Machi, Obierika's brother, who is in the gathering for the occasion, agrees: 'This is very bad ... But what is good in one place is bad in another place. In Umunso they do not bargain at all, not even with broomsticks. The suitor just goes on bringing bags of cowries until his in-laws tell him to stop. It is a bad custom because it always leads to a quarrel' (*AT*: 67). Okonkwo, who is also in attendance at the ceremony, does not wish to be left out of the debate. He wades in, broadening it further as he makes a parody of certain features of matriarchy: 'The world is large ... I have even heard that in some [places] a man's children belong to his wife and her family' (*AT*: 67-68). Machi can barely disguise his incredulity at Okonkwo's intervention: 'That cannot be ... You might as well say that the woman lies on top of the man when they are making the children' (*AT*: 68). Looking at a piece of chalk in his hand, Obierika returns with a vengeance, anticipating a zone of cultural heterogeneity that the Igbo have never had to confront in their history but which now looms ever menacingly from across the seas: 'It is like the story of white men who, they say, are white like this piece of chalk' (*AT*: 68). 'And

---

[36]Elizabeth Isichie, *Junior History of Nigeria* (Lagos and Ibadan: Macmillan Nigeria Publishers, 1981), p. 101.

have you never seen them?' Machi inquires (*AT*: 68), to which Obierika, for once uncharacteristically reticent, asks instead, 'Have you?' (*AT*: 68). Machi replies: 'One of them passes here frequently ... His name is Amadi' (*AT*: 68). Machi's reply draws some laughter from those in the audience who know Amadi. This is because Amadi is a leper and the polite Igbo word for leprosy is 'the white skin' (*AT*: 68). For the rumbustious theorists and publicists on race and humanity, a number of whom we have encountered in this study, this snippet of the Igbo view of skin colour and race must represent a shattering blow indeed! The colour 'white,' which is at the apex of their standard racist hierarchisation of humanity's races, is not only a source for Igbo ridicule but a metaphor for the degenerating disease of leprosy.

Finally, another metaphor from the text associated with the European invasion and its consequences is worth mentioning briefly here. It is instructive to note that in both instances (above) where Obierika mentions which of Umuofia's neighbours exhibits some differences in two spheres of popular cultural practice, he specifically refers to Abame. Umuofia, in this instance, no doubt prides itself as the keeper, the defender, if not the guarantor of the unimitated and unmitigated expression of the culture of the Igbo among neighbours whose standards and commitments it increasingly questions. Besides this perceived cultural preeminence, Umuofia is of course respected, and, in some cases, feared by other states for its military capability and achievements. It is against this dual solid background of cultural and military self-confidence that Umuofia fails to be fully on the alert to the long-term threat posed to its *own* independence when it receives the news that the ever-expanding British invading military force in the region has committed a horrific massacre of people in Abame: '[T]he white man [has] wiped out Abame' (*AT*: 144); 'Abame is no more ... Abame has been wiped out ... It is a strange and terrible story' (*AT*: 115). Okonkwo's response to the news of this tragedy underlines an increasingly-dated, Umuofia-centred balance of power assessment which takes no full account of the very tragic character of the emergency that threatens everybody, including Umuofia:

> Abame people were weak and foolish. Why did they not fight back? Had they no guns and matchets? We would be cowards to compare ourselves with the men of Abame. Their fathers had never dared to stand before our ancestors. We must fight these [European] men and drive them from our land' (*AT*: 144).

A very sceptical Obierika responds to his friend most solemnly: 'It is already too late' (*AT*: 144). Quite clearly, Okonkwo and others in Umuofia who are understandably proud of the latter's renowned socio-cultural and military legacy, will soon realise that in these new times of a grave and catastrophic military aggression from overseas, the culturally-suspect and militarily-weak Abame is paradoxically an arresting metaphor for the unfolding collective experience of *all* African states (including Umuofia, *obodo dike*!) which will lead to eventual conquest and the loss of national sovereignty.

Before Umuofia ultimately confronts this looming emergency though, its politics is preoccupied dramatically with an internal tragedy, namely the mandatory exile of Okonkwo from his homeland to Mbanta. This event appears to be some form of a fulfilment of the fears expressed by Obierika (above) over Okonkwo's participation in the murder of Ikemefuna. Obierika had argued that while he would not dispute a decree from a god ordering the execution of his own child, he would however not carry out the instruction himself! Consequently, he warned Okonkwo: 'What you have done will not please the Earth. It is the kind of action for which the goddess wipes out whole families.' If exile from Umuofia is indeed the eventual retribution that Okonkwo would face over the Ikemefuna saga, then *ani* may have spared him the full range of censure that his friend reflected upon. Or, does she?

'It was as if a spell had been cast. All was silent. In the centre of the crowd a boy lay in a pool of blood. It was the dead man's sixteen-year-old son, who with his brothers and half-brothers had been dancing the traditional farewell to their father' (*AT*: 105). The accidental discharge of Okonkwo's gun during the funeral of the venerable Ogbuefi Ezeudu dramatically shifts the focus of the historic event into a tragedy of staggering proportions. Another '*ill-fated lad*,' Ezeudu's son, is struck dead - killed by Okonkwo, albeit inadvertently. 'The confusion that followed was without parallel in the tradition of Umuofia ... [N]othing like this had ever happened. The only course open to Okonkwo was to flee ...' (*AT*: 105). The killing of a member of the *umunna*, or the integrated grouping of the extended family, is a grave crime indeed. This is against *ani* and the prescribed punishment is clear: exile. Okonkwo must leave Umuofia at once, banished for seven years. He escapes the stiffer punishment of a permanent exile because the shooting is undoubtedly an accident and thus falls within the 'female,' rather than the 'male' category of the crime. Even then, an important feature of this 'lesser' punishment incorporates the destruction of Okonkwo's home, yam barn, and livestock by his people. Significantly, Obierika is a member of the party that storms his friend's homestead for the punishment but Umuofia, pointedly, has 'no hatred in their hearts against Okonkwo ... They are merely cleansing the land which [he] had polluted with the blood of a [relative]' (*AT*: 105). Thus, in death, Ogbuefi Ezeudu embodies the spiritual bridge that links the lives of the two young men - his own 16-year-old son and the 18-year-old Ikemefuna - whose tragic deaths, at the hand of Okonkwo, impact decidedly on the course of the latter's life and destiny. For Okonkwo, the great war hero, it must have been the most unnerving of experiences that that which singularly resonates in his mind after hearing of the death of Umuofia's most esteemed personality concerns the very subject (*AT*: 103) that both men had wrestled with, without resolution, during their last meeting, rather than those celebratory and nostalgic references to Umuofia's military and diplomatic history which would very much have been of mutual interest to both. Again, we should recall that Ezeudu had warned Okonkwo then: 'That boy calls you father ... Bear no hand in his death.' As we know, not only did Okonkwo ignore the warning and partake in the execution of Ikemefuna, but he had as well killed Ezeudu's young son, even though unpremeditatedly, soon after the old man's death. Ogbuefi Okonkwo could not have been engulfed in a greater crisis!

As Okonkwo heads into an uncertain exile, Obierika ruminates pensively over his friend's plight. He wonders: 'Why should a man suffer so grievously for an offence he had committed inadvertently?' (*AT*: 105). He avoids a straightforward answer to this question. Instead, Obierika offers a reply by reflecting on the 'complexities' (*AT*: 105) of society's relationships with the gods/goddesses which often raise bewildering challenges to the position of the individual, their rights and expectations, and the delicate balance that these have to contend with the collective destiny of the community itself. The ultimate survival of the community as a corporate entity is the most overriding plank in this triangular schema of relations. In effect, therefore, an offence committed by an individual against *ani*, for instance, must receive due punishment from society, otherwise 'her wrath was loosed on all the land and not just on the offender' (*AT*: 105). It is precisely to avoid such an eventuality in Umuofia that Okonkwo's exile, tragic as it is on a personal level, acquires the thrust of inevitability which Okonkwo himself and family and friends alike have to live with! Hence, 'before the cock crowed Okonkwo and his family were fleeing to his motherland' (*AT*: 105). Yet, curiously, Obierika does not explore the *Ezeudu-focus* that links the two murders at the centre of the tragedy. He must have found the very thought of such a process depressing, if not frightening. This is because he would have had to contend with *that* speculation that he made whilst discussing the murder of Ikemefuna with Okonkwo. Obierika had suggested then that Okonkwo's involvement in the murder would 'not please the Earth. It is the kind of action for which the goddess wipes out whole families.'

So, does Okonkwo's accidental murder of Ezeudu's son and his subsequent exile represent the beginning of the fulfilment, or, alternatively, the partial fulfilment of those reflections? Understandably, Obierika would hope that neither is the case! After all, his comment on the possible intervention of *ani*, expressed during that conversation with Okonkwo, could at best be described as 'academic,' made by an intellectual 'who thought about things.' In that case, his observations were therefore not intended to be prophetic! Obierika's current anguish over his friend's plight is real enough and would surely be much worse if he were to feel that he had contributed in some way to Okonkwo's dramatic departure from Umuofia. Yet, the possibility that Obierika's observations were prophetic, even if not intended personally, remained. However, the grounds for the grave punishment of 'wip[ing] out whole families' which he envisions from *ani*, namely 'the kind of action for which...' (*AT*: 63), are not as firm as they would otherwise appear. These grounds, on the contrary, are essentially speculative and thus imply some elements of uncertainty or indicate that there might perhaps be some room for a more open and flexible interpretation of the factors available in the case which could lead another person, *or indeed the goddess herself*, to come to a totally different conclusion as to the exact nature of Okonkwo's crime and its consequences! In other words, going by Obierika's observations, *ani* could conceivably come to the conclusion that Okonkwo's crime is *not* 'the kind of action for which [she] wipes out whole families.' Well, we know that Okonkwo does not lose his family in some major catastrophe but is instead sent off on a 7-year exile to Mbanta. This leads us to feel that *ani* in fact arrives at a different conclusion from that suggested by Obierika.[37]

Given what some have described as the 'aggressively masculin[ised]' social environment[38] in which Okonkwo's rise to fame and success is predicated, it is extraordinarily significant, if not ironical, that the outcome of the grave crisis that he faces on the eve of his enforced departure from Umuofia is decided solely by *ani*, the earth goddess. If *ani* for instance were to resolve this crisis by choosing a 'male' category verdict for Okonkwo's crime in the murder of Ezeudu's son, which would invariably be consistent with the seemingly saturated male referencing dynamics of the social environment under review, then the resultant punishment for Okonkwo and his family would be a permanent exile from their homeland. Alas, this would culturally represent the

---

[37] Some scholars lose sight of this subtle but critical difference in the outcome of Okonkwo's plight. See, for instance, JanMohamed, *Manichean Aesthetics*, pp. 164-165.
[38] Florence Stratton, *Contemporary African Literature and the Politics of Gender* (London and New York: Routledge, 1994), p. 37.

dreaded 'wip[ing]-out-of-whole-families' outcome which Obierika refers to during those moments of contemplation! Instead, *ani* opts for the 'female *ochu*' (*AT*: 109), the 'female' category of the murder verdict, which is a 7-year exile, in addition to an exile destination which is also underscored by its *female* implication - Mbanta, Okonkwo's mother's homeland. In essence, the earth goddess's intervention, a feminine intervention, provides the embattled Okonkwo with a new lease on life and vitality which he is sharply reminded of during his exile by none other than his maternal uncle, Uchendu:

> Why is Okonkwo with us today? This is not his [land]. We are only his mother's [people]. He does not belong here. He is on exile, condemned for seven years to live in a strange land. And so he is bowed with grief. But there is just one question I would like to ask him. Can you tell me, Okonkwo, why it is that one of the commonest names we give our children is Nneka, or 'Mother is Supreme'? ... A man belongs to his fatherland and not his motherland. And yet we say Nneka - 'Mother is Supreme'. Why is that? ... A man belongs to his fatherland when things are good and life is sweet. But when there is sorrow and bitterness he finds refuge in his motherland (*AT*: 112-13).

Uchendu's comments here raise a number of important issues that underpin the character of gender relations in *Things Fall Apart*. It is clear that in Igboland the 'female principle' or the foundational interlocking embodiment of motherhood[39] offers the community its source of fertility[40] and the spiritual/social resource that mediates at critical junctures of societal stresses, contradictions and conflicts.[41] Furthermore, the 'female principle' checks or routinises excessive forms of behaviour that threaten or undermine social justice and cohesiveness into manageable and acceptable norms and values of

---

[39]Cf. Ifi Amadiume, *Reinventing Africa* (London & New York: Zed Books, 1997), p. 112.
[40]Uchendu, *The Igbo of Southeast Nigeria* and M.S.O. Olisa, 'Political Culture and Political Stability in Traditional Igbo Society,' *Conch*, 3, 2, pp. 16-19.
[41]Arinze, *Sacrifice in Ibo Religion* and G Parrinder, *African Traditional Religion* (Ibadan: Ibadan University, 1970).

conduct.[42] *Ani*'s prompt intervention in the grave drama surrounding Okonkwo's shooting incident is a case in point. Indeed the *ani* goddess is arguably the most revered deity in the Igbo pantheon as she is the guardian of society's moral order.[43] It is therefore not surprising that the most grievous crime that anyone could commit in Igboland is directly attributable to a clear violation of the sacredness of *ani* and as such an abomination, a taboo-to-earth, or what the Igbo call *nso-ani*. In effect, what the latter example of the 'female principle' attests to is its permanent and pervasive feature in the day-to-day existence of people generally - including, very importantly, those seemingly happy and contented men living in their fatherland who are *not* about to head for a motherland-exile (!) because 'things are good and life is sweet' (*AT*: 113). The determination or the manifestation of the 'female principle' in society does not therefore have to depend or incorporate a sentence of exile or indeed death, except where this is in response to a severe case of violation.

Besides its revered spirituality and dominant ethos in Igbo juridical thought, the 'female-principle' is of course the embodiment of the social existence of Igbo women. Here, 'there is a deeper and historically more enduring level at which the nature and capacity of women are given primacy in the definition of the human condition.'[44] *Things Fall Apart* does not engage on an extensive sociological exploration of the constituent matricentric heritage of Umuofia society but acknowledges its dominance and vitality nonetheless because of the existentialist crucible of the 'female-principle'. It is therefore not without significance that the novel demonstrates clearly that the reason for Okonkwo's precipitous fall in his community - from the exalted position of a successful farmer and respected war hero to that of an enforced exile - is precisely because of his systematic violation of the *sacredness* that his people attach to the 'female-principle'. *Things Fall Apart* could not have demonstrated the validity of this Igbo cultural heritage any more convincingly than it has done! So,

---

[42] Arinze, *Sacrifice in Ibo Religion*; E. Ilogu, *Christianity and Igbo Culture* (New York and London: NOK Publishers, 1974) and E. Metuh, *God and Man in African Religion: A Case Study of the Igbo of Nigeria* (London: Geoffery Chapman, 1981).

[43] Arinze, *Sacrifice in Ibo Religion*; Ilogu, *Christianity and Igbo Culture*, and Metuh, *God and Man in African Religion*.

[44] Wendy James, 'Matrifocus on African women,' in Shirley Ardener, ed., *Defining Females* (London: Croom Helm, 1978), p. 160.

contrary to Florence Stratton's amazing misreading of the novel,[45] *Things Fall Apart* is indeed a *foremost* 'female-principled' critique of Umuofia society. As Okonkwo should have undoubtedly been aware of, and should have acted accordingly right from the incident when he beat his wife during the 'Week of Peace' (*AT*: 36-37) to his exile to Mbanta (*he was duly punished for both incidents by the earth goddess*), Igbo gender relations are anchored firmly on the fulcrum of complementarity between the sexes.[46] To ignore or violate this key feature in society attracts clearly stipulated sanctions. Just as men, women developed and operated their own institutions which covered the broad spectrum of social life - politics, finance/economics, spirituality, welfare, etc.[47] While these organisations operated autonomously from men's control, they still developed crucial linkages which organically complemented those of the men and the greater society.[48] '[C]ollaboration rather than rivalry was the main feature in male-female relations in Igbo politics.'[49]

Blood-count: Abame is no more...

Uchendu's observation on one's motherland rather than their fatherland being a place of sanctuary during periods of adversity appears to be more valid when the focus of the difficulty or the difficulties at stake is more individual-specific rather than the community or the greater society. Okonkwo returns to Umuofia after his 7-year exile at Mbaino (his motherland) at a time when his fatherland is faced with the imminent invasion by the British which already are in control of some parts of Igboland. Going by Uchendu's reflections, Okonkwo would be expected to once again escape to Mbaino for another spell of exile to weather the new emergency ... But not this time round! The new emergency goes well

---

[45]Stratton, *Contemporary African Literature and the Politics of Gender*. For a more comprehensive critique of Stratton's position on this subject, see Femi Nzegwu's illuminating *Love, Motherhood and the African Heritage* (Dakar: African Renaissance, 2001).
[46]For an updated incisive reading of the sociology of this relationship, see also Nzegwu, ibid.
[47]See ibid., for instance, for a fuller discourse.
[48]Ibid.
[49]See U.D. Anyanwu, 'Gender Question in Igbo Politics,' in U.D. Anyanwu and J.U. Aguwa, ed., *The Igbo and Traditions of Politics* (Enugu: Fourth Dimensions, 1993), p. 120. See also Nzegwu, *Love, Motherhood and the African Heritage*.

beyond the fate of one individual, Okonkwo included. To the contrary, it affects the corporate destiny of all of Umuofia. Indeed, the national sovereignty of Umuofia is threatened and this gives rise to calls for a steadfast defence from all its people despite the military superiority and the ruthlessness of the enemy it faces as historian Obierika is keen to stress: 'Have you not heard how the white man wiped out Abame?' (*AT*: 144). He adds, ominously, 'They would go to Umuru and bring the soldiers, and we [Umofia] would be like Abame' (*AT*: 144). For Okonkwo, the obvious overwhelming military odds against Umuofia notwithstanding, the country must defend its sovereignty resolutely: 'We must fight these men and drive them from our land' (*AT*: 144).

Okonkwo's forthright response to Obierika's apparent reticence about how to respond to the impending British invasion of Umuofia shows clearly that years of exile have not in any way diminished the hero's patriotic instincts and distinctions. Okonkwo's position on this subject has been the source and focus of criticism by some scholars who think it is reckless, given Umuofia's weaker military potential. Ernest Emenyonu notes: 'He [Okonkwo] stubbornly clings to his delusion, does not admit defeat until "tied to a stake".'[50] Solomon Iyasere agrees: 'Compelled by his own uncompromising attitudes ... Okonkwo turns to the only means he knows - violence - to solve the problem.'[51] Kalu Ogbaa writes: 'Okonkwo seizes the call to arms as a welcome opportunity to demonstrate once more his patriotism and valor without discretion. He understands how to "root out this evil" without regard to the danger ...'[52] Richard Priebe reflects on what he terms 'Okonkwo's unbending will' which 'inexorabl[y]' leads to the 'tragic end' of the hero's suicide.[53] In the same breadth, Abdul JanMohamed feels that Okonkwo is 'blind to the virtues of flexibility and accomodation' which leads the latter to 'impulsively' kill the envoy sent by the expanding British conquest regime (positioned outside Umuofia at the time) to disband a crucial mass meeting of the Umuofia leadership and the people called to discuss the grave emergency of the impending British invasion.[54] This subject of 'inflexibility' in Okonkwo's response to the emergency at stake is a theme pursued by Abiola Irele who

---

[50] Emenyonu, *The Rise of the Igbo Novel*, p. 123
[51] Solomon Iyasere, 'Narrative Techniques in "Things Fall Apart",' in C.L. Innes and Bernth Lindfors, eds., *Critical Perspectives on Chinua Achebe*, p. 107.
[52] Kalu Ogbaa, *Gods, Oracles and Divinition* (Trenton: Africa World, 1992), p. 46.
[53] Richard Priebe, *Myth, Realism and the West African Writer*
(Trenton: Africa World, 1988), p. 54.
[54] JanMohamed, *Manichean Asthetics*, p. 167.

describes it as a 'tragic flaw' in the hero's character which he also reckons is a 'reflection of his [Okonkwo's] society.'[55] Gareth Griffiths, finally, is particularly contemptuous of Okonkwo's unquestioning disposition to defend his homeland from the British aggression: 'Okonkwo is destroyed because he performs more than is expected of him, and sacrifices his personal life to an exaggerated, even pathological, sense of communal duty.'[56]

The underlining spur for these critics's condemnation of Okonkwo's resolute position to defend Umuofia from a possible British military and political take-over, emanate from their collective awareness of the preponderant military superiority of the invader; nothing else. Yet, bound by the sole preoccupation on the balance of military forces of both sides, these scholars lose sight of the salient features in history that characterise the defence by peoples, any peoples, of their homeland from external invasion whatever the odds - even when this defence might appear 'too obviously suicidal,' to quote from C.L.R. James, a leading philosopher of the African resistance and liberation wars.[57] As history has shown, each and every invader of some other person's lands is potentially militarily superior to their would-be victims. But the latter's response to the event is the defence of the homeland under attack despite the odds and even when these are known by the defenders as overwhelming. As the European invasion got underway in Africa during the period, African armed resistance, expectedly, was the most featured element of Africa's initial or first phase of the defence of its homeland. It is this fact of African history that Chinua Achebe captures so dramatically in Okonkwo's steadfast response to the British invasion of Umuofia which the array of critics referred to surprisingly overlook. It should be stressed that the African historical landscape is extensively and indelibly marked by the peoples's heroism during this defence, a heroism made more pronounced considering the very obvious superiority of the military forces deployed by the invaders as was evident in some of the most outstanding military confrontations of the era: Igboland ... Asante ... Benin ... Ijebu (Yorubaland) ... Niger delta ... Dahomey ... Nupe ... Senegambian states ... Sierra Leone Dwelling Tax War ... Kenedougou ... Bambara ... Mandingo ... Baule ... Chokwe ... Bihe ... Ganguela ... Yaka ...

---

[55] Abiola Irele, 'The Tragic Conflict in the Novels of Chinua Achebe,' in C.L. Innes & Bernth Lindfors, eds., *Critical Perspectives on Chinua Achebe*, p. 14.
[56] Gareth Griffiths, 'Language and Action in the Novels of Chinua Achebe,' in ibid, p. 70.
[57] Quoted in Walter Rodney, 'The African Revolution,' in Paul Buhle, ed, *C.L.R. James: His Life and Work* (London/New York: Alison & Busby, 1986), p. 35.

Bowa ... Budja ... Chikunda ... Humbe ... Cuamato ... Ovimbundu ... Lunda ... Chewa ... Zulu ... Herero ... Ndebele ... Bemba ... Shona ... Mossi ... Quitanghona ... Makua-Swahili coalition ... Ethiopia ... Nandi ... Bunyoro ... Sudan ... Hehe ... Makonde ... Yao ...

Apart from Ethiopia where the Africans routed the invading Italian army in 1895 and thus safeguarded their independence, Europe ultimately won these wars by the first decade of the 20th century largely for the reason already stated, but we should point out that the African resistance was victorious in a number of epic battles fought during the course of these conflicts as the following examples illustrate: the 1824 Asante defeat of the British army; the 1879 Zulu defeat of another contigent of British forces; the 1891 Hehe defeat of German forces in south-east Africa (contemporary Tanzania), and the celebrated defeat, in 1904, of the Portuguese military by a combined force of the Humbe and Cuamato in a famous battle in southern Angola. Subsequently, as Europe started to consolidate the new states it was creating out of its conquest, African resistance would begin to take new dimensions - away from the open or frontal armed response *a la* Okonkwo phase, with its 'too obviously suicidal' implications, to focus, usually more eclectically and at times contradictorily, on other forms of resistance. These would include the following: (1) Campaigns against the imposition of imperial (European) currency on society. (2) Crop-hold ups/switches to new crop production by small-scale farmers. (3) Tax evasions/boycotts. (4) Competing for commercial territories exclusively earmarked for European business interests by the conquest state. (4) Strikes by wage-earners working in plantations and mines and (5) Sporadic revolts/uprisings - usually classified as 'riots' or 'rebellions' in colonial/conquest historiography. Again, given Achebe's adeptness at capturing the crucial moments of African history of the epoch in *Things Fall Apart* (often overlooked by the less alert critic), it could be said that Obierika's general reticence about the ways and means of his people's response to the European invasion (already referred to) *anticipates* these variegated forms of post-conquest African resistance and is not posed as an *alternative* to Okonkwo's course of action on the eve of the emergency.

Okonkwo's suicide which occurs shortly after he kills one of the envoys sent by the British to disband the crucial Umuofia assembly coincides symbolically with the British overrun of Umuofia, itself the loss of Igbo national sovereignty. The British account of these great events of history is conspicuously a limited one, if not fragmentary ... This is clear in the outline of the extent of the official record envisaged by the District Commissioner or the head of the evolving occupation regime in the country. The District Commissioner's account represents the birth of *anthropology* which erases the African Presence from the central corpus of reality, consigning it conveniently to a 'reasonable paragraph,' or even less (*AT*: 168), as the narrative voice in *Things Fall Apart* alerts us as the novel draws to a close. Essentially, the twin-track orthodoxy of the 'nonsense of Hegel' and the distortionism and ahistoricity of Trevor-Roper that dwell on the great lie on African History is inaugurated. For the British, therefore, the title of its field Commissioner's text detailing its conquest of Umuofia dovetails triumphantly into the parameters of this orthodoxy: *The Pacification of the Primitive Tribes of the Lower Niger (AT*: 168). With this, Africans make it into the accounts of the conquest historiography (which now proclaims that it rules the waves) as 'primitive' and 'tribes' - dehistoricised epithets inscribed in darwinian evolutionist construct that would act as the benchmark of reference in academia and elsewhere subsequently.

As a student of literature and history at Ibadan's London University College of the late 1940s/early 1950s, Chinua Achebe would have been confronted with endless shelf-rows of these africophobist literature of lies, triumphalism and denial. It is no coincidence that one of the leading gurus of the British School of these studies, E.E. Evans-Pritchard, was at the ascendancy of his stretched-out career at this time and would go on to publish several books on the subject with well over 10 of them carrying those unmistakable dual benchmark referents to the African humanity in the actual wordings of his texts: 'primitive', 'tribe'. No doubt by his own careful choice of the wordings of the title of the District Commissioner's book of conquest, Achebe is reminding us all of his painful intellectual experience as a young African undergraduate confronting a vast body of academic works that had virtually written him and his humanity out of history. Yet, Achebe's choice of the towering title of imperial self-conceit was in itself a devastating parody of eurocentric ahistoricity. Even though it appears that the District Commissioner has the last word in *Things Fall Apart* with the commanding space of the title of his text, the groundings of his conquest architecture of control and consolidation are at best tenuous. So, contrary to the bombastic title of an anthropological treatise, the future of history is not in fact dependent on the District Commissioner nor his nascent administration nor indeed the headquarters of his imperial state back home in Europe. Unquestionably, Umuofia or Africa still lays claims to this initiative, despite the conquest of the moment. The regenerative seeds of the African reclamation of national sovereignty are sown right there on the ground - *prior* to the crystallisation of the Commissioner's thoughts that give rise to his testimony of doubtful victory. This is evident in the declaration and tactical gasps of silence encapsulated in Obierika's historic statement of recall and recourse made to the

Commissioner as both discuss Okonkwo's suicide:

> Obierika, who had been gazing steadily at his friend's dangling body, turned suddenly to the District Commissioner and said ferociously: 'That man was one of the greatest men in Umuofia. You drove him to kill himself; and now he will be buried like a dog ...' He could not say any more. His voice trembled and choked his words (*AT*: 167).

4
Involution

In January 1966, Chinua Achebe published his fourth novel, *A Man of the People*. This was a highly imaginative satire of the grave socio-economic crisis that plagued Nigeria's immediate post-conquest state and society, six years after the restoration of independence following 60 years of the British occupation. A few days later, the country's military overthrew the inept civilian government of Abubakar Tafawa Balewa that had been in power since 1960. This was followed by yet another military coup six months later and the premeditated campaign of a spate of horrendous massacres of Igbo people across most of Nigeria organised by influential northern Nigerian politicians and officers in the military. A total of 80,000 - 100,000 Igbo were killed during this pogrom. As a result, the Igbo declared themselves independent of Nigeria by proclaiming the Republic of Biafra. Nigeria responded by declaring war on Biafra which lasted for three years and resulted in the defeat of the latter and the death of three million Igbo. Altogether, the Nigerian military was in uninterrupted power for 13 years before a return to some form of civil rule in 1979. In 1983, Achebe published an essay entitled *The Trouble with Nigeria* which is a brief but lucid critique of the politics of Nigeria's Second Republic (1979-1983). A few months later, a military coup d'état toppled the corrupt regime of Shehu Shagari. Thereafter began another epoch of military rule which this time lasted 15 years.

Achebe is of course no clairvoyant even if the publication dates of some of his writings as we have shown have been precursors to major societal upheavals in Africa. He is rather Africa's foremost novelist who has demonstrated conscientiously in his works in the past 40 years a deftness to keep tabs on the continent's pulse. On the problems of contemporary Nigeria, for instance, Achebe is blunt in his portrayal:

> One of the commonest manifestations of under-development is a tendency among the ruling elite to live in a world of make-believe and unrealistic expectations ... Listen to Nigerian leaders and you will

frequently hear the phrase, 'this great country of ours'. Nigeria is *not* a great country. It is one of the most disorderly nations in the world. It is one of the most corrupt, insensitive, inefficient places under the sun. It is one of the most expensive countries and one of those that give least value for money. It is dirty, callous, noisy, ostentatious, dishonest and vulgar. In short, it is among the most unpleasant places on earth![1]

Less critical and quite often opportunistic observers and commentators persistently used such frivolous appellations as 'Africa's giant' and 'Africa's most powerful and influential nation' to describe Nigeria while discussing the politics of the country especially during the decade of the petroleum oil boom (1970-1980).[2] This was when the oil price increased from the paltry US$2 a barrel to US$34 - bringing the enormous sum of US$20 billion to the country's treasury in 1980.[3] Very limited space was often made available to highlight the scandalously profligate fiscal programmes that successive regimes embarked upon which virtually depleted this unprecedented accumulation of the era.[4] State officials lurched ravenously into the public purse in a frenzy. Both central government and regional public officials converted their administrative units into fiefdoms of elaborately constructed network of nepotism and patronage. The businesspeople who the military had contracted to buy arms for the war against the Igbo in Biafra became millionaires overnight, and expanded their range of commercial interests even further in this post-war squandermania as they secured access to lucrative ventures to construct new military bases, sports facilities, expanded infrastructural development (especially the building of new roads), and new towns, each characterised by enormously-inflated financial returns which were shared mutually with government officials responsible for the contract. In one such contract, which would readily be described as far-fetched if it were part of the plot of a children's pantomime, a stadium to be constructed in central Nigeria was initially contracted for US$8 million by the

---

[1] Chinua Achebe, *The Trouble with Nigeria* (Enugu: Fourth Dimension, 1983), pp. 9-10. Subsequent page details of citation made from this book will be quoted directly in the text preceded by *TWN* and a colon.
[2] For an illustrative text that captures this trend of opinion, see for instance Anthony Kirk-Greene & Douglas Rimmer, *Nigeria Since 1970* (London: Hodder and Stoughton, 1981).
[3] Toyin Falola & Julius Ihonvbere, *The Rise and Fall of Nigeria's Second Republic: 1979-84* (London: Zed Books, 1985), p. 87.
[4] For a notable exception, see Falola & Ihonvbere, ibid.

local government authorities but the contract was soon increased dramatically six-fold to US$49.6 million without any economic justification.[5] A prompt local press and public outcry that followed forced the hand of the authorities on the issue, and the latter had to announce that the stadium would hence be built for US$24.8 million![6] - again, without any economic justification rendered. Billions of dollars of the huge foreign earnings from oil were used in the importation of every conceivable consumer product from the West and in the construction of wasteful and prestige projects such as a new capital at Abuja in central Nigeria.[7] Corruption became institutionalised in the matrix of the country's political economy.[8] Personal enrichment, party and regional patronage became indices for the quest or retention of high office. Not surprisingly, leading functionaries who held public office in the country during the period were undisguised millionaires and a few were even billionaires.[9] Indeed in 1974, a leading government official proclaimed to the world that 'Nigeria's problem was not lack of money, but how to spend the "petro-naira".'[10] The concomitant effect of this 'state robbery' on the people generally was a further deterioration of their living conditions. For them, it was precisely an oil doom! Despite the dismal situation, General Olusegun Obasanjo, one of the heads of state of the era and who is currently Nigeria's 'civilianised' president, once boasted: 'Nigeria will become one of the ten leading nations in the world by the end of the century' (*TWN*: 9). Regimes' spokespersons, some academics and commentators alike sympathetic to the view often exaggerated the impact of the thrust of the country's foreign policy especially on the liberation wars in southern Africa.[11] Such was the nature of the illusions and the deceptions of the era under review.

---

[5]Bade Onimode, *Imperialism and Underdevelopment in Nigeria* (London: Zed books, 1982), p. 214.
[6]Ibid.
[7]Falola & Ihonvbere, *The Rise and Fall of Nigeria's Second Republic*, ch. 5.
[8]Edwin Madunagu, *Nigeria: The economy and the people* (London and Port of Spain: New Beacon Books, 1983), p. 10.
[9]*Daily Telegraph* (London), 7 July 1984, *Evening Standard* (London), 6 July 1984 and *The Observer* (London), 22 January 1984.
[10]Onimode, *Imperialism and Underdevelopment in Nigeria*, p. 123.
[11]For the extent of these claims and aspirations, see Olajide Aluko, *Essays on Nigerian Foreign Policy* (London: George Allen & Unwin, 1981) and Ray Ofoegbu, *Foundation Course in International Relations for African Universities* (London: George Allen & Unwin, 1980). For an excellent critique of the illusion of the claims and aspirations, see Amechi Uchegbu, 'The Dialectics of Nigerian Foreign Politics,' in Asikpo Essien-Ibok, ed., *Towards a Progressive Nigeria* (Kano: Triumph Publishing, 1983), pp. 153-162.

Massacres and national politics

The genocidal massacres of the Igbo in 1966 and the expanded recourse by the federal government the following year to wage a devastating 3-year old war against the Igbo, still remained the central feature of politics in this era of post-British conquest Nigeria. The Igbo massacres were organised and co-ordinated by a coterie of northern politicians and local government officials, who later acquired the sobriquet, the *Kaduna Mafia*. This grouping came into existence soon after the death, in the January 1966 coup, of Ahmadu Bello, the prominent Hausa-Fulani leader and premier of the northern region. Initially, it was made up of Bello's very close aides who were anxious to continue the late premier's work in upholding the north's hegemonic political and military control of the Nigerian federation which had been entrenched in the country on the eve of the restoration of independence, thanks to the terms of British insistence which we shall be elaborating on soon. Later, membership of the organisation was expanded to include some influential northerners in government, academia, the civil service, the armed forces, justice, business and industry, as well as a number of princes from the feudalities of the region.

In embarking on the Igbo massacres which began in May (1966) and intensified during July-October (1966), the Kaduna Mafia sought to achieve three principal objectives: (1) they aimed to expel the Igbo who worked in the north's civil service, business and industrial enterprises from their posts; (2) they wanted to destroy the Johnson Aguyi-Ironsi regime which had come to power in January (1966) and neutralise the Igbo influence in the military and (3) they called for the northern secession from the federation. (It is instructive in this regard to note that the clarion call at every manifestation of the waves of attack throughout the five months of the massacre was 'Araba!' - Hausa for 'Let us Secede!' Indeed, for 18 days after the July - 1966 - coup, the flag of an independent northern republic flew over the headquarters of the northern military offices at Ikeja, Lagos.) By mid-August (1966), the Mafia had virtually achieved the first two objectives mentioned above. Apart from the murder of Aguyi-Ironsi, during the pursuit of (2), 300 other Igbo military officers and men were killed, many of them in horrific circumstances.[12] Soon, the Mafia was

---

[12]Scores of Igbo officers were hacked to death in military bases stretching from Abeokuta, Ibadan and Lagos in the south, to Zaria and Kaduna in the north. Several others were rounded up from their apartments and shot. In some gruesome cases, Igbo officers were bound up, thrown into graves and covered up while still alive.

persuaded to abandon its third goal after the intervention made in Lagos by the British and United States's embassies which held direct negotiations with the key northern officers in control of the capital after the overthrow of Aguyi-Ironsi.[13] According to the candid admission of Olusegun Obasanjo who was a senior military officer at the time and currently the president of Nigeria, 'The second coup [July 1966] was actively encouraged if not assisted by some British officials and university lecturers working and living in the north. It was no secret that to the British the north was more amenable and less refractory than the south.'[14] It must have therefore become clear to the Mafia then that after accomplishing objectives (1) and (2) (above), there was little incentive to extend their programme to (c). In fact in a special broadcast made to the north, Colonel Yakubu Gowon, who was one of the leaders of the coup against Aguyi-Ironsi and who had in the meantime declared himself head of state and would spearhead the gruesome military campaign against the Igbo the following year, stressed that 'God, in his power, has entrusted the responsibility of this great country of ours, Nigeria, into the hands of another Northerner.'[15]

Patrick Wilmot concludes his study of the police massacre of 386 small-scale rural farmers in Bakolori (north-west Nigeria) whilst protesting over the construction of an irrigation project in April 1980 by noting the following:

> The northern faction of the ruling class that currently dominates the (Nigerian) political scene has no tradition for managing social change. The only answer to dissent or rebellion is the massacre.[16]

This observation captures succinctly a characteristically enduring trait of a power bloc to defend its control of society with such tenacity and ruthlessness. While the 'tradition' (or the lack of it) which Wilmot alludes to stretches into centuries, incorporating the central role that this 'establishment' has played in the management of the various Hausa-Fulani states that flourished in that part of west Africa prior to British imperialism, it should be stressed that in the contemporary epoch, *ie. since the British conquest of the region*, the Igbo have mainly borne the brunt of massacres engineered by the northern leadership. In

---

[13]Olusegun Obasanjo, *My Command* (Ibadan and London: Heinemann, 1980), p. 146.
[14]Ibid.
[15]Wogu Ananaba, *The Trade Union Movement in Nigeria* (Benin: Ethiope Publishing, 1969), p. 254.
[16]Patrick Wilmot, 'Poverty amidst riches,' *West Africa* (London), 15 August 1988, p. 1489.

the past 60 years, the record has been grim indeed, significantly coinciding with periods of acute social crisis in Nigeria: the 1945 Igbo massacres in Jos; the 1953 Igbo massacres in Kano, and the 1966 Igbo massacres throughout the major towns, cities and villages of northern Nigeria. The Igbo have became a ready target to these wanton massacres because as a nation, they played a prominent part in the politics of Nigeria's re-establishment of independence for its peoples from British rule to which the northern leadership was opposed. For this leadership, the Igbo role in the independence movement, coupled with the latter's more nationally-oriented political drive and assured intellectual and business versatility were regarded as a threat to its age-long control of politics in the north and the ascriptive political hegemony it now exerted nationwide on behalf of British neo-colonialism. In addition, the presence in the north of nearly 1.5 million Igbo immigrants, many of who ran successful commercial, medical, educational and leisure enterprises, was often seen by the northern leadership as a 'symbol' of (national) Igbo ambitions and progress. As a result measures against these immigrants usually featured very high on the set of policy options available to the northern power bloc whilst responding to national politics, especially during emergencies. Hence, the Igbo immigrants in the north were the most vulnerable community in the Nigerian federation during the period.

The 1966 Igbo massacres in the north were undoubtedly the most monstrous and widespread to date, precisely because they occurred in response to the northern leadership's supposition that the Igbo, *as a nation*, were implicated in the January 1966 coup which had (partially) dislodged it from national power. On the contrary, this military action was *not* an Igbo coup as the federal government's *own investigating commission*, chaired by three important northern Nigerians (M.D. Yusuf, head of the Special Branch, Col. Gowon, chief of army staff, and Captain Baba Usman of military intelligence) concluded unambiguously.[17] The inquiry took three months to complete its work. Two hundred officers and men, including the principal leaders of the coup were interrogated. Vital coup documents were exhaustively evaluated. The report on the outcome of the enquiry showed that the plans to overthrow the Balewa government were restricted strictly to the military officers involved; there was no involvement by members of the civilian population. While the majority of officers involved in the action were mainly from the south of Nigeria, and particularly Igbo, there was no evidence whatsoever to suggest or indicate that

---

[17]See John de St. Jorre, *The Brothers' War - Biafra and Nigeria* (Boston: Houghton Miflin, 1972), pp. 29-47.

the coup was a southern nor indeed some machiavellian Igbo conspiracy to seize and control the federation.[18] The officers who carried out the coup acted on their own.[19] It should be recalled that significant sections of the northern leadership were already aware of the conclusions of the commission's findings before ordering the massacres of Igbo immigrants in the north.

Finally, some comments are required here on the study made in 1987 on Major Chukwuma Nzeogwu, the leader of the January 1966 coup, by Olusegun Obasanjo who is presently Nigeria's head of state - a post he also held between 1976 and 1979. Obasanjo's study was published in a book, appropriately entitled *Nzeogwu*,[20] and concluded, just as the 1966 coup investigation commission, that the January 1966 coup was not an Igbo plot to seize political power in Nigeria. Obasanjo had been a very close friend of Nzeogwu's since 1960 and was actively involved in the negotiations between the Aguyi-Ironsi loyalist forces (to which he belonged) and the Nzeogwu insurgents in Kaduna which later led to the latter's surrender. Obasanjo's *Nzeogwu* is therefore a commendable refutation of the gross distortions of the accounts of the coup contained in *Nigeria 1966*,[21] the publication by northern military officers who were responsible for the overthrow of the Aguyi-Ironsi regime in July 1966. The importance of Obasanjo's study on this subject however lies not so much in the conclusions, but rather on the timing of its publication. This occurred 21 years after the coup. Prior to the publication, Obasanjo had been Nigeria's head of state for three years (1976-79). He is the only southerner to have survived in that office in 35 years. But even more importantly, Obasanjo was a federal war hero during the Biafra War, a conflict whose genesis lies in the reaction of northern leaders to the January 1966 coup and the subsequent massacres of Igbo immigrant population in the north. These factors no doubt accounted for the open hostility expressed by northern leaders in 1987 after the publication of *Nzeogwu*.[22] Yet, it still remains inexplicable why Obasanjo had to wait 21 years before making public his position on this crucial event in Nigerian history. It should be useful to know when Obasanjo found out that the Nzeogwu-led coup was not an Igbo conspiracy. Was it whilst he, Obasanjo, negotiated Nzeogwu's surrender on behalf of General Aguyi-Ironsi in mid-January 1966? Was

---

[18]Ibid.
[19]Ibid.
[20]Olusegun Obasanjo, *Nzeogwu* (Ibadan: Spectrum Books, 1987).
[21]*Nigeria 1966* (Lagos: Federal Ministry of Information, 1966).
[22]See Herbert Ekwe-Ekwe, 'Nzeogwu: Notes on a Controversy,' *West Africa* (London), 2 March 1987, p. 418.

Obasanjo aware of the findings of the coup investigating commission which completed its assignment in May 1966? If so, when? Why did Obasanjo remain silent *throughout* 1966 in airing his views publicly on what he knew of the January 1966 coup?

Thirty years on, the memory of the Igbo genocide and the resultant Biafra War maintains a haunting presence in Nigeria and Nigerian affairs. It refuses to dissipate. Hardly a week passes by presently without Olusegun Obasanjo, who became a 'civilian' president of the country in 1999 after 15 years of another stretch of brutal military rule, making pointed references to the war but with astonishingly-reversed, if not 'mischievous[ly]-changed'[23] tune from what we reviewed above. Only recently, during a visit to Yenegoa (southern Nigeria), he told a gathering that the war was caused by what he called 'resource control,'[24] a reference to the current democratic liberatory demand by the oil producing regions and several other circles of political opinion (particularly in the south of the country) to control the appropriation of their human and natural resources as a crucial feature of their membership of the federation. 'If Biafra had won the war,' Obasanjo had intoned, quite enigmatically, 'I would have been dead, your governor [the regional administrator] would not have been in the position he is today.'[25]

No post-Biafra War Nigerian head of state has been so obsessed with this subject as Obasanjo. Not even six previous leaders centrally associated with the conflict (Yakubu Gowon, Murtala Muhammed, Muhammadu Buhari, Ibrahim Babangida, Sani Abacha, Abdulsalami Abubakar), all northerners whose involvement impulses were *dictated and driven largely* by their desire to safeguard the north's hegemonic political and military leadership of Nigeria, have been so transfixed on Biafra. Indeed, one or two of the surviving sextet of leaders just mentioned have shown more reticence over their involvement in the war and a third has at least offered what amounts to an unqualified 'apology' over his own participation.

It is tempting to think that Obasanjo is more ideologically welded to the war than his predecessors, hence the *volte-face* in his position on the cause of the conflict as we have just seen. But what does this actually mean in our understanding of that conflict? Biafra was a war of genocide, a war that was waged in its totality (with all the annihilative indices that this particular war

---

[23]Levi Obijiofor, 'When a president runs out of steam,' *The Guardian* (Lagos), 6 April 2001.
[24]*The Guardian* (Lagos), 17 March 2001.
[25]Ibid.

strategy connotes) in a very limited expanse of territory (Africa's most densely populated area outside the Nile valley) where the victims did not have access to a 'neutral' or friendly contiguous state for refuge and respite. The war was waged to overwhelm and destroy the corporate ability of the Igbo people to resist an aggression triggered, in the first place, because they were simply expressing their inalienable fundamental human right to freely decide to belong or not to belong to a political relationship in the wake of the most horrendous spate of massacres. During the course of four months in 1966 as we have indicated, 80,000-100,000 Igbo were hunted down and killed in several northern towns and cities and elsewhere in the federation. It is therefore utterly disingenuous for anyone to describe what in effect was then an *extended* territorial range of armed attack on a national group, already the target or subject of a sustained pogrom elsewhere in the country, as some war of 'resource control.' As Fred Ohwahwa has argued in his perceptive essay on the controversy, '[f]or the president to claim that resource control led to the ... War is to ignore the crisis in the Western Region; the coup of January 1966 and the ... coup of July of the same year and the subsequent pogrom that took place in the North against Nigerians of Igbo extraction.'[26]

Yet, if 'resource control' was indeed the cause or what the Biafra War was all about, then Obasanjo must answer urgently either of the following two questions which are essentially the same but with the second re-phrased to capture the salient features evident in the thrust of our analysis: (1) Why did the federal military still continue to wage the war against Biafra after the former's June 1968 capture of Port Harcourt (namely 11 months after the start of its military operations in July 1967) which effectively had ensured its *complete* take-over of all the non-Igbo speaking territories of Biafra including the oil fields and installations? (2) Why did the federal military surround and embark upon the siege and devastating attack of the so-called Igbo heartland for a period of 19 months (almost twice as long as the offensive in the non-Igbo provinces) beginning from June 1968 after it had effectively captured from the Biafrans all the non-Igbo speaking territories of Biafra including the oil producing fields and installations?

What must be stressed here is that the 'success' at Biafra in 1970, if that is what is called federal Nigeria's victory over the Biafran resistance, was at best Pyhrric as subsequent events in the past 30 years in Nigeria and further afield in Africa have shown. Three million African lives were destroyed in Biafra.

---

[26]Fred Ohwahwa, 'The President Knows Better,' *The Guardian* (Lagos), 25 March 2001.

This figure is more than the casualties recorded in either the Vietnam War or the Iraq-Iran Gulf War, the much longer duration of the latter conflicts notwithstanding. The three million dead represented a quarter of the Igbo population then. No Igbo family in the world escaped the immediate or long-term impact and consequences of this holocaust. So, besides lodging their case at the hearings of the Justice Chukwudifu Oputa-chaired Human Rights Violations Investigation Commission in Nigeria, Igbo people must exercise their right to seek full restitution for these dreadful massacres beyond Nigeria's territorial jurisdiction, if need be. To ensure that this bloodbath never happens again in Nigeria or elsewhere in Africa, state(s), corporate interests, and persons responsible for it must be made to account including particularly officials who worked on the infamous 'starvation as weapon/quick kill' strategy whose principal architect was Obafemi Awolowo, the deputy-chair of the federal war cabinet and minister of finance. Awolowo, backed by a grouping of influential civil servants, politicians and senior military officers, had argued that 'starvation was a legitimate weapon of war' and that this was an urgent means required then to break the dogged resistance of the Biafran people which had caused too much frustration in the federal military campaign.[27] This strategy had had some noticeable success as a result of the federal military occupation of most of Biafra's food producing provinces at the early stages of the war. But Awolowo and his group still felt that Biafra could overcome its enormous food problems if it continued to receive relief supplies from abroad and if its guerrilla forces (the Biafran Organisation of Freedom Fighters), which had begun to operate behind federal lines, were able to maintain their so-called food corridors through which strings of porters carried food from occupied Biafra to the free republic. In pursuance of this strategy on the ground, Brigadier Benjamin Adekunle, a division commander and a ruthless advocate of the Awolowo doctrine, once made the following chilling remarks to foreign journalists during a press conference in his theatre of military operations:

> I want to prevent even one Ibo having even one piece to eat before their capitulation. We shoot at everything that moves, and when our forces march into the centre of Ibo territory, we shoot at everything, even at things that do not move.[28]

---

[27] De St. Jorre, *The Brothers' War - Biafra and Nigeria*, p. 244.
[28] *The Economist* (London), 24 August 1968 - cited in John Stremlau, *The International Politics of the Nigerian Civil War* (Princeton: Princeton University, 1977), p. 331.

Adekunle returned to the subject 20 years after the war and showed no remorse whatever nor offered any apologies for his views and deeds during the conflict. In an interview, he told the Nigerian news magazine, *ThisWeek*: 'Starvation is a legitimate weapon of war. In war, all is legal. Take the Second World War - thousands of planes flew over Stuttgart alone in one day, dropping bombs. So what's the ... fuss about starvation?'[29] Besides the implicit comparison to the savagery of the land war in Biafra which is conveyed in this quote, Adekunle's reference to Stuggart is a striking reminder of the calculated federal policy of the carpet bombing of Biafran civilian population centres by the Soviet-equipped Nigeria airforce during the period. This was a permanent feature of the war - a crucial component of the federal 'quick kill' strategy. Chinua Achebe had captured the criminality and the devastating consequences of these bombings on Biafrans in the haunting lines of his poem written at the time, aptly entitled 'Air Raid':

> It comes so quickly
> the bird of death
> from the evil forests of Soviet technology
>
> A man crossing the road
> to greet a friend
> is much too slow.
> His friend cut in halves
> has other worries now
> than a friendly handshake
> at noon.[30]

As for Obafemi Awolowo, the sudden collapse of the Biafran resistance in January 1970 became the opportunity for him to shift his much treasured 'starvation as weapon/quick kill' strategy to a new phase with emphasis on the financial/economic strangulation of Igbo assets across the country - such was the virulence of Igbophobia that he championed during the era. As a result, a federal banking edict was soon published invalidating all bank accounts operated by the Igbo during the war with the federal treasury earning £4 million as a result (*TWN: 45-46*). A paltry flat rate of £20.00 was given in exchange for

---

[29] *ThisWeek* (Lagos), 13 July 1987, p. 28.
[30] Chinua Achebe, *Beware Soul Brother* (Oxford: Heinemann International, 1972), p. 15.

the value of Biafran currency held by the head of every Igbo family, a move which further impoverished the nine million Igbo survivors of the war.[31] Igbo entrepreneurs were for all intents and purposes barred from Port Harcourt, the oil refinery town which had been built largely by Igbo merchant capital since the early 1920s. Millions of pounds worth of land, property and financial investments owned by Igbo people were seized by the local state government authorities set up by Lagos, with the connivance of the federal government. And to maintain the serious tension which Lagos was deliberately fostering between the Igbo and the Ijo people in Port Harcourt, a 'divide-and-rule' strategy reminiscent of the European conquest administration of the past, it arbitrarily excised 13 Igbo towns and villages south of the Imo River and transferred these to the Port Harcourt political jurisdiction. This transfer had also been motivated by the fact that these towns and villages were all connected with the petroleum oil industry which entitled local state governments to an annual special federal subsidy. Elsewhere in the national economy, Awolowo speeded up the draft of the federal government economic programme which envisaged the compulsory purchase by Nigerians of stipulated quotas of shares from major foreign-controlled businesses operating in the country. Within two years, the first allocation of these shares were marketed. It was quite clear that the impecunious Igbo stood no chance of participating in this grand financial activity. The prospects of the Igbo individual or family economic recovery were bleak enough. Unlike several other wars where a given financial figure is set for the reparation paid to the victor by the defeated, the Igbo's was more subtle, diffused, and perhaps more pernicious in the long run.

To underscore the point, the federal government has had a policy of no development in Igboland in the past 30 years, a programme which Nnaemeka Ikpeze has categorised appropriately as an 'atrocity.'[32] As the current 2001 federal budgetary allocations to the regions demonstrate,[33] Igboland continues to receive the lowest annual fiscal resource transfers from the central government since 1970 despite its population of 30 million (about a quarter of

---

[31] For an excellent parody of the value of this sum of £20.00 to the head of Igbo family war survivor, see Chinua Achebe, 'Civil Peace,' in Chinua Achebe and C.L. Innes, eds., *African Short Stories* (London: Heinemann, 1985), pp. 29-35.

[32] Nnaemeka Ikpeze, 'Post-Biafran Marginalization of the Igbo in Nigeria,' in Ifi Amadiume & Abdullahi An-Na'im, eds., *The Politics of Memory* (London and New York: Zed Books, 2000), p. 106.

[33] *Vanguard Daily* (Lagos), 4 December 2000 and *Vanguard Daily* (Lagos), 15 December 2000.

Nigeria's total) and its notoriously dilapidated infrastructure. Power stations and other major industrial enterprises destroyed during the war still lie in ruins. To date, Igboland has the worst communication infrastructure in the country. Its roads particularly remain death-traps especially during six months of the annual wet season. The region was conspicuously omitted as a site for the implementation of the mid-1970s nation-wide multifaceted multi-million dollars irrigation and agricultural expansion programme (*TWN*: 49). In view of its obvious implications, it is scandalous that the central government has virtually ignored the extensive erosion of crop land across the north-western stretch of the region (in the Onitsha/Anambra area) which poses a long term danger to the ecology of the district and far beyond. Igboland was also the only part of the country excluded from the near US$4.5 billion national steel construction project which was scheduled to account for the employment of 100,000 people by 1990 (*TWN*: 49). In the mid-1970s, the federal government enacted a regional quota provision for entry into federal colleges and universities as a way of stemming the 'high-level' of Igbo candidates available (severe restrictions in personal economic activities and the 3-year loss of opportunities during the Biafran struggle caused a post-war upsurge in Igbo educational pursuits). The region was also excluded from the multi-million dollars African Festival of the Arts (1976) even though its contribution to Nigeria's political, cultural and intellectual development in the past 60 years is immensely disproportional to its relatively smaller size and population. At the height of this policy of 'atrocity' in the 1980s, Chinua Achebe made the following observations which were as unequivocal as they were prophetic in the light of the virtual collapse of the Nigerian state presently:

> There is no doubt in my mind that the competitive individualism and the adventurous spirit of the Igbo are necessary ingredients in the modernization and development of Nigerian society. It is neither necessary, nor indeed possible, to suppress them. Nigeria without the inventiveness and the dynamism of the Igbo would be a less hopeful place than it is (*TWN*: 49).

Gani Fawehinmi, the influential human rights lawyer and leading political activist, agrees:

> The Igbo, by their contribution to the economic development of this country, are otherwise called the Jews of Nigeria. They are hard working, very industrious, very innovative, and very articulate people.

> The economic development of this country owes much to their contribution. I do not like the way they have been treated since 1970. They still bear the scars of the Biafran crisis and they are still being treated as if the ... War is still nascent, which is wrong.[34]

Thirty years since the fall of Biafra, the Igbo have had to carry out the reconstruction of their war-battered region *largely by themselves*. Apart from the other economic punitive policies we have cited, the reconstruction of the region through the singular efforts of its population has been part of the 'reparations' the people have paid for losing the Biafra War ('the reconstruction of your region is your responsibility'!). Initially, funds for the tortuous process of rebuilding towns, villages, schools, hospitals and some communication infrastructure came from financial receipts made by the Igbo living abroad (especially in Europe and North America) and through contributions by those who had no choice but to seek some employment elsewhere in Nigeria in the years immediately after the war. Later, local entrepreneurship began to establish the industrial and commercial enterprises that have made towns such as Aba, Umuahia, Abakaliki, Okigwe and Onitsha success stories. The local initiative seen here presently is an inevitable extension of the creativity and dynamism of the Biafra War days when the people, under siege for 30 months, constructed their oil refineries, carried out advanced medical surgeries in underground hospitals, invented and deployed a range of defensive weapon systems that extensively stalled the federal military advance, and ran an excellent administrative service. As in Biafra, the Igbo have relied on their own resources in the past 30 years to make sense of their collective existence.

In all, the Igbo had suffered an incalculable catastrophe - the second in 100 years since their defeat by British imperialism, captured so dramatically in Achebe's *Things Fall Apart*. No other African nation had suffered such a grand-scale holocaust and impoverishment in 200 years. King Leopold II of Belgium, 'The Rapist of Congo', had in the 19th century killed three million Africans in the Congo[35] as his troops ravaged the country in search of ivory, diamonds, and the like - enormous wealth that would soon transform the nascent Belgian state into a modern European country. But that scourge at least included peoples from several nations and nationalities that make up contemporary Democratic

---

[34] Quoted in Joe Igbokwe, 'Nigeria still has an Igbo problem,' *The Guardian* (Lagos), 15 December 2000.

[35] Colin Blane, 'Belgian wealth squeezed from Congo,' *BBC News Online*, 18 January 2001.

Republic of the Congo, Republic of Congo, Rwanda, Burundi, Central African Republic and Angola.

Equally reprehensibly, those who ordered and sustained the war against the Igbo between 1967-1970 had the unenviable record, and should we add responsibility, of literally clearing the undergrowth from which the gruesome killing fields that have since littered Africa expanded almost inexorably. The haunting milestones of Uganda, Ethiopia, Somalia, Sudan, Liberia, Zaire/Democratic Republic of Congo, Republic of Congo, Sierra Leone, Rwanda, Burundi, Guinea-Bissau, and Southern Guinea testify to this. Closer home, just as its devastating consequences were overwhelmingly evident in central Africa 200 years ago, the 'Leopold Syndrome' dictates a switch from reckless human destruction to other fronts of pillage and sacrilege (in an often-quoted letter to one of his envoys during the period, Leopold II had insisted: 'I don't want to miss the chance of getting us a slice of this magnificent African cake.'[36]). It is therefore important to note that those who played varying roles in the wanton destruction of Igbo lives 30 years ago (especially in direct military operations and in enunciating and pursuing the Awolowoist strategy of 'starvation/quick kill' and post-war economic strangulation) with scant opposition from any other constituent nations or nationalities of the federation or concerted critical opinion (especially from intellectuals[37]), have since been prominent, if not central, in making up the managing cast of the unfolding drama of the socio-economic tragedy that has characterised Nigeria. In essence, Biafra projects an enveloping shadow across and within which subsequent *crucial* national events and processes in Nigeria become intelligible: the asphyxiation and retarded development of the Nigerian state by the military and their allies within the civilian population especially among some sections of the intelligentsia; the virtual loot and environmental destruction of the Niger Delta; the export by thieving state officials and their allies of staggering sums of national capital to overseas banks and interests; the unmitigated anti-Igbo

---

[36] Ibid.

[37] One of the ugly features of the Igbo genocide was the lack of concern shown to the victims by most Nigerians elsewhere, a situation which had led Okwudiba Nnoli to observe that '[a]t that time, Nigeria seemed morally anesthesized.' (See Okwudiba Nnoli, *Ethnic Politics in Nigeria* [Enugu: Fourth Dimension Publishers, 1978], p. 245.) In what was clearly an obscene postscript to the massacres, a group of Yoruba *obas* (kings) toured northern Nigeria soon after these horrific events during which they thanked the various local authorities for the 'protection' they had rendered to the Yoruba during the period.

course of national politics and development (what Igbo statespeople and intellectuals often euphemistically term 'marginalisation'[38]); the murder of Ken Sara-Wiwa and other Ogoni human rights spokespersons; the blocking of Mashood Abiola's presidency, his detention, and mysterious death whilst in custody; the varied incarceration, without trial, of citizens Agbakoba, Anyanwu, Fawehinmi, Irabor, Obi, Ransome-Kuti, Thompson and numerous others, including, ironically, Olusegun Obasanjo who himself was tried and sentenced to 15 years in jail by the Abacha military junta for apparently planning a coup d'état. It is against the backdrop of the murder of three million children, women, and men that these seemingly arbitrary events become possible.

Contrary to our earlier proposition that Obasanjo could have some ingrained ideological attachment to the war his forces waged in Biafra 30 years ago, the president's current obsession with the subject is perhaps more politically electoral, hemmed unto the tapestry of the discourses associated with the 2003 presidential elections. Whilst it is true that Obasanjo has not openly decided whether or not to seek re-election at these polls, a number of his senior aides have indicated variously in the past few months that he would run. One indeed noted several months ago that there would be 'no vacancy'[39] in the seat of power as the new elections approached. All sorts of organisations have mushroomed all over the place advocating or proffering support for the president's re-election and there is no evidence to date that Obasanjo himself has convincingly distanced himself from some complicity in the operations of these groups including even the bizarre outfit run by Senator Arthur Nzeribe.

Even then, one does not need to wait for Obasanjo's formal declaration of intent to stand for re-election to conclude that it would be extremely unlikely if he didn't run. If anything, his comments on Biafra and the amazingly and unabashedly anti-Igbo tenor therein clearly indicate the evident link to 2003. Interestingly, in this context, it is no coincidence that Obasanjo's references to Biafra have been stepped up since the concerted declaration made during the conference in January 2001 by *ohaneze*, the pan-Igbo cultural group, to work towards the twin-track programme of the election of an Igbo as the president of Nigeria during the next presidential elections and support of the right of constituent states in the federation to control their resources. The attempt by

---

[38]For an informed analysis on this, see, for instance, Ikpeze, 'Post-Biafran Marginalization of the Igbo in Nigeria,' pp. 90-109.
[39]Tony Anenih, minister of works and housing and an Obasanjo confidant, quoted in Wale Akinola & Lekan Bilesanmi, 'Re-election: The odds against Obasanjo,' *Sunday Vanguard* (Lagos), 24 December 2000.

pro-Obasanjo delegates at the meeting (mostly legislators, ministers and presidential aides) to scuttle these expected historic declarations and instead choreograph an *ohaneze* endorsement of their patron's possible 2003 bid was a humiliating failure. Given the obvious facts of the current regional arithmetic of electoral choices, alignment, and opposition across the country for particularly a presidency that is perceived to be completely inept in tackling the country's staggering woes, Obasanjo now knows that were he to run in 2003 against an Igbo candidate, he really would have to contend with a serious contest that couldn't guarantee success. Obasanjo would subsequently become vociferous in his anti-Igbo rhetoric, fighting the Biafra War all over again in intemperate propaganda outbursts even though this war supposedly ended on 12 January 1970.[40] It is this unimaginable politics of hate against one of the very leading nations of the Nigerian federation that informed Obasanjo's outbursts in Yenogoa and, in the same vein, his recent Owerri sergeant-major mode-of-response or rather *Anthills of the Savannah*'s His Excellency-style pugnacious declaratory dismissal of successive federal government anti-Igbo policies of a generation. Here, Obasanjo charged at his hosts, who incidentally responded to the amazing gusto of the theatrical on display with equanimity, 'Show me your Marginalisation!'[41]

In the broader Nigerian political calculations therefore, Obasanjo's politics of anti-Igbo virulence is predicated on constructing an anti-Igbo alliance *à la* Biafra but he must increasingly find it very depressing that this strategy doesn't seem to be working. The historical circumstances that help to create or enhance the creation of alliances or coalitions for a specific political project are ever in a state of flux, ensuring, thankfully, that they are not recreated subsequently as some mathematical construct! So, despite the vehemence of Obasanjo's anti-Igbo tirades in Yenogoa, the Movement for the Survival of the Ogoni People reaffirmed its determination to control *their* resources themselves in a statement it issued soon after the visit: 'Resource control is an inalienable right .... The human right to development also implies the full realisation of the very right of people to self determination which includes the exercise of their inalienable right to full sovereignty over all their natural wealth and resources.'[42] Also, despite the contemptible anti-Igbo tirades, the progressive position of southern governors on 'resource control' and the expansion of other vistas of democratic

---

[40]See Obijiofor, 'When a president runs out of steam' and Dele Shobowale, 'The President in Civil War,' *Sunday Vanguard* (Lagos), 15 April 2001.
[41]*Sunday Vanguard* (Lagos), 15 April 2001.
[42]*The Guardian* (Lagos), 17 March 2001.

participation is holding firm. At their March 2001 Benin conference, the governors defined 'resource control' unambiguously: '[T]he practice of true federalism and natural law in which the federating units [the constituent 36 states of the federation] express their rights to primarily control the natural resources within their borders'[43]

'Though sovereign ... still a colonial state'

Historically, these are breathtaking positions to take by ever-widening spaces of Nigeria's national publics. This is a critical development. It can only augur well for the urgent and far-reaching restructuring needed to transform the debilitating quagmire of the conflictive and murderous European-imposed nation-state in Africa which has since not benefited from an all-embracing autochthonous dialogue and interrogation. It was in Biafra that barely 10 years after the start of the process of the African restoration of independence that African women and men challenged fundamentally the efficacy of a non-deconstructed 'nation-state' to cope with the exigencies of multi-nationality, multi-culturality and re-development in the aftermath of the devastating European conquest and occupation.

We should here recall that frank diary entry (cited earlier) made by one of the commanders of the British army that defeated the Igbo during those early years of the 20th century: 'Igboland had proved the most troublesome area in all Nigeria.' This evidently security-focused judgement from a British official in the field made as a result of the protracted nature of Igbo resistance to the British invasion and the continuing forms of Igbo opposition to the occupation subsequently, became the precursor to the broad anti-Igbo policy and distrust that Britain adopted as it began to construct the Nigerian federation particularly after 1914. Ultimately, this contraption incorporated the Igbo, Yoruba, Ijo, Ibibio, Urhobo, Tiv, Hausa-Fulani, and scores of other nations and nationalities in these easterly part of west Africa. The historic Igbo political spearhead, beginning in the 1940s, to terminate the British occupation would only reinforce the latter's hostility towards the restive Igbo. The British therefore ensured that when eventually Nigerian liberation occurred in 1960, the Igbo were denied political power. Instead, the British worked assiduously to install the Hausa-Fulani (whose leading political party, the Northern Peoples Congress,

---

[43] *Sunday Vanguard* (Lagos), 1 April 2001.

consistently opposed the liberation of the country throughout the struggles of the 1950s) to the position of the new rulers of Nigeria on the morrow of the formal termination of the conquest regime.[44]

Essentially, Hausa-Fulani political hegemony became the crucial *internal* lever through which Britain reinforced its firm grip of the Nigerian economy following the so-called restoration of independence. Apart from South Africa, Nigeria was then the site of Britain's highest economic and industrial investment in Africa with a total worth of £1.5 billion (mainly in the country's leading extractive industries such as petroleum oil, coal and tin, and in banking and insurance). The British government controlled about 50 per cent shares in Shell-BP (the predominant oil prospecting company in Nigeria) and 60 per cent shares in Amalgamated Tin Mining Nigeria, a major prospecting tin, cobalt and iron ore mining company.[45] In the non-mining sector of he economy, John Holt Company, owned by a British family, was one of the two largest in the country with branches located in the principal towns and cities. The United Africa Company (UAC), another British enterprise, accounted for 41.3 per cent of Nigeria's entire import and export trade. The UAC is the major African subsidiary of the British transnational group, Unilever. It developed from the Royal Niger Company, which, in association with the entrepreneur Taubman Goldie, and Frederick Lugard, the first principal British administrator of occupied Nigeria, harnessed the British conquest of a number of nations and states in this south-eastern territorial stretch of west Africa, and converted these into the political agglomeration presently called the Nigerian federation

---

[44]It is often ignored by scholars interested in the comparative politics of the era that while major liberation wars would break out in British-occupied Kenya, Portuguese-occupied Guinea Bissau and elsewhere in Africa during the period, there was a major political party in British-occupied Nigeria which *was not* opposed to the continuation of European conquest rule in this part of West Africa. The Northern Peoples Congress worked feverishly between 1951 and 1957 particularly to oppose Nigeria's liberation. It was only prepared to alter its position in late 1957 after the British had guaranteed it that it would head the first post-conquest government.

[45]For a discussion of the background to the British exploitation of Nigeria's tin mines and the extensive range of workers' resistance during the period, see William Freund, 'Theft and social protest among the tin miners of northern Nigeria,' in Donal Crummey, ed., *Banditry, Rebellion and Social Protest in Africa* (London/Portsmouth: James Currey/Heinemann, 1986), pp. 49-63.

between 1886-1941.[46] The UAC, for its part, had wholesale and retailing enterprises run in most parts of Nigeria by its numerous subsidiaries, among which the following three were most prominent: Kingsway Chemist, G.B. Ollivant, and African Timber and Plywood.[47] In addition, the UAC had part interest in other well-established companies in the country such as Gulf Oil of Nigeria, Nigerian Prestressed Concrete, Nigerian Breweries, Taylor Woodrow Nigeria, and Nigelec. Ikenna Nzimiro's often quoted aphorism, 'UAC was Nigeria and Nigeria was UAC,'[48] does not therefore exaggerate UAC's strategic control of Nigeria's economy at the time. Finally, in the finance sector, Barclays Nigeria (a subsidiary of the British Barclays Bank) and the Standard Bank of Nigeria (owned largely by Lloyds Bank and the Westminster Bank) controlled 90 per cent of Nigeria's effective banking system. Once again, these institutions had branches throughout the regions in the country. About 20,000 Britons resident in Nigeria were employed in this extensive network of businesses and related services in the economy.

Forty years on, Britain still maintains its dominant position in both the ownership of capital and trade in the country. Britain has always enjoyed a fantastically more advantageous balance of payment position in its trade with Nigeria. Figures for the first six months of 1995 show that British exports to Nigeria stood at £250 million while its imports from Nigeria amounted to £77 million.[49] As for figures for the first six months of 2000, Britain's impressive all time performance on this score remains unchallenged: it exported £230.8 million worth of goods and services to Nigeria while the total worth of its Nigerian imports during the same period was just £31.8 million.[50] Given this entrenched British role in the Nigerian economy, British banks and other

---

[46]For an account of Unilever's strategic interests in Nigeria during the period, see Ikenna Nzimiro, 'The Political Implications of Multinational Corporations in Nigeria,' in Carl Widstrand, ed., *Multi-National Firms in Africa* (Dakar/Uppsala: African Institute for Economic Development and Planning/Scandinavian Institute for African Studies, 1975), pp. 210-243. See also Margery Perham, *Mining, Commerce and Finance in Nigeria* (London: Faber and Faber, 1948), Claude Ake, ed., *Political Economy of Nigeria* (Harlow and Lagos: Longman Group, 1985), especially chs. 1-4, Robert Shenton, *The Development of Capitalism in Northern Nigeria* (London: James Currey, 1986) and Toyin Falola, ed., *Britain and Nigeria* (London and New Jersey: Zed Books, 1987).
[47]Nzimiro, 'The Political Implications of Multinational Corporations in Nigeria,' pp. 212-214.
[48]Ibid., p. 217.
[49]*The Guardian (London)*, 11 November 1995.
[50]*Vanguard Daily* (Lagos), 20 October 2000.

financial services have emerged as favoured conduits used by corrupt Nigerian leaders and officials to siphon and transfer millions of capital assets from Nigeria overseas. In just one example, assets worth £600 million looted from the Nigerian treasury during the course of the 1990s by General Sani Abacha, the late Nigerian dictator, were initially deposited in British banks[51] before subsequent transfers of part of the haul to Swiss banks and elsewhere. The British Financial Services Authority (FSA) has been very critical of the role of British banks to this effect, openly accusing 15 banks of 'significant control weaknesses' in their anti-money laundering controls.[52] The FSA found out that at least 40 personal and corporate accounts linked to Abacha's family and associates existed in Britain.[53] For the Hausa-Fulani leaders and their allies who have been in supreme political power in Nigeria since 1960, Nigeria's relationship with Britain is dictated pivotally on the premise that 'though sovereign, [it] behave[s] as if it were still a colonial state.'[54]

It would therefore appear that no imperial state which has access and control of such a vast fiefdom of fortune as Nigeria would fail to keep this estate under its constant, unflinching gaze for obvious reasons. As a result, the politics of the 'troublesome' Igbo is always of particular interest to British policy in the country. Not surprisingly, the 1967 Igbo declaration of independence from Nigeria in response to the genocide against its people was completely unacceptable to Britain. London promptly supported the federal government war effort to crush the independence movement. Britain was probably the only country in the world that could not maintain a neutral position in the Biafra War. Michael Stewart, its foreign secretary at the time, said as much during a contribution to one of the several debates on the conflict in the British parliament.[55] Britain stepped up its arms supplies to the federal military despite mass popular protests at home and some opposition in parliament.[56] On the eve

---

[51] *The Financial Times* (London), 9 February 2001.
[52] *The Guardian* (Lagos), 10 March 2001.
[53] Ibid.
[54] Billy Dudley, *An Introduction to Nigerian Government and Politics* (London and Basingstoke: Macmillan, 1982), p. 283.
[55] Suzanne Cronje, *The World and Nigeria* (London: Sidgwick and Jackson, 1972), p. 38.
[56] For an updated insight on this, based on recently declassified British state papers, see Michael Leapman, 'While the Biafrans starved, the FO moaned about hacks,' *The Independent on Sunday* (London), 3 January 1999.

of the war, Britain accounted for 38 per cent of Nigeria's arms imports.[57] Six months after, this had jumped to 48 per cent. In 1968, it was 80 per cent and by December 1969 (one month before Biafra's capitulation), Britain accounted for 97 per cent of total federal arms imports.[58] Britain had readily filled in the gap created in federal arms imports as a result of the early embargo placed on all weapons' sales to both belligerents by those countries which hitherto made up 62 per cent of Nigeria's arms exporters. These included the then Federal Republic of Germany, Italy, Israel, The Netherlands, Canada, Belgium, Switzerland, India and Sweden. Apart from military aircraft which Britain did not as a matter of policy sell to independent Africa, London supplied Lagos with an assortment of sophisticated weaponry which guaranteed the federal military the capacity to sustain a 30-month offensive in Biafra. British military experts were at hand in Lagos to give advice throughout the war.

The British intervention on the federal Nigeria side of the Biafra War was not just restricted to military or diplomatic pursuits of the government or its officials. Some ex-conquest administrators who served in Nigeria including a few who had retired as academics in British universities (and other institutions of higher learning) were often more coherent spokespersons of the federal government cause in Britain than visiting envoys from Lagos. These ex-administrators published in academic and popular journals arguing the case on behalf of the federal government, lobbying members of parliament and other interested parties accordingly, and offering specialist advice to members of the federal government especially in ways of confronting the broad British public opposition to the war and their government's intervention. One of them, Margery Perham, who was a fellow in African Studies at Oxford University, even went as far as calling on Biafrans to abandon their resistance to the Nigerian military in September 1968.[59] Perham had made her call in a special broadcast to Biafra from radio facilities provided generously by the federal government in Lagos. It seemed that these former imperial field officials who spent most of their adult lives constructing a haven for British economic and strategic interests in Nigeria were traumatised by the prospects of watching so soon the Nigerian edifice cascading to an abyss due to the popular, defiant and determined resistance organised by the 'troublesome' Igbo.

It would take another 10-15 years after the capitulation of Biafra for students of conflicts (and interventions) in the Southern World to popularise the concept

---

[57] Cronje, *The World and Nigeria*, p. 393.
[58] Ibid., pp. 385-393.
[59] Obasanjo, *My Command*, p. 150.

of 'war-by-proxy.' This describes the extent to which a Northern World power bloc may have to rely on a local client in a war in the South to fight in defence of the former's interests (economic, strategic, whatever). Yet, the Biafra War was Britain's war-by-proxy, essentially fighting its Igbo adversary all over again since their previous encounter 40-70 years earlier. As Chinua Achebe recalls that late 19th century/early 20th century confrontation, with evident understatement, 'Britain never... quite forgave'[60] the Igbo for the continuing resistance the latter posed during the consolidation of the conquest state in Nigeria nor the Igbo spearhead of the termination of the imperial occupation beginning 40 years later. In this new conflict in the mid-1960s, Britain was *actively* involved in the critical phases of the political developments that led to the war. It was highly unlikely that the federal government would have ordered the invasion of Biafra by the Nigerian armed forces without seeking some guarantee of British support. That support was given soon after the outbreak of hostilities. It ensured that Britain emerged from a position where it supplied 38 per cent of Nigeria's weaponry on the eve of the war to 97 per cent one month to the Biafran capitulation 30 months later. While the *rest* of Nigeria's arms exporting countries placed embargoes on both belligerents as we indicated earlier, Britain readily filled in the short-falls in the federal armoury. In turn, the Nigerians were able to sustain a ferocious offensive on a population of 14 million people encircled in 29,500 square miles of territory that was Biafra. By the time Biafra fell, just about 6,000 square miles of that territory was under the effective control of the Biafran military.

In the absence of British weaponry, what is presently known as the Biafra War would have been a highly unlikely event. Federal Nigeria *did not* produce any weapons of its own. For the federals to have contemplated attacking Biafra in the wake of the 1966 genocidal massacres of the Igbo meant that they had to rely on an *external* source for their acquisition of weaponry. Not only did Britain provide the arms generously, it also mobilised its governmental, political, and diplomatic machinery for the support of the Nigerian war effort. Short of introducing direct combat troops, British intervention in Biafra was at par with British interventionism in two other Southern conflicts in the post-1939-1945 War epoch - Malaysia and Kenya. Yet, seen from another perspective, Britain's proxy war in Igboland was indeed not new in the African experience. In the past, particularly prior to the formal 19th century seizure of Africa, it was a common feature among invading European states and interests

---

[60] Achebe, 'Words of anxious love,' p. 21.

to arm one African nation against the other in pursuance of their mission to conquer the continent of Africa. Chancellor Williams, the distinguished African American historian, recalls this trajectory of a tragic history:

> Now the shadows lengthened. The Europeans had also been busily building up and training strong African armies. Africans trained to hate, kill and conquer Africans. Blood of Africans was to sprinkle and further darken the pages of their history ... Indeed, Africa was conquered for the Europeans by the Africans [themselves], and thereafter kept under colonial control by African police and African soldiers. Very little European blood was ever spilled.[61]

Deconstruction

As we have already stated, three million Igbo people were killed in Biafra during three years of bitter fighting in 1967-1970. Since Biafra, nine million additional Africans have been slaughtered in the other extended eerie killing fields of the continent stretching from Guinea-Bissau, Guinea, Liberia and Sierra Leone in the west to Uganda, Ethiopia, Somalia and Eritrea in the east, and Sudan, Rwanda and the Congos in the centre to Angola in the south. These conflicts have erupted as a result of the continuously thunderous demands made by desperately deprived and exploited nations in the European-created artificial states of the continent for the construction of decentralised and decentring alternative political structures and institutions which empower people at their locale. As Nigeria shows, and typifies, the African 'nation-state' in question is a murderous political and economic contraption or a residual conurbation of empire that serves the interests of the imperial European state creator which 'carefully and laboriously put it together.'[62] This is to ensure that the latter continues to exercise influence in the politics of Africa *indefinitely* in furtherance of its own historical economic and strategic imperatives. In this context, the claims by former French President Mitterand (cited earlier) about the importance of who controls Africa in the 21st century are indeed no exaggeration. Presently, the imperatives at stake are such that while 12 million Africans have been killed in the last 40 years to prop up the essential character

---

[61]Chancellor Williams, *The Destruction of Black Civilization* (Chicago: Third World, 1987), p. 218.
[62]Achebe, 'Words of anxious love,' p. 21.

of this state and while there has been a virtual collapse of socio-economic development in most of the continent, the state nonetheless fulfils its historic role as the agency through which the European World and countries elsewhere extract gargantuan surplus product from Africa as we have demonstrated clearly in this study. It should never escape the attention of the observer that the flip side of the coin that tells the tale of Africa's staggering capital transfers to the Western World, day in, day out, is the emaciated, starving and dying African child, woman or man that has for long been the abiding image on television screens across the world.

It is now evident that there is no future for African progress, especially in ensuring that the people themselves exercise unfettered self-governing ability to develop their lives and environment, except Africans totally dismantle the European-created state on the continent which, thankfully, has all but collapsed as these lines are being written. The ultra-centralising ethos of this state which feeds on its genocidal proclivity cannot respect not to talk of safeguard the human rights of peoples in the multi-national and multi-cultural milieu that typify contemporary Africa.[63] On the contrary, the future for Africa should revert to extensive socio-political decentralisation where communities, however 'small', have the right to control and develop their human and natural resources as they deem fit, and decide freely on the nature of the relationship that they wish to establish with their neighbours and those further afield.

---

[63] This observation extends, even more so, to cover the concept of the supranational 'African Union' as envisaged by some African leaderships presently. Apart from the very limited exchange of ideas on the subject among the leaders themselves, this concept has not been subjected to any extensive democratic debate, whatsoever, by the varying publics of the African population. This 'Africa Union', essentially a social club of leaders who have failed Africa, is therefore extremely anti-democratic. It goes against the grain of the African liberation proffered here.

5
Reconfiguration

The total world population is [now] 3 billion human beings, while [US citizens] number 200 million. This is one-to-fifteen odd. If force comes to prevail against right, the US can be taken over, and all that we have will be snatched away by the hungry masses of the world.
US President Lynden Johnson, 1966

The gap between rich and poor countries is continually widening. As of the 1970s, more than one-half of the world population will be living in independent countries in the southern hemisphere. These people will be hungry and will have access to less than one-tenth of the stock of goods and services produced by mankind.
Robert McNamara, US Defence Secretary, 1966; later, president of the World Bank

Folk forms

The African 'nation-state' has now run the course of its bloody trail in history. The greatest challenge facing Africans in the new millennium is to dismantle this state and create new state forms based on Africa's critical re-engagement with its rich cultural heritage. This is to enable them to safeguard the lives of their people and embark on the vast topography of reconstruction of society after a depressing and devastating history. This task must be a cardinal facet of the African renaissance. On the eve of the restoration of African independence almost 40 years ago to the day, Frantz Fanon, one of the leading theorists of the African resistance had warned Africa about the future course of direction:

> Let us decide not to imitate Europe; let us combine our muscles and brains in a new direction ... not pay tribute to Europe by creating states,

institutions and societies which draw their inspiration from her. If we want to turn Africa into a new Europe ... then let us leave the destiny of our countries to Europeans. They will know how to do it better than the most gifted among us ... If we wish to live up to our peoples' expectations ... we must work out new concepts ... and try to set afoot a new [people].'[1]

Fanon's profound analytical insight into the fast-changing developments of the African liberation during the period could not have alerted even him to anticipate the dire consequences to Africa of its leadership ignoring his 'not to imitate Europe' stricture. Successive African leaderships across the continent have since operated a death state machine that has dispatched 12 million fellow Africans to their untimely deaths in the last 40 years, adding to the 'avalanche of murders'[2] that were the hallmarks of the preceding African holocaust and occupation. What is clear now is that Africa has no other choice than to abandon and dismantle this machine of terror. This European-'scissors and paste job,' as Richard Dowden has described it, has indeed caused Africa 'much blood and tears.'[3] To attempt to 'perfect it' through all sorts of bogus constitutionalism as we have seen in recent years under the aegies of 'globalisation' is at best to dress up the character and consequences of its existentialist mission to appear 'more humane'.[4] Africa's alternative path of survival and reconstruction is clearly a path that emerges from the people *reconnecting* to the continent's enduring cultural precepts and institutions

---

[1] Frantz Fanon, *The Wretched of the Earth* (Harmondsworth: Penguin Books, 1967), pp. 252-255
[2] Ibid, p. 252.
[3] Richard Dowden, 'Redrawing the outmoded colonial map of Africa,' *Independent* (London), 10 September 1987. Thomas Pakenham has also noted: 'One has only to think of the bloody ... wars that followed decolonisation to see the craziness of these lines drawn on maps in Europe by men ignorant of African geography and history.' (See Thomas Pakenham, 'The European share-out of the spoils of Africa,' *Financial Times* [London], 15 February 1988.)
[4] In the past 10 years, several ex-African military dictators in west and central Africa particularly have followed in the footsteps of Flt-Lt Rawlings of Ghana and General Eyadema of Togo in 'civilianising' themselves into state presidents where they oversee the implementation of damaging IMF/World Bank socio-economic programmes on their populations. An important example to note is that of General Obasanjo who is currently president of Nigeria after having served in that post in the 1970s as head of a military junta.

emplaced in its ancient nations or in 'real Africa',[5] as Femi Nzegwu has aptly categorised them. Chinua Achebe anticipates this historic path of African renaissance in the name *Amaechina* (may-the-path-never-close),[6] given to the daughter of Elewa, the priestess of the redemptive *idemili* goddess and Ikem Oshodi, the revolutionary author-poet, in the novel *Anthills of the Savannah*, published in 1987 - 30 years after *Things Fall Apart*. Amaechina is at once an African philosophical/spiritual prayer of reclamation and an affirmative quest for societal reconstruction. This prefigures a future 'that springs eternal' (*AS*: 222). Amaechina is a unisex name. With this reclamatory name-share between the sexes, Achebe gives notice of the priority he attaches to the resuscitation of the treasured position of the family in African community affairs and the full operation of the ethos and institutions of the dual-sex complementarity that has for centuries defined the central tenets of African social existence. These spheres of African life have come under sustained assaults and, in some fronts, have had considerable fractures during the course of the European occupation of the continent and the last 40 years of disastrous African overseeing-management. One such emergency zone of fracture has been the outrageous marginalisation of African women from participating actively in the key institutions of the state and society. This has been an historical setback for women who in the past controlled and exercised extensive rights and authority over their own affairs as well as those of the rest of society.[7] The re-positioning of women in the shared complementary spaces of responsibility, power and authority must be at the epicentre of the reconfiguration of African fortunes in these new state forms of decentralisation.

On relationships further afield, Amaechina operates from the crucial premise that following the liberation of South Africa and the formal end of the direct political and military occupation of Africa by extra-continental powers, arms confrontation is not a viable option to resolve Africa's outstanding problems - especially those affecting constituent peoples in the current state. Amaechina therefore insists that arms should henceforth be removed from the African continental scene as the vehicle for the settlement of disputes. All Africa's problems, however complex and intractable they may appear presently, can and should be resolved through painstaking negotiation even if this seems or becomes protracted. As it was generally in pre-conquest times, there should be

---

[5]Nzegwu, *Love, Motherhood and the African Heritage*, p. 41.
[6]Chinua Achebe, *Anthills of the Savannah* (London: Pan Books, 1988), p. 222. Further references of the text will be made in the text, abbreviated as *AS*.
[7]Nzegwu, *Love, Motherhood and the African Heritage*, *passim*.

no time limits or ultimatums placed on negotiations and conflict resolutions in Africa: the talking went on and on until some resolution was achieved ... The mutual bombardment of ideas, not bullets and shells, was the driving impetus for the avoidance and overcoming of conflicts. Thus, the battlefield, whether it is Angola, Sierra Leone, Congo or Sudan, should no longer be an option for the settlement of Africa's extant problems. On this score, the ethos that governs the African journey of recovery is the commitment of all Africans and a demand they make on the rest of the world to place a mandatory embargo of all arms sales and transfers to Africa as well as a complete demilitarisation of the continent. Real Africa needs peace for, and with itself, to enable it embark on this much-vaunted era of renaissance. Given the devastating impact of arms, arming, armies and armed conflicts on Africa's tragic history, Franz Schurmann has correctly reminded us:

> The warlords of Africa are not traditional but rather a phenomenon of modernity. They are fighting for power in a Western-type state with its armies, police, bureaucracies, control over economic institutions ...[8]

The new Africa therefore has a commanding signpost for the world's attention: *Africa Is An Arms-Free Zone. No More Arms Sales Or Transfers to Africa.*

Amaechina also rejects any existing structures or exchange relations of the past that act as obstructions to the actualisation of the goals of the African renaissance. It rejects out of hand the enslaving politics and economics of the IMF/World Bank-'structural adjustment programme'. New Africa will tear up this package right away and replace it with an African-centred discourse and strategy of (re)development. Never again will Africans allow themselves to be *active participants* of policies or programmes devised to harm their people as has been the shattering epoch of the past 40 years. Finally, Amaechina will reject the so-called debt that the West claims currently that Africa owes it. Amaechina will instead demonstrate, as we shall make available soon, that it is the West which owes Africa a fortune that goes back to the tragic era of the African holocaust. In the meantime, some notes are required here to examine and respond to an array of topics including food, population and health which a number of critics have argued in recent times, quite often in apocalyptic

---

[8]Franz Schurmann, 'Africa is Saving Itself,' *Choices: The Human Development Magazine*, Volume 5, Number 1, pp. 4-5, June 1996.

exegeses,[9] constitute an urgent task for Africans to overcome if indeed they have a future in the world today!

Food, population, reproductive health

In 1987, the United States Commission on Demographic Crisis (CDC) published its report on a study it carried out to determine an International Suffering Index.[10] This research focused on most of the world's sovereign states. Utilising a number of socio-economic indices such as population growth, gross national product, infant mortality, illiteracy and food consumption, and measuring these on a 0-10 scale indicating a deficiency-sufficiency range, the CDC concluded by classifying these states in two main groups: (1) Least Suffering Rates (LSR) - these included the United States, the then Soviet Union, Cuba, Britain, the former West Germany and Japan, and (2) Highest Suffering Rates (HSR) which included Somalia, Ethiopia, Burkina Faso, Central African Republic, Ghana, Mali and Nigeria. In summarising the outcome of the study, Joseph Spidel, the CDC vice-president, stressed that the HSR countries were generally those with highest levels of population growth,[11] even though he did not demonstrate how this particular index was related to the rest, except of course to underline how serious a problem it was, reflecting very similar fears expressed 20 years before by the two leading US public figures quoted in the epigraphs above. Generally, there was scant analysis in the report of the 'background' political and economic factors which produced these contradictory results. This was clearly a case where empirical indicators, instead of helping to enlighten us in our understanding of social development, further obfuscate reality.

The concern of leading Western officials and institutions on the population of countries in the Southern World acquired a bizarre, if not obscene dimension in 1990 when a member of the British parliament advocated that condoms should be sent to Bangladesh and the Sudan as a method of limiting the population growth rate of the two countries. Both countries had just experienced extensive deaths and socio-economic dislocations caused by a cyclone in the

---

[9]See, for instance, Desmond Cohen, 'Responding to the Socio-Economic Impact of the HIV Epidemic in Sub-Saharan Africa,' *Issues Paper*, No. 32 (New York: UNDP, February 1999).
[10]*West Africa* (London), 25 May 1987, p. 1007.
[11]Ibid.

former and a crop failure in the latter. It was not evident anywhere in this call for condom-intervention that a lower population growth rate, or indeed a population tally lower than the number in either of the two countries at the time would have prevented any of the tragedies. In parallel vein, the so-called environmental pressure group, Earth First!, sees the current spread of the HIV/AIDS epidemic, and the calamity of famine in a number of African countries as the 'Earth's salvation, ridding the planet of a particularly destructive life-form (human beings).'[12] Earth First! has reinforced its position on the subject by specifically calling for a denial of any external food shipment to the African famine victims because the 'problem of African starvation [is] merely a question of human numbers moving beyond the carrying capacity of the land, and seeing the solution as just a population crash.'[13]

If the above outbursts amount to a silly use of the size of the population of a people as a red herring to explain social phenomenon, or indeed verge on what Rudolph Bahro would describe as 'eco-fascism,'[14] these charges may not be as obvious in the next example. In a special feature article on Africa published in September 1991, the British historian Roland Oliver makes the following observation on African population:

> Africa's population problem by itself offers almost a sufficient explanation of the continent's growing poverty, as compared even with the rest of the [Southern] World. In the 1960s, the annual rate of population growth in Africa was roughly similar to that in Southern Asia and Latin America, at around 2.5 per cent. During the 1970s and 1980s, the Southern Asian and Latin American rates decreased, while that of Africa increased dramatically to 3.5 per cent.[15]

There is however no evidence shown in this article on how population growth affects, as in this case, what Oliver refers to as Africa's 'growing poverty.' Despite this, Oliver concludes his piece by stating:

> With its overriding population problem, Africa can hardly expect to achieve First World standards of economic development within the next

---

[12] Bill Weinberg, *War on the Land* (London and New Jersey: Zed Books, 1991), p. 162.
[13] Ibid.
[14] Ibid., p. 163.
[15] Roland Oliver, 'The condition of Africa,' *Times Literary Supplement* (London), 20 September 1991, p. 8.

century, but with just a little more day-to-day accountability, it could at least recover the confidence to continue the uphill struggle with more success.[16]

Ignoring the gratuitous racism and paternalism evident in this quote, we shall soon demonstrate how the cynical use of population by some Western officials and publicists to explain the crisis of exploitation in Africa (and elsewhere in the Southern World) is pointedly diversionary. It is in fact a continuing effort made by the West to deny its *instrumental* role in creating the barbarism of contemporary African political economies. The result has been that whilst the West represents just about 20 per cent of the world's population, it appropriates nearly 90 per cent of the annual stock of goods and services produced by all of humanity. This is the converse of the striking revelation made by Robert McNamara on the critical subject of the pattern of the consumption of the world's resources cited above. We shall be returning soon to elaborate on our position established towards the end of the last chapter that Africa's future lies in the creation of new state forms to replace the existing murderous entities. Before that though, it is pertinent to demonstrate that neither the size of Africa's population nor its rate of growth is an adequate factor in explaining either the drastic fall in Africa's food production, particularly in the last 20 years, or indeed the current continent's generalised socio-economic tragedy.

Africa's population is presently about 645 million, approximately a 3-fold increase since 1900. Not until the beginning of the last century did Africa record an appreciable increase in its population after 300 years of stagnation caused by the mass transportation of millions of its peoples to the Americas to work the mines and plantations, and build the cities and economies of a continent that had just been pillaged and conquered by European imperialism. Between 1650 (approximately 100 years after the start of this exportation of Africans) and 1850, Africa's population remained roughly at 100 million.[17] This was a period that showed high increases in Europe (from 103 million to 274 million) and Asia (from 257 million to 656 million). In the subsequent 50 years, Europe's population increased by about 70 per cent (from 274 million to 423 million) and Asia's increased by about 50 per cent (from 656 million to 857 million). In contrast, Africa's population increased from 100 million to 120 million, a rise of just 20 per cent! While it is true that rapid increases in

---

[16]Ibid., p. 9.
[17]Rodney, *How Europe Underdeveloped Africa*, p. 106. The rest of the population statistics below are also derived from this source.

population growth could affect the food balance in a given human society, an increase in the number of the hungry and/or starving is *not* a direct consequence of population growth. Africa's current population is, for instance, less than one-half that of China which is 1.5 billion. While anything between 60-70 per cent of Africans are malnourished, less than 5 per cent of Chinese could be categorised as such.

Capacities despite holocaust

It should be obvious in this discussion that our goal is definitely not to contribute to the 'politically correct' rhetoric bandied about incessantly which calls for the decrease in African population because we do not believe that Africa, in the first instance, is overpopulated. We must now examine this issue. The population argument is usually advanced on a number of fronts. First, there is a 'theory' that the given landmass which presently defines Africa and its various 'nation-states' cannot sustain the existing populations, but, more critically, the 'projected populations' in years to come. We shall examine the degree to which this 'theory' is able to stand up to serious scientific scrutiny first by comparing Africa's landmass *vis-à-vis* its population and those of countries of the Western World.

Africa's population is currently estimated at approximately 645 million people[18] covering an incredibly vast landmass. Ethiopia's landmass is five times the size of Britain at 471,775 sq miles as compared to Britain's 94,226 sq miles, yet both support similar populations at 60 million and 58 million, respectively. As for Somalia, it is 2.6 times the size of Britain but has a population of only 10 million. Sudan provides an even more fascinating comparison. Whilst Sudan is 10 times the size of Britain, it supports a population of just 27 million - about half the size of Britain. In fact Sudan has a land mass equal to that of India which is populated by one billion people! Britain is one-tenth the size of the Congo Democratic Republic (CDR) which has a land mass of 905,562 sq miles, similar to Sudan and India. In other words, the CDR is about ten times the size of Britain but with a population of 48 million, it has a smaller population than the latter.

Second, let us examine similar sized countries. France has a landmass of

---

[18] All the statistics here on countries' population, land mass and the like are derived from The World Bank, *The Development Report 2001* and United Nations Development Programme, *Human Development Report 2001*.

211,206 sq miles similar to Somalia. However, France's population of 58 million is about five times the population of Somalia. Similarly, Botswana is slightly larger than France at 254,968 sq miles but with a population of 1.5 million which is a minuscule proportion of France's population. Belgium and Rwanda have similar landmasses; Belgium's is about 11,781 sq miles while Rwanda's is 10,169 sq miles. Uganda's landmass at 91,135 sq miles is similar to Britain's 94,226 sq miles. Yet with a population of only 20 million, Uganda is less than half of the size of Britain. Similarly, Ghana's landmass of 92,099 sq miles makes it approximately equal to the size of Britain. Ghana is however populated by only 18 million people, i.e. one-third the size of Britain on roughly the same landmass size. South to South comparisons can also prove useful in exposing the fallacy of either Africa's 'large population' or 'potential explosive population.' Iran's size of 636,292 sq miles is about the same as Sudan's. Yet, its population, unlike Sudan's 27 million, is three times as large at 71.5 million. Pakistan and Nigeria provide illuminating comparisons. Pakistan's landmass of 310,402 sq miles is slightly less than Nigeria's 356,667 sq miles but with a population of 143 million it is significantly higher than Nigeria's 118 million. Bangladesh's 55,598 sq miles makes it one-sixth the size of Nigeria but with a higher population of 122 million. Namibia has a population of 1.6 million on a landmass of 333,702 sq miles which is comparable to Nigeria's size. Angola and South Africa are significantly bigger than Nigeria at 481,350 sq miles and 471,442 sq miles respectively, yet Angola's population is a mere 11.5 million and South Africa's 43 million. In both cases, if we return to our earlier comparisons, these two countries are about 4-5 times the size of Britain but with one-fifth and two-thirds respectively of the latter's population.

Finally, we should turn to the question of resource, its availability or lack of it, and therefore its ability or inability to support the continent's population - another component of Africa's 'over-population' fallacy. Eighty per cent of Uganda's arable land, some of the richest in Africa, remains uncultivated. Were Uganda to expand its current food production by just 50 per cent, not only would it be completely self-sufficient, but it would be able to feed all the countries contiguous to its territory without difficulty. The overall statistics of the African situation is even more revealing as with regards to the continent's long-term possibilities. Just a quarter of the potential arable land of Africa is being cultivated presently.[19] Even here, an increasingly high proportion of the cultivated area is assigned to the so-called cash-crops (cocoa, coffee, tea,

---

[19]See 'Africa's Development Disaster,' *Comment* (London: Catholic Institute for International Affairs, 1985), p. 19.

groundnut, sisal, floral cultivation, etc.) for exports mainly to the Western World at a time when there has been a virtual collapse, across the board, of the price of these crops in the West's commodity markets. In the past 20 years, the average real price of these African products in the West has been about 20 per cent less than their worth during the 1960s-70s period which was soon after the restoration of independence. As for the remaining 75 per cent of Africa's uncultivated land, this represents *66 per cent* of the entire world's potential.[20] The world is aware of the array of strategic minerals such as cobalt, copper, diamonds, gold, industrial diamonds, iron ore, manganese, phosphates, titanium, uranium, and of course petroleum oil found in Nigeria, Sudan, DRC, Namibia, South Africa, Angola, Zimbabwe and elsewhere on the continent. These countries are among Africa's most wealthy and potentially some of the world's wealthiest. However, what is not always or simultaneously associated with the wealth profiles of these countries is that they have vast acreage of rich farmlands with capacity to optimally support the food needs of generations of African peoples. In addition, the famous fish industry in Senegal, Cote d'Ivoire and Ghana for instance, Botswana's rich cattle farms, west Africa's yam and plantain belts extending from southern Cameroon to the Casamance province of Senegal, the continent's rich rice production fields, etc., all highlight the potential Africa has for fully providing for all its food needs.

Thus, what the current African socio-economic situation shows is extraordinarily reassuring, provided the acreage devoted to cultivation is expanded and expressly targeted to address Africa's own *internal* consumption needs. Land use directed at agriculture for food output, as *opposed* to the calamitous waste of 'cash crop' production for export, must become the focus of agricultural policy in the new Africa. It is an inexplicable tragedy that any African child, woman, or man could go without food in the light of the staggering endowment of resources on this continent. Africa constitutes a spacious, rich and arable landmass that can support its population, which is still one of the world's least densely populated and distributed, into the indefinite future. There is only one condition though for the realisation of this goal - Africa must utilise these immense resources for the benefit of its *own* peoples within newly negotiated, radically decentralised political dispensations which must abandon the current murderous European-created 'nation-states'. We now no longer require any reminders that the primary existence of these states is to destroy or disable as many enterprisingly resourceful and resource-based

---

[20]Ibid.

constituent peoples, nations and publics within the polity that are placed in their genocidal sights. The example of the Igbo in contemporary Nigeria grimly illustrates this fact.

It is abundantly clear that the factors which have contributed to determining the very poor quality of life of Africa's population have to do with the non-use, partial use, or the gross mis-use of the continent's resources year in, year out. This is thanks to an asphyxiating 'nation-state' whose strategic resources are used largely to support the Western World and an overseer-grouping of local forces which exists solely to police the dire straits of existence that is the lot of the average African. As a result, the broad sectors of African peoples are yet to be placed and involved centrally in the entire process of societal reconstruction and transformation. Surely, factors such as improved health and education, full integration of women and men in the running of their societies, justice, peace and security, better physical infrastructure, improved technologies, and, above all, an urgently restructured *culturally supportive political framework* that enhances the quality of life of Africans are really the pressing issues of focus for Africa.

As we have shown in this study, to live in the typical African 'nation state' presently is to live in the most oppressively centralised state in the world that denies most peoples in constituent nations their fundamental human rights. This has been a debilitating legacy for most Africans since this state was created by Europeans during their occupation of the continent. It was, and still remains a conqueror's and a conquest state, having clobbered together peoples of varying political, cultural, religious and ideational heritage with no identifiably-embracing organic 'national' sensibility, save an ensemble to rationalise the exploitation of critical resources for transfers to the Western World. The centralised state was a boon to the European project as can be expected. It was the instrument to harness and enforce the African occupation in its entirety and maximise the expropriation of the spoils of conquest. The African take-over of this state in the 1960s witnessed a new era of even greater centralisation with cataclysmic consequences, creating what C.L. Innes has described as 'a deeply diseased society'[21]: the slaughter of 12 million, colossal decapitalisation of the economy, degenerative poverty.

As a result, as we have indicated, the future of Africa lies in relocating all political and economic power to the constituent nations and peoples - the Igbo, the Urhobo, the Yoruba, the Ijo, the Ogoni, the Bakongo, the Bambara, the

---

[21]C.L. Innes, *Chinua Achebe* (Cambridge: Cambridge University, 1990), p. 151.

Ibibio, etc. These constitute 'real Africa' and not the collapsing and impoverished infrastructure and institutions of the European conquest which are often mistaken for the former in many a superficial discourse.[22] Real Africa is thus the crucible of Africa's much vaunted rebirth and not those residual outposts of European empires with their very alienating and deadly profiles of history that go by the names Nigeria, Sierra Leone, Liberia, Sudan, Rwanda, etc, etc, which, for all intents and purposes, have served their time and space in the reckoning of history. Already, the Ogoni, whose principal leaders including writer Ken Saro-Wiwa were executed a few years ago by the notorious Nigerian state for demanding direct African grassroots control and management of their human and natural resources, have composed the anthem for this new Africa as evident in that crucial declaration which we cited earlier: 'Resource control is an inalienable right. The human right to development also implies the full realisation of the very right of people to self determination which includes the exercise of their inalienable right to full sovereignty over all their natural wealth and resources.' It should be pointed out that the population of the Ogoni nation is just one-half of a million ... In Real Africa, 'small is beautiful' is indeed the mantra of progress. Along with the Igbo, as we have shown, the Ogoni have joined the ever-increasing number of peoples who have borne the brunt of the African central state's ruthlessness; another restive and rebellious province of Abazon in the Nigeria-style Republic of Kangan from the breath taking panoramic canvass of *Anthills of the Savannah* ...

This new Africa, Real Africa, has the capacity to spearhead, within its locale, the vast tapestry of African reconstruction after a very battered history by critically engaging with the rich reservoir of the continent's cultural heritage. It has an immense human and natural resource base to feed, clothe, house, educate, provide the peace and security, and build an advanced civilisation for its people. It will embark on this journey of regeneration by emphasising a fundamental assumption of its being - namely, *an inward-looking confidence of its ability to carry out this transformation itself.*

Just as some commentators bemoan the misleading notion of Africa's 'overriding population problem,' others, ever getting into a bigger pool of observers, have been focusing their minds on the crisis in health in Africa and the devastating impact of HIV/AIDS epidemic (particularly in southern Africa) on the continent's (projected) population growth and figures and the general

---

[22]See, for instance, Karl Maier, *This House Has Fallen: Midnight in Nigeria* (New York: Public Affairs, 2000).

levels of life-expectancy.[23] Already, sharp falls in life expectancy in Zambia, Malawi, Zimbabwe and elsewhere in recent years have led some to question the very quality of life in the future in these parts of Africa.[24] Africa's reproductive health needs and the HIV/AIDS upheaval cannot be studied in isolation of its present socio-economic crisis. The lack of adequate reproductive health services and its limited uptake have always been more the victim of the socio-economic circumstances rather than its cause. In other words, the gross misuse of resources in Africa is directly implicated in the large family sizes and the inadequate supportive resources which currently define African realities. Without those large family units with their vast structures, which Earth First! (as we quoted earlier) has vilified as the culprit of 'human numbers moving beyond the carrying capacity of the land,' the African humanity may not be existing presently. Indeed, it is precisely because of these large family units with their intensive and extensive supportive structures that the inept African 'nation-state' has been able to divest itself of its primary and minimal responsibility of social support of its populations especially in the critical areas of health, education, housing and general economic opportunity. The 100,000-strong African émigrés of mostly intellectuals in North America and Europe send back to Africa the average sum of £1 billion annually to shore up this critical role of support - and survival. As the crippling crisis of the African 'nation-state' intensifies, there has emerged a highly erroneous theoretical assumption which permeates the work of many an agency or institution involved in the field of reproductive health care. This is that African cultural institutions and references are an obstacle rather than a *prerequisite* to 'modernisation'.[25] This assumption is made on an equally erroneous premise that African cultural heritage is

---

[23] See for instance the annual *UNAIDS/WHO Report on the global HIV/AIDS epidemic* publications, Elizabeth Reid, ed., *HIV & AIDS: The Global Inter-Connection* (Connecticut: Kumarian, 1995), and D.A. Feldman, ed., *Global AIDS Policy* (Connecticut: Berigen & Garvey, 1994).

[24] Cohen, 'Responding to the Socio-Economic Impact of the HIV Epidemic in Sub-Saharan Africa,' and UNDP, *Living Positively with HIV/AIDS: Supporting the involvement of people living with HIV/AIDS in the response to the epidemic* (Dakar, November 1995).

[25] See UNAIDS, *Gender and HIV/AIDS: Taking stock of research and programmes* (Geneva, 1999), UNAIDS Technical Update, Gender and HIV/AIDS (Geneva, 1998), K. Rivers and P. Aggleton, *Adolescent Sexuality, Gender and the HIV Epidemic* (New York: UNDP HIV Development Programme, 1999), K. Rivers and P. Aggleton, *Men and HIV Epidemic* (New York: UNDP HIV and Development Programme, 1999) and Feldman, ed., *Global AIDS Policy*.

'unchanging and unevolving.' Once such a conclusion is made, what follows becomes tragically predictable: the continuing demonisation of the cultural heritage of a people is a *sine qua non* for the provision of services and the provision of services is a *sin qua non* for the demonisation of the cultural heritage of a people. It is a vicious cycle of stagnation. Consequently, an immensely minuscule amount of energy, time, and resources have been devoted to understanding how new technologies can be woven/integrated into an African cultural milieu where the role of motherhood is highly valued and celebrated.[26] Little research, for instance, has been centred on interrogating how 'cultural receptivity' can be understood, responded to, let alone enhanced to accommodate the technological progress that this field has yielded, bringing immense benefits to both men and women.

The glaring lack of progress as defined by 'population agencies' in the last 40 years in Africa attests to this fact. A basic knowledge of 'African cultural life' would have made evident the fact that the central focus of African life is the family and that ways of understanding the internal dynamics of African social structures must precede serious attempts to influence behaviour in any direction. Scholars need to investigate and understand the centuries of tried and tested value systems, structures, and processes that have been, and in large part remain the mainstay of African society.[27] This affords us the means of opening up wider channels of information and access to care. Here, once again, practitioners need to shed the extremely prescriptive manner they have adopted in dealing with communities. Instead, communities should be engaged in dialogue about how they themselves can, *given the strengths of their own human resource*, use the technologies available to protect themselves and their families from ill-health and lost opportunity.

So, 40 years after the restoration of independence for most Africans, it is perhaps beginning to dawn on providers of health care that the methods they have been advocating for decades are deficient. But the manner of its deficiency still remains to be investigated. The purpose and one purpose alone in advocating the availability and accessibility of reproductive health care facilities to every African man and woman is to ensure an enhanced quality of life for the people of the continent - to ensure the survivability of mothers, aunts, sisters and daughters and thus ensure the preservation of the African family in a manner that empowers rather than debilitates motherhood. Furthermore, it is to

---

[26] See Nzegwu, *Love, Motherhood and the African Heritage, passim.*
[27] Achebe, *Home and Exile,* especially ch. 1. See also J.A. Sofola, *African Culture and African Personality* (Ibadan: African Resources, 1973).

ensure that every young woman and man realise their emotional, psychological and intellectual potential, thus creating for the next generation - their children - limitless opportunities. It is finally to eliminate the spectre of unhappiness and illness invariably created by an unwanted child.

It is therefore important to ensure that we differentiate between the contentious and sensational politics of population and the very real need of women and men all over Africa (especially young women and men) to become accurately informed about and receive appropriate contraceptive care as a human right. This is so for many reasons including the relatively large sizes of Africa's youth population, and the epidemic levels of HIV/AIDS and other sexually transmitted diseases. There is unquestionably a need to make very accessible quality, safe, cost-effective, and innovative reproductive health services to both women and men. Undoubtedly, there is a dearth of accurate, scientifically factual, culturally sensitive information around the reproductive health needs of Africans.[28] It is shrouded in myth and nonsense.[29] The impact of much of this inaccuracy is reflected in the internal country-based programmes with little questioning occurring about how fundamental African *indigenous* systems can be built upon to ensure the preservation of the quality of life of millions of people. Historically, Africans have provided reproductive health services for their populations. They have for centuries carried out reproductive education of boys and girls in separate spaces and references. This has involved puberty-related subjects, hygiene, antenatal, natal, and postnatal education, gender-specific responsibilities within the family unit, etc. Africans have dispensed services such as midwifery, contraceptives, and carried out a host of other puerperal services obtained in most other societies across the world. Whether by contemporary standards these procedures are considered safe is not really the issue. What is at stake is that the history of reproductive health activity exists that can be built upon. But this building process needs to acknowledge the value, the very relevance of this heritage, in order to deliver state-of-the-art services which have meaning and acceptability within the African population.

Some pressing examples best illustrate this point. Of recent there has been an increased call for the creation of 'male-friendly' (especially adolescent male) centres delivering reproductive health services because programmes have, by

---

[28]Cf. Charles Geshekter, 'The Epidemic of African Aids Hysteria,' *The Citizen* (Johannesburg), 16 September 1998.
[29]Ibid.

and large, ignored the needs of African men in their design.[30] In particular clinics providing contraceptive services, it is claimed, 'must be more comfortable and welcoming to men.'[31] A rudimentary knowledge of African cultural life would have made evident the fact that Africans have for centuries been carrying out reproductive health education separately by gender and age in an environment that was designed to put clients at ease, promote mutual support within the group and facilitate learning. Thus, this valuable legacy of education should have been strengthened to incorporate much of the wide variety of information and services necessary and of relevance in contemporary society. Another example concerns the publicity on the use and accessibility of condoms. There is tremendous cultural sensitivity around being seen purchasing condoms amongst both men and women in Africa. And yet, this valuable piece of information has made no impact whatsoever on the method adopted by providers in ensuring both the availability and accessibility of the product. Thus, the same condom, *the* most common contraceptive and *the* most heralded mechanism for the prevention of HIV/STDs often remains locked out of view in the pharmacist's storage/drug dispensing room, awaiting a 'simple' request from a member of the public whereupon it is then retrieved and dispensed! Little wonder that condom uptake levels remain so low in most African societies!

HIV/AIDS: the facts beyond the figures

Two decades of HIV/AIDS globally have created a world defined and ranked by the impact of the epidemic and the capacity of countries to address, react to, and contain its spread. Not surprisingly, the ranking of these countries coincides invariably with 'global indices of development' used by development institutions.[32] Hence, at one end of this spectrum the Western World appears to remain virtually untouched by the impact of the HIV/AIDS epidemic whilst at the other end lies Africa - ravaged and decimated in almost every aspect of its social existence by the disease. It is impossible to deny the tragic impact of

---

[30] See for instance *Proceedings, ECA Conference on African Women and Development*, Addis Ababa, 28-31 May 1997.
[31] Ibid.
[32] See the annual *UNAIDS/WHO Report on the global HIV/AIDS epidemic* publication.

HIV/AIDS in Africa. The statistics,[33] however debatable, certainly point to a highly traumatised society in the wake of the epidemic as the following points indicate:

1. 23 million adult Africans and a further 1 million children live with HIV/AIDS.
2. Life expectancy at birth for many Africans has dropped dramatically.
3. 50 per cent of infections occur in people aged 15 to 24 years.
4. Greater numbers of women than men are currently being infected and women disproportionately bear the burden of the epidemic.
5. Morbidity rates are predictably higher throughout the continent with HIV/AIDS heavily implicated in infant, child and adult morbidity and mortality.

Variations

We should however examine, less superficially, and perhaps less emotionally, what these statistics mean. Presently, the countries most affected by the epidemic are located in the east and southern regions of the continent. In contrast, west Africa, the home of about one-half of Africa's total population of 645 million, shows a comparatively low infection profile. Contrary to the sweeping and usually hysterical statistics available on Africa, there in fact exist extensive variations across the continent's regions, and indeed within regions, which desperately need to be interrogated and understood. Statistically transposing unevenly-high levels of HIV/AIDS infection rates from one African sub-region/region to another, or unto a continent-wide profile, is surely scientifically objectionable. Such sweeping statistics do not permit an informed understanding of the nature of the factors impacting on the spread of the disease within individual country (and region), especially given the fact that besides Uganda there has been no aggressive state intervention across Africa designed to stem the epidemic. Indeed the statistics are presented in such a manner as to almost overwhelm or paralyse the observer particularly when juxtaposed with other emergencies on the continent such as conflicts, capital flight and transfers, and hunger and starvation. This has major implications for Africa's capacity to embark upon useful courses of action in addressing the HIV/AIDS crisis in

---

[33] UNAIDS, *Report on the Global HIV/AIDS epidemic* (Geneva, 1998). Subsequent statistical references here emanate from this publication.

Africa. Additionally, and perhaps more seriously, it prevents us from genuinely acknowledging and building on the actions being taken by Africans, *themselves*, especially through their institutions in families, communities, villages and towns, to stem the spread of the disease. Seen from its blanket universal application across Africa, the current statistics and the discourse on HIV/AIDS on the continent can indeed be very misleading. Researchers and other practitioners in the field should instead focus, very seriously, on interrogating these statistics in order to understand the very basis for the extremely dramatic *intra-* and *inter*-regional variations that exist, thus creating opportunities for learning, shared knowledge, and support within and across the regions of Africa.

A consideration of the two tables below further highlight this position. On the west coast, the average number of adults living with HIV/AIDS as a proportion of the population is estimated at about 3.4 per cent, with a range from 10.1 per cent in Cote d'Ivoire (highest) to 1.2 per cent in Equatorial Guinea (lowest). West Africa contains approximately 42 per cent of the population of Africa - in other words, nearly one-half of African peoples live in the region. As the country in the region with the highest infection rate, Cote d'Ivoire, with its population of 14.3 million (third most populous country in the region after Nigeria and Ghana), is a significant country from which to begin our analysis.

Cote d'Ivoire is a major centre of economic activity where population movements/migrations occur routinely between itself and its neighbours, but especially amongst the contiguous states of Burkina Faso to the north, Mali to the north-west, and Ghana to the east. The relationship between Ghana and Cote d'Ivoire is defined more by cross-border trade than seasonal migration. Migration of whatever category has been heavily implicated in the spread of HIV/AIDS across borders.[34] Thus, given the relationship amongst these four west African states, one would expect to find equally high adult HIV infection in all the states. This proposition holds true only for Burkina Faso with an infection rate of 7.2 per cent (population: 11.1 million) but not in Ghana with its population of 18.3 million and infection rate of 2.4 per cent nor indeed Mali which has a population of 11.5 million and an infection rate of 1.7 per cent. It would therefore be important to establish what exactly is happening in Cote de'Ivoire that is not occurring in Ghana despite, for instance, the same cultural antecedents shared by the Akan peoples in both countries who continue to

---

[34] Cf. east and southern Africa.

maintain close ties across the border. The same question could also be posed in relation to Ghana's eastern neighbour, Togo, both of which have the Ewe-speaking people contiguously across their common frontier. Togo, a country which only recently enjoyed the region's second highest economic growth rate, has a comparatively high infection rate of 8.3 per cent for its 4.3 million people. What comparable socio-political factors prevalent in both economically vibrant Cote d'Ivoire and Togo account for the two countries' highest HIV/AIDS rates of infection in west Africa?

	Population (millions)	Adults living with HIV (%)
Benin	5.7	2.1
Burkina Faso	11.1	7.2
Cameroon	13.9	4.9
Chad	6.7	2.7
Cote d'Ivoire	14.3	10.1
Equatorial Guinea	0.4	1.2
Gabon	1.2	4.3
Gambia	1.2	2.2
Ghana	18.3	2.4
Guinea	7.6	2.1
Guinea Bissau	1.1	2.3
Liberia	2.5	3.7
Mali	11.5	1.7
Niger	9.8	1.5
Nigeria	118.4	4.1
Senegal	8.8	1.8
Sierra Leone	4.4	3.2
Togo	4.3	8.5

Table 1: Adult rate of People living with HIV/AIDS in countries in western Africa, end 1997 *(Source: UNAIDS/WHO, Report on the global HIV/AIDS epidemic – June 1998, Annexe, pp. 64-65)*

Shared destiny

The nature of spread of HIV/AIDS in Nigeria, to the east, provides an important focus for our discussion. With a population of 118.4 million (both the region's and continent's highest) and an adult prevalence rate of 4.1 per cent, Nigeria's total infection figure of 2.2 million is undoubtedly one of Africa's highest. A figure of this enormity which is assessed in the context of the size of the country and which also incorporates the indices of the political instability that have plagued the country in its recent history, creates the immense potential of an incalculable catastrophe in Nigeria (and the continent at large) if this current infection rate is not slowed down or indeed if an increase were to occur. Yet, given Nigeria's relatively low infection rates presently and compared to infection rates elsewhere in the region, not to mention the situation further afield in east and southern Africa, it is evident that people in Nigeria, as distinct from the Nigerian state, must be responding somewhat successfully to the challenges of the HIV/AIDS epidemic. Another point to note is that it serves no useful purpose and is indeed macabre to suggest (as has been done in certain circles[35]) that Nigeria's 4.1 per cent prevalence rate is a greater human catastrophe than say Togo's 8.5 per cent (in a population of 4.3 million) or Botswana's 25.1 per cent (population: 1.5 million - see Table 2) because of the absolute figures involved in the former. The societal implications for the latter two countries are just as devastating as in Nigeria - in the short, but especially in the long term. Obviously, the depth and impact of HIV/AIDS devastation is greater in societies where large proportions of the population (however low the absolute numbers may be) are affected. In effect, the current HIV/AIDS situation in Togo is just as urgent and potentially catastrophic to the Togolese and their society as the situation in Botswana is to the people of Botswana and that in Nigeria to Nigerians.

---

[35] Cf. Paul Nwabuikwu, 'AIDS is not our identity,' *The Guardian* (Lagos), 21 February 2001.

	Population (millions)	Adults living with HIV (%)
Angola	11.6	2.1
Botswana	1.5	25.1
CAR	3.4	10.8
Congo	2.7	7.8
Congo DR	48	4.4
Eritrea	3.4	3.2
Ethiopia	60.1	9.3
Kenya	28.4	11.6
Malawi	10.1	14.9
Mozambique	18.3	14.2
Namibia	1.6	19.9
South Africa	43.3	12.9
Tanzania	31.5	9.4
Uganda	20.8	9.5
Zambia	8.5	19.1
Zimbabwe	11.7	25.8

Table 2: Adult rate of People living with HIV/AIDS in countries in Southern Africa, end 1997 *(Source: UNAIDS/WHO, Report on the global HIV/AIDS epidemic – June 1998, Annexe, pp. 64-65)*

Most countries in west Africa have known little political stability in the past 40 years. Besides Senegal,[36] few states have pursued, let alone implemented credible countrywide AIDS prevention programmes since the outbreak of the epidemic. Yet, their HIV/AIDS infection rates remain low. Scientific inquiry into the reasons for this situation is urgently needed. Nigeria's seeming success to hold somewhat at bay the disease to date would appear to be due largely to the efforts that the people themselves have embarked upon rather than the state which has in the last 15 years overseen the virtual collapse of the strategic institutions of contemporary society. Anecdotal evidence from Nigeria shows

---

[36] See Ofeibea Quist-Arcton, 'Interview of President Abdoulaye Wade,' *AllAfrica* (Washington), 7 February 2001.

that communities particularly in the south of the country have since mobilised independently of the state to initiate HIV/AIDS publicity and preventative programmes through town, village and family unions including mandatory HIV-virus testing for would-be married couples. Such grass-roots initiatives would need to be reinforced across the country not only to stem the spread of the disease but also to radically cut the number of those being infected. Furthermore, these and similar experiences in other countries should be shared with the rest of Africa. Could the seemingly critical role being played by African indigenous institutions in Nigeria and elsewhere in HIV/AIDS prevention be enhanced upon? Are there lessons to be learnt and perhaps applied in other parts of the continent especially in the east and south where the epidemic is more severe? After all, the combined population of east and southern Africa is 324 million - home to slightly over half of Africa's total population. It has an HIV/AIDS average infection rate of 11.6 per cent ranging from Botswana's 25.1 per cent in a population of 1.5 million to Eritrea's 3.2 per cent in a population of 3.4 million. Contrary to the west African situation where there is no uniform infection spread across contiguous states, countries in the southern Africa cone with common frontiers all share high double-digit infection rates - namely Botswana (25.1%), Namibia (19.9%; population: 1.6 million), Zambia (19.1%; population: 8.5 million) and Zimbabwe (11.7%; population: 25.8 million).

What is important about these regional variations of the HIV/AIDS data is that they provide an important launching pad for scientific inquiry about those factors internal to societies which could explain intra- and inter-regional variations. Our aim is not to construct some league table-ranking of the spread of HIV/AIDS in Africa. Rather, it is to place these statistics in perspective and to push scientific inquiry on the continent along more useful, enlightening, and less sensationalist paths, thus providing the world with a clearer understanding of the patterns of this epidemic and strategies for real solutions. Our intention also is to ensure that African scientists and practitioners do not become overwhelmed and incapacitated with the sheer magnitude of quite often non-interrogated and therefore un-enlightening statistics regularly reeled out by individuals and institutions from around the world. Our purpose is therefore to pursue an understanding of those factors that could explain the relatively low rates of infection, the slow spread of the disease, and the variations (also) present in the west African region. Two critical key questions need to be posed especially in the light of the oddities, paradoxes and trends that do not conform to 'established wisdom' in the discussion on HIV/AIDS in Africa:

1 What factors account for the vast differences in prevalence rates between the west and east/southern regions of Africa, even among countries that appear to have similar socio-economic and political experiences in the recent past?

2 If indeed west Africa remains relatively uninfected by the epidemic, are there crucial lessons which need to be learnt from (1) above in order to ensure that the epidemic in this region is kept at these minimal rates of infection and even further reduced? Do these lessons have any relevance for Africans in the east/southern regions?

Question 1 is particularly important primarily because an understanding of the situation in west Africa could conceivably lead to the implementation of effective preventative measures which would ensure a non-repetition of the east/southern African experience and provide effective tools for addressing the epidemic in those high prevalence areas. The present low rate of infection in west Africa therefore must not give way to a feeling of complacency either on the part of HIV/AIDS practitioners or indeed by the population at large. To do this could result in future tragedy. In the end, it is important to establish what, if any sociocultural, political and/or economic factors have contributed to the emergence of such differing regional patterns in the spread of the epidemic across Africa.

Just who owes whom what?

As we have already indicated, Amaechina, Real Africa, or new Africa will sever immediate links with any residual tentacles of the oppression of the past that will pose as a hindrance to its goals of the African renaissance. Top on the list will obviously be a repudiation of all outstanding debts which the West claims Africa owes it. Real Africa will insist, as we shall now show, that it owes the West nothing. To the contrary, the West owes Africa trillions of dollars in debt. Real Africa will insist that this debt is recovered.

The mere notion of Africa owing the European World something, even the huge sum of US$350 billion claimed by the IMF, the World Bank and the other European World-controlled 'international' financial institutions, is outrageous - an affront to the African humanity, given the continuing and relentless pillaging of Africa by individuals, institutions and states of the European World during the course of the past 500 years as we have demonstrated in this study. No

Orwellian use of language could be comparable to such a proposition of African indebtedness except of course a likely intelligibility is reserved for those in politics, academe and media who believe that Africa is 'owned by Europeans in perpetuity.' For instance, it was no other than former French President Francois Mitterand, who, at that intensely reflective occasion we cited above, observed that 'without Africa, France will have no history in the 21st century.'

To suggest that Africa owes the European World anything is like suggesting that Jews are indebted to Nazi Germany, but much worse. Unlike the six million who died during the Jewish holocaust, 25 times more Africans perished during the latter's own carnage. Africans who survived were universally appropriated and utilised for Europe's construction of the new 'frontier spaces' of the post-conquest territories of the Americas and the Caribbean to which it had equally taken over during its mid-15th century march across the globe's lands and seas. Coupled with its subsequent seizure and formal occupation of Africa, Europe soon found, to its eternal unenviable credit, that its perpetration of the African holocaust laid the very foundation of the European World's hegemonic control of the socio-economic heritage of the world as we know it presently. The Jews have received billions of dollars in reparations from Germany since the end of the 1939-45 war. They are guaranteed such payments by Berlin into the indefinite future, in addition to expecting fresh payments soon from other states and interests implicated in that holocaust - United States corporate interests in Germany during the period, Swiss banks, British state/banks which sequestrated victims' saving accounts lodged in British banks, French pro-German Vichy regime responsible for the transportation of French Jews to the German gas chambers, Russian/East and Central European governments who have in their possession invaluable looted Jewish art treasures. In contrast, Africans whether in Africa, the Americas/Caribbean or anywhere else have yet to be paid anything by any European World state for the African holocaust which remains the worst crime ever committed against humanity. We should recall that every Western state and principality of the day (including every religion and faith) was actively involved in the perpetration of this holocaust with Britain, the United States, Portugal, France, Spain and Germany being the pre-eminent beneficiaries - in that order. The European World owes Africans trillions of dollars in recompense for this crime and its devastating aftermath.

Thanks to a feeble and disconcerted African political leadership, Africa lost an historic opportunity during the recent Genoa G-8 summit to problematise dramatically a debt 'debate' whose perspectives and parameters of discourse have long been one-sidedly fashioned, dictated, and presented by Western spokespersons and institutions who have a vested interest in employing this subject as a giant eraser to wipe off from collective consciousness the memory of the West's staggering indebtedness to Africa just stated. In effect, the West currently employs its claim of Africa's 'debt' to it as a means of trying to reverse the underlying oppressor-subjugated moral imperative that characterises its relationship with Africa. Thus, instead of going to Genoa to ask the West to cancel 'the debt' or seek 'forgiveness,' to refer to the disingenuous position of Jubilee 2000 movement on the subject, the African leaders should have tabled a position paper at the summit entitled 'Just Who Owes Whom What?' In this, they would have shown, most dispassionately, the haunting expanse of human and material acquisition and exploitation that has defined the European World-Africa relationship from 1492 to 2001 - not just between 1960 and 2001 or the 1970s/80s-2001 which is the epoch that the West conveniently prefers. We emphasise the adverb 'conveniently' because this Western preference focuses on the epoch of the restoration of African independence after its age long direct occupation of Africa. This epoch also doubles as the era of Fraudulent Developmentalism during which, again thanks to the naivety of the African leaders at the time, European leaderships and states that had committed such heinous crimes of conquest in Africa were overnight entrusted with a role, a central role for that matter, in contributing to Africa's seeming project of societal reconstruction.

In its Genoa memorandum to settle once and for all the outstanding debt between the West and Africa, African leaders should have called for the establishment of an impartial international body of adjudicators to handle the settlement based on examining the records of the past 500 years during which the most horrific crimes against humanity were perpetrated. In that case, each party, including Africa, must agree in advance to pay the other if found to be the outstanding debtor. Yes, Africa must commit itself to paying off the West, if, in the very unlikely outcome, it is found guilty by the adjudicators as a debtor. There is no question of asking for forgiveness as one must be responsible for their decision, consciously embarked upon or executed. One must pay for their indebtedness and this applies to Africans just like any other peoples.

A critical examination of the West's preference of the African post-conquest epoch for accounting for West-Africa socio-economic relationship is fraught with immense difficulties which must be clarified and here an illustration with Nigeria will suffice. The West currently claims that Nigeria owes it about US$30 billion even though the maximum original principal of this sum of money was never more than US$6 billion. According to President Obasanjo, 'All that we had borrowed up to 1985 or 1986 or thereabout was around $5 billion and we have paid about $16 billion yet we are still being told that we are owing about $28 billion.'[37] This 'debt' originates from the 1970s/80s and given the ever spiralling dynamics of Western interest rates over the period and also considering the multiplicity of the contending currencies of procurement (British pound sterling, US dollars, Canadian dollars, French francs, Swiss francs, deutchmark, yen, etc), it has since increased five fold. Yet, Nigeria has paid off this principal several billion dollars over on interest payments alone as the records show. Just as the rest of Africa since the early 1980s, Nigeria has been a net exporter of capital to the West based chiefly on this mandatory 'debt servicing' transfers but also on the unnerving billions looted from the country's treasury and routinely deposited in Western banks by furacious heads of state and other thieving public officials. From this channel alone, the awesome sum of US$60 billion has been transferred from Nigeria to the West since 1972, with US$54 billion dollars of this leaving the country between 1983 and 1999 particularly.[38] These were the years of the Babangida and Abacha military dictatorships. During this period, the whole of Africa made a total net-capital transfer of US$400 billion to the West. This amounts to four times the original US$100 billion principal of the 'debt' the whole of Africa supposedly 'owed' it or one and half times the current total of US$350 billion which we cited earlier. Clearly, when it comes to its relation with Africa, the West's age-old dictum remains heavily entrenched as ever: 'We eat our cake and have it.'

Assuming that Nigeria has not, after all, paid off this 'debt,' contrary to our just stated assertion, and assuming that we push back the genesis of its procurement to the year 1960 (from October 1960 to be exact to coincide with the date of the restoration of independence) rather than the 1970s/80s, we can still demonstrate that the people of Nigeria, excluding their leaders or those who claim or arrogate to themselves that role during the 40-year period in question, can hardly be held responsible for either the original US$6 billion or the phenomenally-inflated US$30 billion 'debt' currently bandied about. Apart from just 11 years of 'democratically elected' civilian governments, Nigeria has been run by an agglomeration of military juntas during the period headed by the following: General Aguyi-Ironsi, General Gowon, General Muhammed, General Obasanjo, General Buhari, General Babangida, Mr Shonekan-General Abacha civilian-military dyarchy, General Abacha, General Abubakar. None of these men was elected to office by anybody in Nigeria. Each came to power through

---

[37]Rotimi Ajayi, 'Nigeria's foreign debt illegal - Obasanjo,' *Vanguard Daily* (Lagos), 15 August 2000.
[38]Yinka Olusanya, 'Nigeria loses N7.2 trillion ($60 billion) to capital flight,' *Sunday Vanguard* (Lagos), 24 December 2000.

a coup d'etat or in the cases of two of the lot by assuming power after the sudden death in office by an incumbent who had seized power earlier. Each of these men who, we must recall, characteristically described themselves whilst in office with the flamboyant epithet, 'Head of State of the Federal Republic of Nigeria and the Supreme Commander/Commander-in-Chief of the Armed Forces,' was an absolutist leader who ran their regime as they deemed fit. During the life of their regime, each of them was therefore literally responsible personally for the fate of Nigeria with the grim consequences all too familiar presently. Part of that responsibility and its obvious consequences was economic policy and this is where the so-called debt subject is lodged.

Quite simply, the records are straightforward. If any of these 10 junta leaders whilst in power contributed to this sum of US$6 billion or US$30 billion or whatever sum the West quotes as 'owed' to it, then they, individually or collectively should pay up. They can't hide under the canopy of the state, not to talk of the constituent publics of Real Africa that make up the polity who bear the overwhelming burden of the current tragedy. No such publics authorised anyone of them to enter into any financial/economic deals on their behalf during the period and whoever did that, including the West who now cry 'foul,' did that at their own risk. The West should pursue these self-appointed leaders and recover its money if it so desires despite the amazing irony of the situation for it is the same West which cheered on these ruthless dictators (and their other league cohorts elsewhere in Africa) at the height of their misrule with the blazing extravagance of its most-often repeated thesis, 'The African Military is an Agent of Modernisation.'[39] The West must have a pretty good idea of the range of outlandish assets deposited in several of its banks and other financial institutions and assets by these Nigerian dictators including those who have since died. They should recover their money accordingly but we must insist that the mechanism for that payback cannot be extended to the people in Nigeria or indeed elsewhere in Africa. The people, on the contrary, reserve the right to press to recover from these dictators the matching compensation for the extensive damage to national life inflicted on them during 29 years of arbitrary

---

[39]See S.E Finer, *The Man on Horseback* (London: Pall Mall, 1962), W.F. Gutteridge, *Armed Forces in the States* (London: Oxford University, 1962), W.F. Gutteridge, *Military Institutions and Power in the New States* (London: Pall Mall, 1964), M. Janowitz, *The Military in the Political Development of New Nations* (Chicago: Chicago University, 1964), J.J Johnson, ed., *The Role of the Military in Under-developed Countries* (New Jersey: Princeton University, 1967) and Samuel Huntington, *Political Order in a Changing Society* (New Haven: Yale University, 1968).

rule. This right also extends to an extensive inquiry of the three civilian governments of the era (Balewa, Shagari, Obasanjo - again!) despite the so-called 'constitutionality' of their mandates.

The constituent publics in Nigeria cannot and must not pay for the 'debt' accumulated by the military. Such payments intrinsically negate the hard won freedom from the juntas and constitute a dishonour to those who lost their lives in the course of the resistance, not to mention the millions who have become destitute with the virtual destruction of the economy. If such payments are currently being made, they should be stopped forthwith. For a country that cannot even pay the monthly minimum wage of US$75 which its government promised on its own volition and where, according to a recent statement by its president, '65 per cent of the ... population is living below the poverty line with about 40 per cent wallowing in abject poverty,'[40] it is nothing short of a sentence of death to subject this hapless citizen with the burden of owing the West US$250, being his/her individual share of this 'debt'. Following from this, for every child born in Nigeria today, he or she has a debt stamp on their head equivalent to US$250. By the time they are five, if past Western interest rate increases are a guide and if there are possible delays or re-scheduling of existing Nigerian 'payment servicing' which are often the norm, the value of this debt mark is likely to quadruple to US$1000. According to Jerry Gana, the country's minister of information, Nigeria's annual 'debt service of about $1.5 billion is nine times our budget for health, and three times our budget for education.'[41] Is it therefore really surprising that besides other contributing factors, this 21st century peonage does in itself ensure that those 50 million people in Nigeria referred to in the statistics above are 'wallowing in abject poverty'?

No one has the right to mortgage the future of their people including most importantly their children and those still unborn in so flagrant and reckless a manner. No conscientious parents for instance would countenance telling their children that they couldn't provide crucial parental care and support for them because of obligations they have to some bank manager. Their children, their family, must compulsorily come first. In the case of the people in Nigeria and the rest of Africa, they do not even have such obligations to any bank official as we have shown here. Any attempt to foist such an obligation on them should therefore be vigorously resisted. As President Obasanjo's quoted remarks above indicate, African leaders do know that what the West and 'international'

---

[40]*The Guardian* (Lagos), 28 July 2000.
[41]Quoted by Mustapha Ogunsakin et al, 'Debt question tops Obasanjo-Blair talks,' *The Guardian* (Lagos), 13 September 2000.

financial organisations describe as the 'African debt to the West' is clearly bogus. Yet, if African leaders know of this, why do they play the role of overseers in the expropriation of their vital capital resources for export to the West? Equally enigmatically, how does someone who knows that some debt is 'bogus' seek from their dubitable creditor to be 'forgiven' for this same fraudulent indictment? Why are African leaderships currently mortgaging the very survival of their own peoples by daily authorising the transfers of critical resources from their homelands to the West?

African leaderships must now realise that they constitute the immediate source of the grave emergency that Africa faces presently. They indeed bear the primary responsibility. As we have shown, the West will always wish to expropriate the rich strategic resources of Africa given the opportunity which, currently, African leaders provide for their own personal benefits as we have variously illustrated in this study. It has taken 10 generations of Western governments to accomplish their control of Africa and no future government and associated interests there would voluntarily abandon such a lucrative harvest of conquest. The fulcrum of control which the West has deployed on the ground to ensure that it realises its goals in Africa is of course the deadly machinery of the African 'nation-state' which we have argued must now be dismantled. Trapped in this contraption, Africa and Africans have no possibility of a future of meaningful progress. African choices for the future could therefore not be clearer, for lodged in the vast cultural crucible of its peoples lie the intellectual resources and commitment of Africa's timely liberation from this quagmire. Chinua Achebe has observed:

> We are ... committed to reclaiming the rich heritage of Africa, every inch of it, and redrawing the contours of African history which in the hands of others has been drawn, and is drawn, with great malice and lurid falsehood ... The perspectives will be many, reflecting the complexity of the problem but out of the welter will emerge a sound, clear vision of the way forward.[42]

There is no more appropriate time than the present for the future direction of a people to be determined by the people themselves. Amaechina ...

---

[42] Chinua Achebe, 'Our Mission,' *African Commentary*, 1, October 1989, p. 4.

Bibliography

Achebe, Chinua, *A Man of the People*, London: Heinemann, 1966.
Achebe, Chinua, *Girls at War and Other Stories*, London: Heinemann Educational Books, 1972.
Achebe, Chinua, *Morning Yet on Creation Day*, London: Heinemann Educational Books, 1975.
Achebe, Chinua, *The Trouble with Nigeria*, Enugu: Fourth Dimension, 1983.
Achebe, Chinua, 'Civil Peace,' in Chinua Achebe and C.L. Achebe, eds., *African Short Stories*, London: Heinemann, 1985.
Achebe, Chinua, *Anthills of the Savannah*, London: Pan Books, 1988.
Achebe, Chinua, *Hopes and Impediments*, Oxford: Heinemann, 1988.
Achebe, Chinua, *Beware Soul Brother*, Oxford: Heinemann International, 1988.
Achebe, Chinua, *The African Trilogy*, London: Pan Books, 1988.
Achebe, Chinua, 'Our Mission,' *African Commentary*, 1, 1, October 1989.
Achebe, Chinua, 'African Literature as Restoration of Celebration,' *Kunapipi*, Vol XII, No 2. 1990.
Achebe, Chinua, 'Words of anxious love,' *The Guardian*, London, 7 March 1992.
Achebe, Chinua, *Home and Exile*, Oxford: Oxford University, 2000.
Adamson, Alan, *Sugar without Slaves*, New Haven: Yale University, 1972.
Ade-Ajayi, J.S. and Robert Smith, *Yoruba Warfare in the nineteenth century*, Cambridge: Cambridge University, 1964.
Afigbo, A.E., *The Igbo and their Neighbours*, Ibadan: Ibadan University, 1987.
Ajayi, Rotimi, 'Nigeria's foreign debt illegal - Obasanjo,' *Vanguard Daily*, Lagos, 15 August 2000.
Ake, Claude, ed., *Political Economy of Nigeria*, Harlow and Lagos: Longman Group, 1985.
Akinola, Wale and Lekan Bilesanmi, 'Re-election: The odds against Obasanjo,' *Sunday Vanguard*, Lagos, 24 December 2000.
Aluko, Olajide, *Essays on Nigerian Foreign Policy*, London: George Allen & Unwin, 1980.
Amadiume, Ifi, *Reinventing Africa*, London & New York: Zed Books, 1997.

Ambrose, Soren, 'Challenging the IMF, Intellectually and Politically,' *International Herald Tribune*, Paris, 25 April 1998.

Ananaba, Wogu, *The Trade Union Movement in Nigeria*, Benin: Ethiope Publishing, 1969.

Anyanwu, U.D., 'Gender Question in Igbo Politics,' in U.D. Anyanwu and J.U. Aguwa, eds., *The Igbo and Traditions of Politics*, Enugu: Fourth Dimension, 1993.

Arinze, Francis, *Sacrifice in Ibo Religion*, Ibadan: Ibadan University, 1970.

Asante, Molefi Kete, *Kemet, Afrocentricity and Knowledge*, Trenton: Africa World, 1990.

Asante, Molefi Kete, 'On the Wings of Nonsense,' *Black Books Bulletin*, 16, 1&2, Winter 1993-94.

Asante, Molefi Kete, 'Finally, Afrocentricity Operationalised,' *African Peoples Review*, Vol III, No 3, October-December 1994.

Beaud, Michel, *A History of capitalism*, New York: Monthly Review, 1983.

Bhabha, Homi, *The Location of Culture*, London and New York: Routledge, 1994.

Blane, Colin, 'Belgian wealth squeezed from Congo,' *BBC News Online*, 18 January 2001.

Busia, Abene, 'Manipulating Africa: the buccaneer as "liberator" in contemporary fiction,' in David Dabydeen, ed., *The black presence in English literature*, Manchester: Manchester University, 1985.

Castel, Carol, 'Clinton's Historic Visit,' *West Africa*, London, 6-26 April 1998.

Catholic Institute for International Affairs, 'Africa's Development Disaster,' *Comment*, 1985.

Chinweizu, Jemie, Onwuchekwa and Madubuike, Ihechukwu, *Toward the Decolonization of Literature*, Enugu: Fourth Dimension, 1980.

Chinweizu, *Decolonisng the African Mind*, Lagos: Pero, 1987.

Chinweizu, *Voices from Twentieth-Century Africa*, London & Boston: Faber and Faber, 1988.

Chukwukere, B.I., 'Chi in Igbo Religion and Thought: The God in Every Man,' *Anthropos*, 78, 1983.

Clairemonte, Frederick and John Cavanagh, 'Impossible debt on road to global ruin,' *The Guardian*, London, 9 January 1987.

Clemetson, Lynette, 'Caught in the Cross-Fire,' *Newsweek*, New York, 14 December 1998.

Cohen, Desmond, 'Responding to the Socio-Economic Impact of the HIV Epidemic in Sub-Saharan Africa,' *Issues Paper*, No 32, February 1999.

Cole, Bill, *John Coltrane*, New York: Da Capo, 1993.

Conrad, Joseph, *Heart of Darkness and Other Tales*, London: Pickering and Chatto, 1993.

Cronje, Suzanne, *The World and Nigeria*, London: Sidgwick and Jackson, 1972.

Dabydeen, David, 'This land is our land,' *New Statesman & Society*, London, 1 November 1991.

Davidson, Basil et al, *Southern Africa: The New politics of Revolution*, Harmondsworth: Penguin Books, 1976.

Davidson Basil, *Africa in History*, London: Granada Publishing, 1978.

Davidson, Basil, *The Search for Africa*, London: James Currey, 1994.

De st. Jorre, John, *The Brother' War - Biafra and Nigeria*, Boston: Houghton Miflin, 1972.

Diop, Cheikh Anta, *Precolonial Black Africa*, New York: Lawrence Hill Books, 1987.

Diop, Cheikh Anta, *The Cultural Unity of Black Africa*, London: Karnak House, 1989.

Dove, Nah, 'Contra Marxism,' *African peoples Review*, Vol. IV, No. 3, July-December 1995, p. 3.

Dowden, Richard, 'Redrawing the outmoded colonial map of Africa,' *Independent*, London, 10 September 1987.

Drechsler, Horst, *'Let Us Die Fighting': The Struggle of the Herero and Nama against German Imperialism, 1994-1915*, London: Zed, 1980.

Dudley, Billy, *An Introduction to Nigerian Government and Politics*, London and Basingstoke: Macmillan, 1982.

Dyall, Lorna, 'The tangata whenua: Maori people and their health,' *Radical Community Medicine*, No. 28, Winter 1986/7.

Edwards, Paul, ed., *Equiano's Travels* London: Heinemann Educational Books, 1967.

Eagleton, Terry, *Criticism & Ideology*, London: Verso, 1978.

Eagleton, Terry, *Walter Benjamin or Towards a Revolutionary Criticism*, London: Verso Editions and NLB, 1981.

Ekundare, R. Olufemi, *An Economic History of Nigeria: 1860-1960*, London: Methuen, 1973.

Ekwe-Ekwe, Herbert, 'Nzeogwu: Notes on a Controversy,' *West Africa*, London, *2 March 1987*.

Ekwe-Ekwe, Herbert, 'The antimonies of Mazrui's worldview,' *West Africa*, London, 11 May 1987.

Ekwe-Ekwe, Herbert, 'Africans and the European Wars of the 20th Century,' *African peoples Review*, July-December 1995.

Emenyonu, Ernest, *The Rise of the Igbo Novel*, Ibadan: Oxford University, 1978.

Ezekwugo, Christopher, *Chi: The True God in Igbo Religion*, Alwaye: Pontifical Institute of Philosophy and Theology, 1987.

Ezenwa-Ohaeto, *Chinua Achebe: A Bibliography*, Oxford: James Currey, 1997.

Falola, Toyin & Julius Ihonvbere, *The Rise and Fall of Nigeria's Second Republic: 1979-84*, London: Zed Books, 1985.

Falola, Toyin, ed., *Britain and Nigeria*, London and New York: Zed Books, 1987.

Fani-Kayode, Femi, 'The Nigerian Question,' *The Guardian On Sunday*, Lagos, 21 September 1997.

Fanon, Frantz, *The Wretched of the Earth*, Harmondsworth: Penguin Books, 1967.

Feldman, D.A., ed., *Global AIDS Policy*, Connecticut: Berigan & Garvey, 1994.

Finer, S.E., *The Man on Horseback*, London: Pall Mall, 1962.

Fitch, Bob and Mary Oppenheimer, *Ghana: End of an Illusion*, New York and London: Monthly Review, 1966.

Frady, Marshall, 'The Life and legacy of Malcolm X,' *The Sunday Times Magazine*, London, 14 February 1993.

Freund, William, 'Theft and social protest among the tin miners of northern Nigeria,' in Donal Crummey, ed., *Banditry, Rebellion and Social Protest in Africa*, London/Portsmouth: James Currey/Heinemann, 1986.

Fryer, Peter, *Black People in the British Empire: An Introduction*, London: Pluto, 1989.

Gakwandi, Shatto, *The Novel and the Contemporary Experience in Africa*, London: Heinemann Educational Books, 1977.

Galeano, Eduardo, *Open Veins of Latin America: Five Centuries of the Pillage of a continent*, London and New York: Monthly Review, 1973.

Geshekter, Charles, 'The Epidemic of African Aids Hysteria,' *The Citizen*, Johannesburg, 16 September 1998.

Gikandi, Simon, *Reading Chinua Achebe*, London: James Currey, 1991.

Gikandi, Simon, 'Chinua Achebe and the Poetics of Location: The Uses of Space in *Things Fall Apart* and *No Longer at Ease*,' in Abdulrazak Gurnah, *Essays on Africa Writing*, Oxford: Heinemann Educational, 1993.

Gilroy, Paul, *The Black Atlantic*, London and New York: Verso, 1993.

Goulbourne, Harry, *Ethnicity and nationalism in post-imperial Britain*, Cambridge: Cambridge University, 1991.

Gray, Chris, *Conceptions of History: Diop and Obenga*, London: Karnak

House, 1989.

Griffiths, Gareth, 'Language and Action in the Novels of Chinua Achebe,' in C.L. Innes and Bernth Lindfors, eds., *Critical Perspectives on Chinua Achebe*, London: Heinemann Educational books, 1979.

Griffiths, Gareth, 'Writing, literacy and history in Africa,' in Mpalive-Hangson Msiska and Paul Hyland, eds., *Writing and Africa*, London and New York: Addisom Wesley Longman, 1997.

Gutteridge, W.F., *Military Institutions and Power in the New States*, London: Oxford University, 1962.

Hammond, Dorothy and Atla Jablow, *The Africa that Never Was: Four Centuries of British Writing About Africa*, New York: Twayne Publishers, 1970.

Hill, Christopher, 'Lies about crimes,' *The Guardian*, London, 29 May 1989.

Hirsh, Michael, 'Dirty Business,' *Newsweek*, New York, 14 December 1998.

Holder, Robyn and John Holliday, '"People been dying today": The Politics of Aboriginal health in Australia,' *Radical Community Medicine*, No. 28, Winter 1986/7.

Huntington, Samuel, *Political Order in a Changing Society*, New Haven: Yale University, 1968.

Hymas, Charles and Lesley Thomas, 'Africans move to the top of British educational ladder,' *The Sunday Times*, London, 23 January 1994.

Igbokwe, Joe, 'Nigeria still has an Igbo problem,' *The Guardian*, Lagos, 15 December 2000.

Ihekweazu, Edith, ed., *Eagle on Iroko*, Ibadan: Heinemann Educational Books, 1991.

Ikpeze, Nnaemeka, 'Post-Biafran Marginalization of the Igbo in Nigeria,' in Ifi Amadiume & Abdullahi An-Na'im, eds., *The Politics of Memory*, London and New York: Zed Books, 2000.

Ilogu, E., *Christianity and Igbo Culture*, New York and London: NOK Publishers, 1974.

Innes, C.L., *Chinua Achebe*, Cambridge: Cambridge University, 1990.

Irele, Abiola, *The African Experience in Literature and Ideology*, London: Heinemann Educational Books, 1981.

Irele, Abiola, 'The Tragic Conflict in the Novels of Chinua Achebe,' in C.L. Innes and Bernth Lindfors, eds., *Critical Perspectives on Chinua Achebe*, London: Heinemann educational Books, 1991.

Isichie, Elizabeth, *Junior History of Nigeria*, Lagos and Ibadan: Macmillan Nigeria Publishers, 1981.

Iyasere, Solomon, 'Narrative Techniques in "Things fall Apart",' in C.L. Innes and Bernth Lindfors, eds., *Critical Perspectives on Chinua Achebe*, London: Heinemann Educational Books, 1979.

Izevbaye, Dan, 'History's Eye-Witness: Vision and Representation in the works of Chinua Achebe,' in Edith Ihekweazu, ed., *Eagle on Iroko*, Ibadan: Heinemann Educational Books, 1991.

James, Wendy, 'Matrifocal on African women,' in Shirley Ardener, ed., *Defining Females*, London: Croom Helm, 1978.

JanMohamed, Abdul, *Manichean Aesthetics*, Amherst: University of Massachusetts, 1983.

Janowitz, M., *The Military in the Political Development of the New Nations*, Chicago: Chicago University, 1964.

Jacques, Martin and Stuart Hall, 'Les enfants de Marx et de Coca-Cola,' *New Statesman*, London, 28 November 1997.

Jeyifo, Biodun, 'For Chinua Achebe: The Resilience and the Predicament of Obierika,' *Kunapipi*, Vol XII, No 2, 1990.

Johnson, J.J., ed., *The Role of the Military in Under-developed Countries*, New Jersey: Princeton University, 1967.

Keegan, John, 'Why men of Jewish blood shed it for Adolf Hitler,' *The Daily Telegraph*, London, 28 November 1997.

King, Tom, 'Jews who wore a Nazi uniform,' *The Daily Telegraph*, London, 2 December 1996.

Kirk-Greene, Anthony and Douglas Rimmer, *Nigeria Since 1970*, London: Hodder and Stoughton, 1981.

Ki-Zerbo, Joseph, 'Which Way Africa,' *Development Dialogue*, 1995:2.

Larkin, Philip, *All What Jazz* London: Faber and Faber, 1985.

Larson, Charles, *The Emergence of African Literature*, London and Basingstoke, 1978.

Leapman, Michael, 'While the Biafrans starved, the FO moaned about hacks,' *The Independent on Sunday*, London, 3 January 1999.

Lenin, Vladimir, *Selected Works*, Moscow: Progress Publishers, 1977.

Lindqvist, Sten, *'Exterminate All the Brutes'*, London: Granta Books, 1997.

Macebuh, Stanley, 'Poetics and the Mythic Imagination,' *Transition*, 50, 1975-76, pp. 79-84.

Madunagu, Edwin, *Nigeria: The economy and the people*, London and Port of Spain: New Beacon Books, 1983.

Magdoff, Harry, *Imperialism: From the Colonial Age to the Present*, New York and London: Monthly Review, 1978.

Mahood, M.M., *The Colonial Encounter*, London: Rex Collins, 1976.

Maier, Karl, *This House Has Fallen: Midnight in Nigeria*, New York: Public

Affairs, 2000.

Mannsaker, Frances, 'The dog that didn't bark: the subject races in imperial fiction at the turn of the century,' in David Dabydeen, ed., *The black presence in English literature*, Manchester: Manchester University, 1985.

Marby, Marcus, 'The Tough Go Shopping,' *Newsweek*, New York, 14 December 1998.

Marx, Karl, *the Revolutions of 1848: Political Writings, Volume I*, Harmandsworth: Penguin Books, 1973.

Marx, Karl, *Capital, Volume 1*, Harmandsworth: Penguin Books, 1976.

Marx, Karl and Frederick Engels, *Selected Works (In one volume)*, London: Lawrence Wishart, 1977.

Masland, Tom, 'African Duel,' *Newsweek*, New York, 30 March 1998.

McClure, John, 'Problematic presence: the colonial other in Kipling and Conrad,' in David Dabydeen, ed., *The black presence in English literature*, Manchester: Manchester University, 1985.

Mcgreal, Chris, 'Claire Short letter riles Zimbabwe,' *The Guardian*, London, 22 December 1997.

Metuh, E., *God and Man in African Religion: A Case Study of the Igbo of Nigeria*, London: Geoffrey Chapman, 1981.

Mintz, Sidney, 'Descrying the Peasantry,' *Review*, VI, 2 Fall 1982.

Moore, Carlos, 'Conversation with Cheikh Anta Diop,' *Presence Africaine*, Nos 3/4, 1993

Moore, Gerald, *Seven African Writers*, Oxford: Oxford University, 1962.

Morrison, Toni, *Beloved*, London: Pan Books, 1988.

Morrison, Toni, *Playing in the dark: Whiteness and the literary imagination*, London and Basingstoke: Picador/Pan Books, 1992.

Nehusi, Kimani, 'Why "Ethnic Minority" is Racist,' *African Peoples Review*, Vol. V, No. 2. May-August, 1996.

Ngara, Emmanuel, *Stylistic Criticism and the African Novel*, London: Heinemann Educational Books, 1982.

Ngara, Emmanuel, *Art and Ideology in the African Novel*, London: Heinemann Educational Books, 1985.

Ngugi wa Thiong'o, *Writers in Politics*, London: Heinemann Educational Books, 1981.

Njaka, Elechukwu, *Igbo political Culture*, Evanston: Northwestern University, 1974.

Nnoli, Okwudiba, *Ethnic Politics in Nigeria*, Enugu, Fourth Dimension, 1978.

Nnoli, Okwudiba, 'A Short History of Nigerian Underdevelopment,' in Okwudiba Nnoli, ed., *Path to Nigerian Development*, Dakar: Codesria, 1981.

Nwoga, Donatus, *The Supreme God as Stranger in Igbo Religious Thought*, Ekwereazu: Hawk, 1984.
Nzegwu, Femi, *Love, Motherhood and the African Heritage*, Dakar: African Renaissance, 2001.
Nzimiro, Ikenna, 'The Political Implications of Multinational Corporations in Nigeria,' in Carl Widstrand, ed., *Mult-National Firms in Africa*, Dakar and Uppsala: African Institute for Economic Development and Planning/Scandinavian Institute for African Studies, 1975.
Obasanjo, Olusegun, *My Command*, Ibadan and London: Heinemann, 1980.
Obasanjo, Olusegun, *Nzeogwu*, Ibadan: Spectrum Books, 1987.
Obiechina, Emmanuel, *Culture, Tradition and Society in the West African Novel*, Cambridge University, 1975.
Obijiofor, Levi, 'When a president runs out of steam,' *The Guardian*, Lagos, 6 April 2001.
Ofoegbu, Ray, *Foundation Course in International Relations for African Universities*, London: George Allen & Unwin, 1980.
Ogbaa, Kalu, *Gods, Oracles and Divinition*, Trenton: Africa World, 1992.
Ogunsakin, Mustapha, et al, 'Debt question tops Obasanjo-Blair talks,' *The Guardian*, Lagos, 13 September 2000.
Ohwahwa, Fred, 'The President Knows Better,' *The Guardian*, Lagos, 25 March 2001.
Okpewho, Isidore, *African Oral Literature*, Bloomington and Indianapolis: Indiana University, 1992.
Okpong, Jennifer, 'The Asian Sandwich Syndrome,' *African Peoples Review*, Vol. V, No. 3, September-December 1996.
Olisa, M.S.O., 'Political Culture and Political Stability in Traditional Igbo Society,' *Conch*, 3, 2, September 1971.
Oliver, Roland, 'The condition of Africa,' *Times Literary Supplement*, London, 20 September 1991.
Olusanya, Yinka, 'Nigeria loses N7.2 trillion ($60 billion) to capital flight,' *Sunday Vanguard*, Lagos, 24 December 2000.
Omotoso, Kole, *Achebe or Soyinka?* East Grinstead: Hans Zell, 1996.
Onimode, Bade, *Imperialism and Underdevelopment in Nigeria*, London: Zed Books, 1982.
Onwuejeogwu, M.A., *An Outline of an Igbo Civilization*, Nri: Tabansi, 1980.
Osundare, Niyi, 'Words of Iron, Sentence of Thunder: Soyinka's Prose Style,' *African Literature Today*, No. 13, 1983, pp. 24-37.
Owoh, Kenna, 'Fragmenting Health Care: The World Bank Prescription for Africa,' *Alternatives*, 21, 1996.

Pakenham, Thomas, 'The European share-out of the spoils of Africa,' *Financial times*, London, 15 February 1988.
Palmer, Eustace, *The Growth of the African Novel*, London: Heinemann, 1979.
Perham, Margery, *Mining, Commerce and Finance in Nigeria*, London: Faber and Faber, 1948.
Priebe, Richard, *Myth, Realism and the West African Writer*, Trenton: Africa World, 1988.
Porter, A.N. and A.A, Stockwell, *British Imperial Policy and Decolonisation, 1938-1941. Vol I: 1938-51*, Basingstoke and London: Macmillan, 1987.
Quist-Arcton, Ofeibea, 'Interview of President Abdoulaye Wade,' *AllAfrica*, Washington, 7 February 2001.
Reed-Anderson, Paulette, *Rewriting the Footnotes*, Berlin: Die Ausländerbeauftragte des Berliner Senats, 2000.
Reid, Elizabeth, ed., *HIV & AIDS: The Global Inter-Connection*, Connecticut: Kumarian, 1995.
Rivers, K., and P. Aggleton, *Adolescent Sexuality, Gender and the HIV Epidemic*, New York: UNDP HIV Development Programme, 1999.
Rivers, K., and P. Aggleton, *Men and HIV Epidemic*, New York: UNDP HIV and Development Programme, 1999.
Rodgers, Terence, 'Empires of the imagination: Rider Haggard, popular fiction and Africa,' in Mpalive-Hangson Msiska and Paul Hyland, ed., *Writing and Africa*, London and New York: Addison Wesley Longman, 1997.
Rodney, Walter, *How Europe Underdeveloped Africa*, London: Bgle-L'ouverture, 1972.
Rodney, Walter, 'The African revolution,' in Paul Buhle, ed., *C.L.R. James: His Life and Work*, London and New York: Alison and Busby, 1986.
Schurmann, Franz, 'Africa is Saving Itself,' *Choices: The Human Development Magazine*, Volume 5, Number 1, June 1996.
Segal, Ronald, 'The chains of shame,' *The Guardian*, London, 17 December 1997.
Shelton, Austin, 'The offended *Chi* in Achebe's novels,' *Transition*, 13, 1964.
Shenton, Robert, *The Development of Capitalism in Northern Nigeria*, London: James Currey, 1986.
Shobowale, Dele, 'The president in Civil War,' *Sunday Vanguard*, Lagos, 15 April 2001.
Shujaa, Mwalimu and Kofi Lomotey, 'Afrocentric Education,' *African Peoples Review*, Vol. V, No. 2, May-August 1996.
Sofola, J.A., *African Culture and African Personality*, Ibadan: African Resources, 1973.

Soyinka, Wole, *The Open Sore of a Continent* (Oxford: Oxford University, 1996.
Stratton, Florence, *Contemporary African Literature and the Politics of Gender*, London and New York: Routledge, 1994.
Street, Brian, 'Reading the novels of empire: race and ideology in the classic "tale of adventure",' in David Dabydeen, ed., *The black presence in English literature*, Manchester: Manchester University, 1985.
Stremlau, John, *The International Politics of the Nigerian Civil War*, Princeton: Princeton University, 1977.
Tudor, Dean and Nancy Tudor, *Jazz*, Littleton: Libraries Unlimited, 1979.
Uchegbu, Amechi, 'The Dialectics of Nigerian Foreign Politics,' in Asikpo Essien-Ibok, ed., *Towards a Progressive Nigeria*, Kano: Triumph Publishing, 1983.
Uchendu, Victor, *the Igbo of South Eastern Nigeria*, New York: Holt, Rinehart and Winston, 1965.
UNAIDS, *Gender and HIV/AIDS: Taking stock of research and programmes*, Geneva, 1999.
UNAIDS Technical Update, *Gender and HIV/AIDS*, Geneva, 1998.
UNAIDS/WHO, *Report on the Global HIV/AIDS epide*mic, Geneva, 1998.
UNDP, *Living Positively with HIV/AIDS: Supporting the involvement of people living with HIV/AIDS in the response to the epidemic*, Dakar, November 1995.
Van Bueren, Geraldine, 'It's Britain's guilty secret,' *The Guardian*, London, 25 May 2001.
Wallerstein, Immanuel, 'The Three Stages of Africa Involvement in the World-Economy,' in Peter Gutkind and Immanuel Wallerstein, ed., *The Political Economy of Contemporary Africa*, California and London: Sage Publications, 1976.
Weinberg, Bill, *War on the Land*, London and New York, Zed Books, 1991.
Weistock, Donald and Cathy Ramadan, 'Symbolic Stucture in *Things Fall Apart*,' in C.L. Innes & Bernth Lindfors, *Critical Perspectives on Chinua Achebe*, London: Heinemann Educational Books, 1979.
Williams, Chancellor, *The Destruction of Black Civilization*, Chicago: Third World, 1987.
Worsthorne, Peregrine, 'What my new (black) friend told my relatives about their manor house,' *The Spectator*, London, 11 April 1998.
Wills, John, *1688: A Global History*, London: Granta, 2001.
Wilmot, Patrick, 'Poverty amidst riches,' *West Africa*, London, 15 August 1988.

Wren, Robert, *Achebe's World*, Harlow: Longman, 1990.
Wright, Donald, 'Things standing Together: A Retrospective on Things Fall Apart,' *Kunapipi,* Vol XII, No 2, 1990.
Wright, Ronald, *Stolen Continents*, London: Pimlico, 1993.

Index

Aba, 122
Abacha, Sani, 116, 129, 159
Abakaliki, 122
Abeokuta, 112n12
Abiola, Mashood, 124
Abubakar, Abdulsalami, 116, 159
Account of the Regular Graduations in Man, An (White), 25
Achebe, Chinua, 2, 2n4, 17, 17n28, 46n129, 49, 51, 51n142, 63, 63n28, 73-74, 75, 75n1, 76-81, 81n17, 87-89, 89n26, 90, 90n27, 91, 91n30, 92-110, 110n1, 119, 119n30, 120n31, 121, 131, 131n60, 133n62, 136, 136n6, 147n27, 162, 162n42
Achebe or Soyinka? (Omotoso), 76, 77, 78
Adams, Pepper, 84
Adamson, Alan, 22n54
Ade-Ajayi, J.S., 77, 77n10
Adderley, Cannonball, 83
Adekunle, Benjamin, 118-119
    virulence of Igbophobia, 118-119
'Africa' (Coltrane), 84
Africa, African World, 1-24 *passim*
    actors, agents, in history, 1-2
    Africa America, 2, 48
    Africa Caribbean, 2, 3, 52, 72
    African-centredness, 1-2 *passim* 79-80 *passim*
    'African Studies', 2, 24
    'African Union', 133n63
    africophobism, 33, 43, 45, 55, 62, 71, 83, 107
    Arab states in, 4. *See also* Arab, Arab/muslim
    arms-free Africa, commanding signpost for future, 137
    capital, net-capital transfers, 3-7
    casualties in 1914-1918 war, 22
    casualties in 1939-1945 war, 19
    collapse, virtual collapse of economy, state, 3 *passim* 132-133, 134 *passim*
    complementarity, dual-gender comlementarity, 136
    conquest and occupation of, 1-3, 15-17 *passim* 103-108 *passim*
    debt discourses, 156-162. *See also* capital transfers
    double-jeopardy character of holocaust, 34
    east Africa, 16, 33, 153, 154, 155, 166
    'green beans', as metaphor for life-giving, 12-14
    green beans export, 12-13
    health, health services, 146-149. *See also* HIV/AIDS
    HIV/AIDS, 8, 139, 145-146, 149-156
    holocaust, 2, 15, 17-18 *passim*. *See also* pogrom
    intellectuals mass emigration to the Western World, 10
    liberation of, 1-3, 16 *passim* 78-79 *passim*
    marginalisation of women, restoration of women's independence, 136
    'nation-states' as killing fields, 132-133, 134, 135, 143-144, 162
    north Africa, 4, 16, 32
    pogrom, 15, 36, 38, 66
    population, 140-144
    pre-conquest, independent, 2, 16
    role in world economy, 7 *passim*
    resistance, 1-3
    resource capacities, contemporary,

Index 175

141-145, 158-162
restoration of independence, *see* liberation
south, southern Africa, 16, 38, 40, 67-68, 153, 155, 156
'sub-Sahara Africa', as racist typology, 4
'The Burden Prize for Western Wealth', 7
west Africa, 16, 67, 151-153, 155, 156

Africa/Brass (Coltrane), 84, 85
Africa in History (Davidson), 66
Afro Blue Impressions (Coltrane), 84
Agbakoba, Olisa, 124
Aggleton, P., 146n25
Aguwa, J.U., 103n49
Aguyi-Ironsi, Johnson, 112, 115, 116, 159
'Air Raid' (Achebe), 119
Ajayi, Rotimi, 159n37
Akan, 77, 151-152
Ake, Claude, 128n46
Akinola, Wale, 124n39
Algeria, 4, 16
Ali, Rashied, 85
'All The Things You Could Be By Now If Sigmund Freud's Wife Was Your Mother' (Mingus), 83
Allan Quatermain (Haggard), 43
Allan's Wife (Haggard), 43
Aluko, Olajide, 111n11
'Amaechina', as concept of reclamation and reconstruction, 136-137, 156, 162
Amadiume, Ifi, 101n39, 120n32
Ambrose, Soren, 11, 11nn17, 18, 53
  50 Years Is Enough, 11
  America, Americas, 2, 3, 14, 15, 18, 28, 29, 31, 32, 33, 34, 39, 41, 157
  Caribbean, 2, 3, 18, 19, 28, 48, 51n143, 157
  Latin America, *see* south America
  north America, 30, 64
  south America, 2, 30-31, 139

'Americanisation', as metaphor for conquest and occupation, 33, 34
American Enterprise Institute, 50
Ananaba, Wogu, 113
Anenih, Tony, 124n39
Angola, 9, 16, 31, 106, 123, 137, 154
Animal Kingdom, The (Cuvier), 25
An-Na'im, Abdullahi, 120n32
Annenkov, P.V., 64
Anthills of the Savannah (Achebe), 125, 136, 145
Anyanwu, Chris, 124
Anyanwu, U.D., 103n49
'Appointment in Ghana' (McLean), 83
Arab, Arab/muslim, Arab World, 4, 32-34
  conquest and occupation of Africa, 32-34
  precursor of Europe invasion of Africa, 33
  racist rationalisation of conquest and occupation of Africa, 33
Arinze, Francis, 89n26, 101n41
Asante, 105, 106
Asante, Molefi Kete, 1, 1nn1, 2, 3, 3n5, 48, 48nn136, 137, 63n30, 86, 86n23
Ascension (Coltrane), 84, 85
Asia, 19, 28, 32, 39, 41, 45, 51, 51n143, 52-54, 139
  'miracle', economy, 54
  pliant middle stratum, 51-53
  population, 140-143
  mirage, economy, 54
  'sandwich privilege', 52
  'tiger economies', 51
Atlantic, The, 32
Attlee, Clement, 57
Auschwitz, 29, 40
Australasia, 28, 31, 33, 34, 39, 41
'Australasianisation', as metaphor for conquest and occupation, 33
Australia, 29, 30
Avant-Garde, The (Coltrane), 84
Awolowo, Obafemi, 118, 119-120

176 African literature in defence of history

financial/economic strangulation of Igbo assets, exponent of, 119-120
'starvation as weapon/quick kill' Biafra War doctrine, exponent of, 118-120, 123
virulence of Igbophobia, 119-120
Ayler, Albert, 82

Babangida, Ibrahim, 116, 159
Bahamas, 49
Bahro, Rudolph, 139
Bakalori, 113
Bakongo, 144
Balewa, Abubakar Tafawa, 109, 161
Ballantyne, R. M., 42
Bambara, 105, 141
Bangladesh, 49, 138, 142
Baule, 105
Beaud, Michel, 14, 14n23, 17
Beaumont, Joseph, 22
Belgium, 14, 18, 35, 36, 59, 63, 66, 122-123, 130, 142
  conquest and occupation of Africa, see Europe, European World
Bello, Ahmadu, 112
Beloved (Morrison), 49
Bemba, 106
Benin, 105
Benin, Republic of, 152
Berg Damara, 36, 37, 38
Berlin, 28, 157
Bhabha, Homi, 48-49, 49nn139, 140, 50, 54
Biafra, Biafra War, 109, 110, 116-124, 129-132
Biafra Organisation of Freedom Fighters, 118
  casualties in, 109, 118
  enveloping shadow, 124
  war of genocide, 116-117, 118
Bihe, 105
Bini, 86
Bilesanmi, Lekan, 124n39
Birmingham, 12

'Black, Brown and Beige' (Ellington), 82
Black Fire (Hill), 83
Black Skins, White Masks (Fanon), 49
Blair, Tony, 56-57
Blane, Colin, 123nn35, 36
Blixen, Karen, 42, 43, 50
Blues and the Abstract Truth (Nelson), 83
Boers, 36
Borroughs, Edgar, 42
Bosnia-Herzegovina, 9, 12
Botswana, 4, 142, 153, 154, 155
Bowa, 105
Brazil, 64
Brazilia (Coltrane), 84
Bristol, 12
Britain, 7, 8-10, 11-15, 18, 19-27, 29-30, 35, 36, 38, 41-44, 45, 47-48, 49, 51-53, 55, 56-57, 58, 59-65, 66-68, 71-73, 94, 95, 96, 97, 103-105, 106-108, 109, 113-114, 122, 126, 127, 127nn44, 45, 128-132, 138, 141, 142, 159
  Angola land mine production, 9
  arms to federal Nigeria, Biafra War, 130, 131-132
  Barclays Bank, 128
  British Financial Services Authority, 129
  'centre of world science', 22
  Channel 4 Television service, 13
  conquest and occupation of Africa, see Europe, European World
  creator, codifier, publicist of racism as ideology, 42
  'cultural and scientific backwater', 22
  diplomatic and adminstrative support to federal Nigeria, Biafra War, 130-131
  Dumblane massacres, 9
  'ethical' foreign policy relations, 72
  hegemonic control, Nigerian

economy, 127-129
Hungerford massacres, 9
foot-and-mouth epidemic, 9
Labour party, 56-57, 71
Lloyds Bank, 128
'mad cow' epidemic, 9
Marks & Spencer food stores, 13
Northern Ireland War, 9
'nuclear-war biscuits', as metaphor for state(s) scorched earth policy, 12-14
nuclear-war biscuits to Africa, 11-12
Safeway food stores, 13
Sainsbury's food stores, 12-13
Tesco food stores, 13
writers of empire, 42-54, 59
Buchan, John, 42, 43, 44, 45, 50
Budja, 106
Buhari, Muhammadu, 116, 159
Buhle, Paul, 105n57
Bunyoro, 106
Burkina Faso, 138, 151, 152
Burundi, 35, 123
Busia, Abena, 59, 59n14
Bye Bye Black Bird (Coltrane), 84
Bygrave, Michael, 65

Cabral, Amilcar, 23, 23n57
Camdessus, Michel, 10-11
Cameroon, 35, 66, 143, 152
Canada, 130, 159
Cape Verde, 16, 31
Cardiff, 12
Cary, Joyce, 42, 43, 76
Castel, Carol, 58n11
Cavanagh, John, 3n6
Central African Republic, 123, 138, 154
Chad, 19, 152
Change Of The Century (Coleman), 83
Charles, Prince, 8n13
Chase, Chase Manhattan, 56
Chewa, 106
Chikunda, 106

China, 141
Chinweizu, 31n86, 32nn87, 89, 33nn91, 92, 75n2
'season' of foreign aggression in Africa, 31-32
Chokwe, 105
christians, 34, 45, 93
Chukwukere, B.I., 89n26
Churhill, Winston, 57, 57n10
Clairmonte, Frederick, 3n6
Clemetson, Lynette, 56n8
Clinton, Bill, 8n13, 58
Cohen, Desmond, 138n9, 146n24
Cold War, 11
Coleman, Ornette, 82, 83
Coltrane, Alice, 83, 85
Coltrane, John, 82, 83-85
  themes on Africa, African essence, African reality, 85
Coltrane Jazz (Coltrane), 84
Columbus, Christopher, 65-66
condom, condom intervention, 139, 149
'Configuration' (Coltrane), 85
Congo, Democratic Republic of, 4, 123, 132, 137, 138, 141, 143, 154
Congo, River, 33, 62, 63, 66, 67
Conrad, Joseph, 2, 42, 43, 44, 45, 48-49, 50, 59-63, 63nn26, 27, 86
Coupland, Reginald, 23
Coquery-Vidrovitch, Catherine, 66
Côte d'Ivoire, 151, 152
Cronje, Suzanne, 130nn55, 57, 58
Cry the Beloved Country (Paton), 44
Cuamato, 106
Cuba, 38, 138
Cuvier, Georges, 25

Dabydeen, David, 42n121, 44n125, 59n14, 70, 70n47
Dahomey, 105
'Dahomey Dance' (Coltrane), 84
Darwin, Charles, 23, 26, 38, 107
Davenant, Charles, 22
Davidson, Basil, 18n30, 23, 23n56, 65,

65n35, 66, 66nn36, 37, 38, 39, 67, 67nn40, 41, 68, 68n42, 69, 69nn44, 45, 70, 70n46
challenge of scholarship of, 65-71
Davis, Miles, 83
de St. Jorre, John, 114n17, 115nn18, 19, 118n27
Deeds Not Words (Roach), 83
Demerara, 22-23
Der Lebensraum (Ratzel), 39
Descent of Man, The (Darwin), 26
Development Report 2001, The (World Bank), 5
'development studies', 2, 158. *See also* African Studies
Diana, Princess, 8-9
Dial Africa (Harden), 84
Diop, Cheikh Anta, 15n27, 32n88, 34n93, 69, 78
loss of national sovereignty, implications of, 78-79
Disneyland, 49
Dolphy, Eric, 83, 85
Dove, Nah, 64-65, 65n33
Dowden, Richard, 135, 135n3
'blood and tears/scissors and paste job', 135
Drechsler, Horst, 37nn101, 102, 103, 38n106
D'Souza, Dinesh, 50-51, 55
Dudley, Billy, 129n54
Dyall, Lorna, 29n77

Eagleton, Terry, 59, 59n15, 60, 60nn16, 17, 18, 19, 20, 61, 61nn21, 22, 62, 86, 86nn22, 23
Earth First!, 139, 146
Eboue, Felix, 18-19
Edinburgh, 28
Edwards, Paul, 81nn15, 16
Egerton, Hugh, 23
Egypt (contemporary), 4
Egypt (Kemet), 32, 51
Ekundare, R. Olufemi, 20nn38, 39, 42, 43
Ekwe-Ekwe, Herbert, 19n31, 22n50, 115n22'end of history' interpretation, African Holocaust, 79. *See also* 'mere episode, catalytic episode only' interpretation
Ellington, Duke, 82, 83
Emenyonu, Ernest, 92, 92n32, 104, 104n50
End of Racism, The (D'Souza), 50
Equiano, Olaudah, 74, 81
Equatorial Guinea, 16, 151, 152
Eritrea, 132, 154, 155
Essien-Ibok, Asikpo, 111n11
Ethiopia, 11-12, 18, 106, 123, 132, 138, 154
Europe, European World, Western World, 1-8, 9, 10, 11, 13, 14, 15-19, 20 *passim* 122-123 *passim*
academy on African conquest and holocaust, 2-3, 18, 21-22, 23-29, 38-40, 41-54, 55-56, 59-74, 75-76, 78, 79
African military, 'agent of modernisation', 160
animalisation of African subject of history, 8n13, 43
capital, net-capital imports from Africa, 3-7
conquest and occupation of Africa, 1-3, 14-18 *passim* 103-108 *passim*
connecting thread, of historic crimes, 56, 73
debt claims from Africa, critique of, 156-162. See also capital imports from Africa
'deny-the-African Presence' trope, 18. *See also* eurocentric packaging of African phenomena
eurocentric packaging and typecasting of African phenomena, 4, 9-10, 18, 21-29, 34, 37, 38-40, 42-54, 55-56, 59-74, 75-76, 78, 79, 107, 138, 139-140, 145, 146-147, 148, 150-151,

155, 156, 160
genocide, 24-32, 35-40, 55-56, 58-59
genocidist(s), genocidist scholars and scholarship, 24-29, 34, 37, 38-40, 42-45, 55-56, 59, 61-65, 66, 67, 68, 70-74
   intellectuals from Africa, 11
   juvenalisation of African subject of history, 43
   mass emigration of peoples to conquered lands, 40-41
   population, 140-143
   racist language of rationalisation of African conquest, see eurocentric packaging and typecasting of African phemomena.
   silence, evasion, rationalisation of African holocaust, 17-54, 55-56, 75, 86-87
   triumphalism and claims of being actuating source in history, 43, 59
   typologisation of peoples, 44-46. See also euorocentric packaging and typecasting of Africa phenomena
Evans-Pritchard, E.E., 107
Evidence (Monk), 83
Ewe, 152
'*Exterminate All the Brutes*' (Lindqvist), 24, 63
Eyadema, Gnassingbé, 135n4
Ezekwugo, Christopher, 89n26
Ezenwa-Ohaeto, 49n138
Ezz-thetics (Russell), 83

'Fables of Faubus' (Mingus), 83
Falola, Toyin, 110nn3, 4, 111n7, 128n46
Fani-Kayode, Femi, 27nn74, 75
Fanon, Frantz, 49, 49n140, 134-135, 135n1
Farrar, Frederick, 23
Fawehinmi, Gani, 122, 124
Feldman, D. A., 146nn23, 25
Finer, S.E., 160n39

Fitch, Bob, 19n34, 20nn35, 36, 21, 21nn47, 48, 49
Ford, 56
foundational holocausts, 29
Frady, Marshall, 18n29
France, 14, 18, 19, 25, 27, 30, 35, 36, 48, 54n150, 58, 59, 63, 66, 69, 141-142, 157
   conquest and occupation of Africa, see Europe, European World
   Free French Forces, 19
Frankfurt, 53
Free At Last (Waldron), 83
Freedom (Shepp), 83
Freedom Suite, The (Rollins), 83
Fryer, Peter, 42, 42n122
Fuller, Curtis, 84

Gabon, 152
Galeano, Eduard, 30nn81, 82, 31n84
Gambia, 19, 152
Gana, Jerry, 161
Ganguela, 105
Garrison, Jimmy, 85
Geldof, Bob, 6-7
Geldofmania, 7
General Motors, 56
Genoa, G-8 summit at, 157-158
Germany, 14, 18, 21, 23, 25, 34-40, 55, 58-59, 66, 67, 71, 157, 159
   Aryan, 23
   conquest and occupation of Africa, see Europe, European World
   Federal Republic of, 130, 138
   Teutonising occupation strategy, 38
Geshekter, Charles, 148n28
Ghana, 19, 21, 48, 57, 135n4, 138, 151, 152
Giant Steps (Coltrane), 83
Gikuyu, 67
Gillepsie, Dizzy, 83
Gilroy, Paul, 47, 47n133, 48
Godfrain, Jacques, 54n150
Gold Coast, see Ghana

Goldie, Taubman, 128
Goulbourne, Harry, 51n143, 52n146, 53n148
Gowon, Yakubu, 113, 114, 116, 159
Griffiths, Gareth, 44n125, 105, 105n56
Guinea, 123, 132, 152
Guinea Bissau, 16, 31, 123, 127n44, 132, 152
Gutkind, Peter, 35n97
Gutteridge, W.F., 160n39
Guyana, 2, 22-23, 48

Haggard, Rider, 42, 43, 44, 44n125, 45, 50, 55
Hall, Stuart, 47, 47nn131, 132, 48
Hamburg, 35
Hamlet, 85
Hammond, Dorothy, 24, 24n59
Harden Wilbur, 84
Hausa-Fulani, 112, 127, 129
Heart of Darkness (Conrad), 2, 43, 44, 59, 60, 61, 62, 63
Hegel, Georg, 23, 107
Hehe, 106
Henty, G.A., 42
Herero, 36, 37, 38, 66 106
Hill, Andrew, 83
Hill, Christopher, 22, 22nn51, 52, 53, 65
Hirsh, Michael, 56n6
Hitler, Adolf, 15, 37
Hobsbawm, Eric, 65
Hodges, Johnny, 83
Holder, Robyn, 30nn79, 80
Holland, 30, 59, 130
Holliday, John, 30nn79, 80
Holy Bible, The, 92n31
Home and Exile (Achebe), 74
Howe, Darcus, 47, 48
Humbe, 106
Hume, David, 23
Huntington, Samuel, 169n39
Huxley, Elspeth, 42, 43, 44
'hybridisation', critique of, 47-51

Hyland, Paul, 44nn124, 125
Hymas, Charles, 52

Ibadan, 112n12
Ibadan, University College, 107
Iberia, 22
Ibibio, 67, 127, 145
Igala, 96
Igbo, 67, 76-77, 80-82, 86, 87-108, 109, 112, 112n12, 113-127, 129, 144
ani, 91, 100, 101, 102
chi, 87, 89, 89n26, 90
efulefu, 95
holocaust, grand-scale holocaust, 118, 122
idemili, 136
kotma, 95, 96
mba, 80
non-development, 'marginalisation', as atrocity, 120, 121
obodo dike, 98
ochu, 101
ohaneze, 125
ozo, 94, 95
pogrom against, genocide of, massacres of, 109, 112-123, 123n37, 124
resistance, British invasion, 96, 105, 106-108, 126-127, 129, 131
'troublesome', 96, 126, 129, 131
umunna, 98
Igbokwe, Joe, 122n34
Ihekweazu, Edith, 55n2
Ihonvbere, Julius, 110nn3, 4, 111n7
Ijebu, 105
Ijo, 120, 127
Ikpeze, Nnaemeka, 120, 120n32, 124n38
Imo, River, 120
Impressions (Colrane), 84
India, 48, 130, 141
Indian, The, 33
Innes, C.L., 93n33, 104n51, 105n55, 120n31, 144, 144n21

Interesting Narrative of the Life of Olaudah Equiano or Gustavus Vassa the African, The (Equiano), 74, 81
International Monetary Fund, 5-7, 10-11, 53-54, 156
  'structural adjustment programme', 5-6, 10-11, 53-54
Interstellar Space (Coltrane), 85
'Invitation', 83
Irabor, Nduka, 124
Iran, 142
Iraq-Iran Gulf War, 118
Ireland, 7
Irele, Abiola, 104-105, 105n55
'Iris' (Coltrane), 85
Iroquois, 86
Israel, 9, 130
Italy, 14, 18, 35, 59, 130
  conquest and occupation of Africa, *see* Europe, European World
Iyasere, Solomon, 104, 104n51
Izevbaye, Dan, 55n2, 79, 79n14

Jablow, Atla, 24, 24n59
Jacques, Martin, 47
James, C.L.R., 105
JanMohamed, Abdul, 87n25, 100n37, 104, 104n54
Janowitz, M., 160n39
Japan, 18, 19, 21, 138, 159
jazz, African American classical music, 82-85
  further africanisation, liberatory thrust, 82-85
Jemie, Onwuchekwa, 75n2
Jews, Jewish, 29, 34, 36-37, 39, 45, 55-56, 58-59, 71, 72-73, 77, 92-93, 122, 157
  holocaust, 28-29, 36-37, 55-56, 58-59, 71, 72-73, 77
Jeyifo, Biodun, 90n28
John Olin Foundation, 50
Johnson, J.J., 160n39
Johnson, Lynden, 134

Jos, 114
'Jupiter' (Coltrane), 85

Kaduna, 112n12
Kanem-Bornu, 32
Kano, 114
Keegan, John, 58nn12, 13
Kemet, Afrocentrality and Knowledge (Asante), 1
Kenedougou, 105
Kenya, 12-13, 16, 31, 33, 51, 66, 127n44, 132, 154
Kind of Blue (Davis), 84
King, Tom, 58nn12, 13
King Solomon's Mines (Haggard), 43, 44
Kipling, Rudyard, 42
Kipsigi, 67
Kirk-Greene, Anthony, 110n2
Ki-Zerbo, Joseph, 10n16, 11n19
Knox, Robert, 23
Korzeniowski, Teodor Josef Konrad, *see* Conrad
'Kulu Se Mama' (Coltrane), 84

Lagos, 112, 112n12
Larkin, Philip, 82, 82n18, 83,
Larson, Charles, 75-76, 76n3
Lee, Richard, 23
Legend, The (Coltrane), 84
Lenin, Vladimir, 41n119
'Leo' (Coltrane), 85
Leopold II, King, 122-123
  'Leopold Syndrome', 123
  'The Rapist of Congo', 123
Let Freedom Ring (McLean), 83
Liberia, 132, 145, 152
'Liberia' (Coltrane), 84
Libya, 4
Lindfors, Bernth, 93n33, 104n51, 105n55
Lindqvist, Sven, 15, 15nn25, 26, 24, 25nn61, 62, 63, 64, 26, 26nn65, 66, 67, 68, 69, 27nn70, 71, 72, 73,

29nn76, 78, 36nn98, 99, 100, 38nn104, 105, 107, 39, 39nn108, 109, 110, 111, 40, 40n112, 63
Little, Booker, 83
Live at Birdland (Coltrane), 84
Live at Seattle (Coltrane), 84
Live at Village Vanguard (Coltrane), 84
Liverpool, 12
Location of Culture, The (Bhabha), 49
'Lock 'Em Up' (Mingus), 83
Lomotey, Kofi, 47, 47n130
London, 11, 13, 19, 27, 28, 29, 40, 42, 53, 129
Love Supreme, A (Coltrane), 84, 85
Lugard, Frederick, 128
Lunda, 106
Luo, 67
Lyell, Charles, 25-26, 26n65

Macebuh, Stanley, 76n6
Madubuike, Ihechukwu, 75n2
Madunagu, Edwin, 111n8
Magdoff, Harry, 40nn113, 114, 115, 116, 41n120
Maghrib, 32
Maier, Karl, 145n22
Mail on Sunday (London), 11-12
Makonde, 106
Makua, 106
Malawi, 4, 146, 154
Malaya, Malaysia, 21, 132
Malcolm X, 18, 34
Mali, 32, 138, 151, 152
'Man from South Africa' (Roach), 83
Man of the People, A (Achebe), 109
Manchester, 12
Mandingo, 105
Mannsaker, Frances, 44n125
Maori, 29-30
Marby, Marcus, 56n7
'Mars' (Coltrane), 85
Marx, Karl, 23, 62, 62nn23, 24, 25, 63, 63n29, 64, 64nn31, 32
marxist discourses, 59-65

Masland, Tom, 54n150
Massai, 67
Mayer, Arno, 55-56
McClean, Jackie, 83
McClure, John, 44n123, 68, 68n43
McGreal, Chris, 56n9
McNamara, Robert, 134, 140
Meditations (Coltrane), 85
Meditations on Integration (Mingus), 83
Mein Kampf (Hitler), 39
Meinhof, Carl, 23
Meline, Jules, 27
Milestones (Davis), 83
Milner, Alfred, 68
Mingus, Charles, 83
Mintz, Sidney, 23
Miravale, Herman, 23
Mister Johnson (Carey), 43
Misterioso (Monk), 83
Mitford, Bertram, 42, 43, 44
Mitterand, Francoise, 19, 54n150, 133, 157
Money Jungle (Ellington), 83
Monk, Thelonious, 83
Monsarrat, Nicholas, 42
Moore, Carlos, 78nn11, 12
Morgan, Lee, 83
Morocco, 4, 32
Morris, Bill, 72
Morrison, Toni, 46n129, 49, 49n140, 50, 50n141
Mossi, 106
Mozambique, 16, 31, 32, 154
'Mr Kenyatta' (Morgan), 83
Msiska, Mpalive-Hangson, 44nn124, 125
Muhammed, Murtala, 116, 159
Museveni, Yoweri, 58
Mutwa, Vusamazulu Credo, 33, 33n92
My Favorite Things (Coltrane), 84

Naipaul, V.S., 51, 51n142
Naipaulists, 51
Nama, 36, 37-38, 66

Namibia, 4, 16, 31, 35, 36-37, 66, 142, 154, 155
Nandi, 106
Naples, 32
Ndebele
Nehusi, Kimani, 45, 45n127
Nelson, Oliver, 83
Netherlands, The, *see* Holland
New York, 53
New Zealand, 29
Newsweek (Washington), 56
Ngugi wa Thiong'o, 33, 33n90, 87n25
Nietzsche, Friedrich, 38
Niger, River, 105, 124, 152
Nigeria, 19-20, 57, 96, 109-127, 127nn44, 45, 128-133, 138, 142, 143, 145, 151, 152, 153, 154-155, 158-162
   African Timber Plywood Company, 128
   Amalgamated Tin Mining Nigeria, 127
   Barclays Nigeria, 128
   corruption, ostentention, profilgacy, 110-111
   coup d'état, 109, 112-116, 117
   G.B. Ollivant, 128
   Gulf Oil of Nigeria, 128
   John Holt Company, 127
   Kaduna Mafia, 112-117
   Kingsway Chemist, 128
   Nigerian Breweries Company, 128
   Nigerian Prestressed, 128
   Northern Peoples Congress, 127, 127n44
   Royal Niger Company, 128
   Standard Bank of Nigeria, 128
   Taylor Woodrow Nigeria, 128
   United Africa Company, 127-128
Nile, River, 33, 117
Njaka, Elechukwu, 89n26
Nnoli, Okwudiba, 21n44, 123n37
Nobel Prize, The, 7,
North, Northern World, 131
'Now's The Time' (Parker), 82

Nubia, 33
Nupe, 105
Nwabuikwu, Paul, 153n35
Nwoga, Donatus, 89n26, 93, 93nn34, 35
Nzegwu, Femi, 103nn45, 46, 47, 48, 49, 136, 136nn5, 7, 147n26
   'Real Africa', site for reclamation and reconstruction, 136, 137, 145, 156, 160
Nzeogwu (Obasanjo), 115
Nzeogwu, Chukwuma, 115-116
Nzeribe, Arthur, 124
Nzimiro, Ikenna, 128, 128nn46, 47, 48

Obasanjo, Olusegun, 111, 113, 113n13, 115, 115n20, 116-117, 124, 124n39, 125-126, 130n59, 135n4, 158-159, 161-162
   anti-Igbo virulence, 125
Obi, Godwin, 124
Obijiofor, Levi, 116n23
Ofoegbu, Ray, 111n11
Ogbaa, Kalu, 104, 104n52
Ogoni, 124, 144, 145
   Movement for the Survival of the Ogoni People, 125-126
'Ogunde' (Coltrane), 84
Ogunsakin, Mustapha, 161n41
Ohwahwa, Fred, 117, 117n26
Okigwe, 122
Okpong, Jennifer, 52n144
Olisa, M.S.O., 101n40
Oliver, Roland, 139, 139n15, 140, 140n16
Olusanya, Yinka, 159n38
Omaheke desert, 37
Omotoso, Kole, 76, 76nn6, 7, 8, 77, 77n9
   'mere episode, catalytic episode only' interpretation, African holocaust, 76-78, 79
Onimode, Bade, 20nn37, 40, 41, 111nn5, 6, 10
Onitsha, 121, 122

Oppenheimer, Mary, 19n34, 20nn35, 36, 21, 21nn47, 48, 49
Oputa, Chukwudifu, 118
  Human Rights Violations Investigation Commission in Nigeria, 118
Osundare, Niyi, 76n6
Out Front (Little), 83
Out of Africa (Blixen), 43, 44
Out To Lunch (Dolphy), 83
Outer Thoughts (Russell), 83
Ovimbundu, 106
Owerri, 125
Owoh, Kenna, 5n10
Oxford, Oxford University, 18, 21, 22, 130

Pacific, The, 28, 29
Pakenham, Thomas, 135n3
Pakistan, 141
Paris, 9, 27, 28, 53
Parker, Charlie, 82, 83
Parrinder, G., 101n41
Paton, Alan, 44
Payne, Cecil, 84
People of the Mist, The (Haggard), 43
Perham, Margery, 128n46, 130-131
Peters, Karl, 36
Petty, William, 25
Philippines, 53
Philosophy of the Unconscious (von Hartmann), 25
Pithecanthropus Erectus (Mingus), 83
Point of Departure (Hill), 83
Poland, 48, 49, 60, 61
Port Harcourt, 117, 120
  Igbo merchant capital, built by, 120
Porter, A.N., 57n10
Portugal, 14, 22, 30, 33, 35, 36, 58, 59, 66, 71, 106, 127, 157
  conquest and occupation of Africa, see Europe, European World
Poverty of Philosophy, The (Marx), 64
Powell, Colin, 6

Prester John (Buchan), 43
Prichard, J.C., 23, 26-27
Priebe, Richard, 104, 104n53
Principles of Geology (Lyell), 25, 26
Prussia, see Germany
Ptah The El Daoud (Coltane), 83

Quest, The (Waldron), 83
Quist-Arcton, Ofeibea, 154n36
Quitanghona, 106

Ramadan, Cathy, 93n33
Ransome-Kuti, Beko, 124
Ratzel, Friedrich, 38-39
Rawlings, Jerry, 135n4
Reade, W. Winwood, 27
Red Strangers, The (Huxley), 43, 44
Redding, Don, 11
Reed-Anderson, Paulette, 34n94, 35n95
Reid, Elizabeth, 146n23
Rhodes, Cecil, 40-41
Right Now (Mingus), 83
Rimmer, Douglas, 110n2
Rivers, K., 146n24
Roach, Max, 83
Rodgers, Terence, 44nn124, 125, 55, 55nn1, 3, 4
Rodney, Walter, 19, 21nn45, 46, 35n96, 40nn117, 118, 76n4, 105n57, 140n17
Rollins, Sonny, 82, 83
Romany, 39
Ruark, Robert, 42
Russell, George, 83
Russia, 12, 39, 60, 157
Rwanda, 35, 123, 132, 142, 145

Sahara, The, 4
Sahel, The, 32
Salisbury, Lord, 14-15
sankofa, 50
São Tomé and Princípé, 16, 31
Saro-Wiwa, Ken, 124, 145
'Saturn' (Coltrane), 85
Save the Children, 11-12

Saxon, *see* Germany
Scale of Creatures, The (Petty), 25
Schurmann, Franz, 137, 137n8
Scotland, 86
Search For The New Land (Morgan), 83
Segal, Ronald, 14n24
Seligman, C. G., 23
Senegal, 143, 152, 154
Senegambia, 105
'Seraphic Light' (Coltrane), 85
Shades (Hill), 83
Shagari, Shehu, 109, 161
She (Haggard), 43, 44
Shenton, Robert, 128n46
Shepp, Archie, 82, 83
Shona, 106
Shonekan, Ernest, 159
Short, Clare, 56
Shujaa, Mwalimu, 47, 47n130
Siberia, 39
Sierra Leone, 19, 21, 57, 105, 123, 132, 137, 145, 152
Slav, 61
Smith, Robert, 77, 77n10
'So What' (Davis), 83
Sofola, J.A., 147n27
Somalia, 13, 32, 132, 138, 141, 142
Songhai, 32
South, Southern World, 3, 10-11, 36-37, 41, 131, 132, 138, 139, 140
  'war-by-proxy', 131, 132
South Africa, 16, 31, 45, 51, 55, 68, 127, 136, 142, 143, 154
  world racism conference, 71
South Korea, 53
Soviet Union, 119, 138
Soyinka, Wole, 76, 76n6, 77-78
Spain, 14, 22, 30, 35, 36, 38, 58, 59, 157
  conquest and occupation of Africa, *see* Europe, European World
Spawn, John, 84
Spencer, Herbert, 24-25, 25n60, 38
Spidel, Joseph, 138

Spring (Williams), 83
Stella Regions (Coltrane), 85
'Stella Regions' (Coltrane), 85
Stengers, J., 35n97
Stewart, Michael, 129-130
Stockwell, A.A., 57n10
Straight Ahead (Nelson), 83
'Straight, No Chaser' (Monk), 83
Stratton, Florence, 100n38, 103, 103n45
Street, Brian, 42n121, 44n123
Stuttgart, 119
Sudan, 13, 32, 106, 132, 137, 141, 143, 145
'Sun Star' (Coltrane), 85
Surharto, T. N. J., 53
Surinam, 2, 64
Swahili, 106
Sweden, 24, 130
Switzerland, 13, 59, 130, 157, 159

tangata whenua, *see* the Maori
Tanganyika, *see* Tanzania
Tanganyika Strut (Harden), 84
Tanzania, 7, 33, 106, 154
Tasmania, 29
Thing to Love, A (Huxley), 43
Things Fall Apart (Achebe), 74, 75, 76, 79, 87, 94, 95, 101, 102, 103, 106, 107, 122, 136
Thomas, Lesley, 52n145
Thompson, E.P., 65
Thompson, Tunde, 124
Tille, Alexander, 38
Tiv, 127
Togo, 35, 135, 152, 153
Tokyo, 53
Tomorrow Is The Question (Coleman), 83
Toward the Decolonization of African Literature (Chinweizu et al), 77-78
'Tranesonic' (Coltrane), 85
Transition (Coltrane), 84
Trevor-Roper, Hugh, 18, 21-22, 23-24, 107

Trinidad, 48
Trouble with Nigeria, The (Achebe), 109
'Truth is Marching In' (Ayler), 83
Tudor, Dean, 83n19
Tudor, Nancy, 83n19
'Tunji' (Coltrane), 84
Tunisia, 4
Turner, George, 72-73

Uchegbu, Amechi, 111n11
Uchendu, Victor, 89n26, 101n40
Uganda, 51, 123, 132, 141, 142, 154
Umuahia, 122
United Nations, 4, 8n13, 10
United States, 6, 8n13, 10-11, 13, 18, 21, 38, 51, 58, 59, 71, 82-85, 86, 138, 157
    Commission on Demographic Crisis, 138
    International Suffering Index, 138
    Least Suffering Index, 138
    Oklahoma bombings, 9
Urhobo, 127, 144
Usman, Baba, 114

Vagogo, 36
Van Bueren, Geraldine, 71n49
'Venus' (Coltrane), 85
Vietnam, Vietnam War, 118
von Bismarck, Otto, 35
von Hartmann, Eduard, 25, 25n61
von Trotha, Lother, 37

Wahehe, 37
Wallace, A. R., 23
Wallerstein, Immanuel, 35n97
war, 1914-1918, 21-22, 67
war, 1939-1945, 18-21, 67, 157
Washington, 53

We Insist!: Freedom Now Suite (Roach), 83
Weinberg, Bill, 139nn12, 13, 14
Weird of Dealy Hollow, The (Mitford), 43, 44
Weistock, Donald, 93n33
White, Charles, 25
Why Did the Heavens Not Darken? The 'Final Solution' in History (Mayer), 55
Widstrand, Carl, 128n46
Williams, Chancellor, 132, 132n61
Williams, Prince, 8n13
Williams, Tony, 83
Wills, John, 31n85
Wilmot, Patrick, 113, 113n16
Wilson, Harold, 57
Wolof, 48, 69
World Bank, 5-7, 10-11, 156
Worsthorne, Peregrine, 47, 47n134, 48, 48n135
Wren, Robert, 76n5
Wretched of the Earth, The (Fanon), 49
Wright, Derek, 91, 91n29
Wright, Ronald, 30n83
Yao, 106
Yasmina/Poem For Malcolm (Shepp), 83
Yenogoa, 125
Yoruba, 67, 76-77, 123n37, 144
Yusuf, M.D., 114

Zambia, 33, 146, 154, 155
'Zambia' (Morgan), 83
Zanzibar, 32-33
Zaria, 112n12
Zimbabwe, 4, 16, 31, 45, 56-57, 143, 146, 154, 155
Zulu, 33, 106
Zurich, 53

www.ingramcontent.com/pod-product-compliance
Lightning Source LLC
Chambersburg PA
CBHW021406290426

44108CB00010B/410